D1645837

6
11

# THE CULTURAL INTERMEDIARIES

## INTERMEDIARIES

### ★★★ Reader ★★★

# THE CULTURAL INTERMEDIARIES

## Reader

★★★ ★★★

EDITED BY

JENNIFER SMITH MAGUIRE

AND

JULIAN MATTHEWS

Los Angeles | London | New Delhi
Singapore | Washington DC

Los Angeles | London | New Delhi
Singapore | Washington DC

SAGE Publications Ltd
1 Oliver's Yard
55 City Road
London EC1Y 1SP

SAGE Publications Inc.
2455 Teller Road
Thousand Oaks, California 91320

SAGE Publications India Pvt Ltd
B 1/I 1 Mohan Cooperative Industrial Area
Mathura Road
New Delhi 110 044

SAGE Publications Asia-Pacific Pte Ltd
3 Church Street
#10-04 Samsung Hub
Singapore 049483

Editor: Chris Rojek
Editorial assistant: Gemma Shields
Production editor: Katherine Haw
Copyeditor: Solveig Gardner Servian
Marketing manager: Michael Ainsley
Cover design: Lisa Harper
Typeset by: C&M Digitals (P) Ltd, Chennai, India
Printed in India at Replika Press Pvt Ltd

Editorial Matter © Jennifer Smith Maguire and Julian Matthews 2014
Introduction © Julian Matthews and Jennifer Smith Maguire 2014
Chapter 1 © Jennifer Smith Maguire 2014
Chapter 2 © Toby Miller 2014
Chapter 3 © Sean Nixon 2014
Chapter 4 © Liz McFall 2014
Chapter 5 © Giselinde Kuipers 2014
Chapter 6 © Aidan Kelly 2014
Chapter 7 © Liz Moor 2014
Chapter 8 © Caroline E.M. Hodges and Lee Edwards 2014
Chapter 9 © Victoria Durrer and Dave O'Brien 2014
Chapter 10 © Lise Skov 2014
Chapter 11 © Charles Fairchild 2014
Chapter 12 © Tania Lewis 2014
Chapter 13 © Julian Matthews 2014
Chapter 14 © Jennifer Smith Maguire 2014
Chapter 15 © Lynne Pettinger 2014
Chapter 16 © David Wright 2014
Chapter 17 © Richard E. Ocejo 2014

First published 2014

**Library of Congress Control Number: 2013956845**

**British Library Cataloguing in Publication data**

A catalogue record for this book is available from the British Library

ISBN 978-1-4462-0132-9
ISBN 978-1-4462-0133-6 (pbk)

At SAGE we take sustainability seriously. Most of our products are printed in the UK using FSC papers and boards. When we print overseas we ensure sustainable papers are used as measured by the Egmont grading system. We undertake an annual audit to monitor our sustainability.

To – and for – our families.

# CONTENTS

Notes on Contributors     ix

Introduction: Thinking with Cultural Intermediaries     1
*Julian Matthews and Jennifer Smith Maguire*

**PART I  CONCEPTUAL AND METHODOLOGICAL
FOUNDATIONS**     **13**

1  Bourdieu on Cultural Intermediaries     15
*Jennifer Smith Maguire*

2  Cultural Work and Creative Industries     25
*Toby Miller*

3  Cultural Intermediaries or Market Device? The Case of Advertising     34
*Sean Nixon*

4  The Problem of Cultural Intermediaries in the Economy of Qualities     42
*Liz McFall*

5  Ethnographic Research and Cultural Intermediaries     52
*Giselinde Kuipers*

**PART II  CULTURAL INTERMEDIARY CASE STUDIES**     **65**

6  Advertising     67
*Aidan Kelly*

7  Branding     77
*Liz Moor*

8  Public Relations Practitioners     89
*Caroline E.M. Hodges and Lee Edwards*

9  Arts Promotion     100
*Victoria Durrer and Dave O'Brien*

10  Fashion     113
*Lise Skov*

11   Popular Music                                              125
     *Charles Fairchild*

12   Lifestyle Media                                            134
     *Tania Lewis*

13   Journalism                                                 145
     *Julian Matthews*

14   Fitness                                                    156
     *Jennifer Smith Maguire*

15   Clothing                                                   168
     *Lynne Pettinger*

16   Book Retail                                                180
     *David Wright*

17   Food and Drink                                             192
     *Richard E. Ocejo*


References                                                      202
Index                                                           237

# NOTES ON CONTRIBUTORS

**Victoria Durrer** is Lecturer in Arts Management and Cultural Policy at Queen's University Belfast and has over ten years of international experience in the field of arts management. She is member of the Editorial Team of the new *Irish Journal of Arts Management and Cultural Policy*. Her research and work focuses on access and participation in the arts and the co-production of cultural provision and policy at local level.

**Lee Edwards**, University of Leeds, teaches and researches on PR as a socio-cultural occupation. A critical scholar, her primary focus is on the operation of power through PR both within the occupational field and in wider society. As well as making theoretical contributions to the understanding of PR, she has published on the exercise of symbolic power through PR as a cultural intermediary, and on diversity in PR.

**Charles Fairchild** is an Associate Professor of Popular Music at the University of Sydney, Australia. He is the author of *DJ Danger Mouse's The Grey Album* (Bloomsbury Academic, 2014), *Music, Radio and the Public Sphere* (Palgrave, 2012) and *Pop Idols and Pirates* (Ashgate, 2008).

**Caroline E.M. Hodges**, Bournemouth University, teaches and researches on the relationship between communication and culture, with a particular focus on the promotional industries. Sympathetic to ethnographically inspired approaches, her doctoral work studied the lifeworlds of a group of PR practitioners in Mexico City and their occupational role as cultural intermediaries. She is currently involved in collaborative research studying the marketization of subaltern popular culture within the rapidly transforming cities of Lima, Peru and Rio de Janeiro, Brazil.

**Aidan Kelly** is a Senior Lecturer in Marketing at Royal Docks Business School, University of East London. His research interests are in the areas of advertising theory, socio-cultural brand research, marketing practice and consumer research. His work has been published in the *Journal of Marketing Management*, *Advertising & Society Review*, *Advances in Consumer Research* and other edited volumes.

**Giselinde Kuipers** is Professor of Cultural Sociology at the University of Amsterdam. She has published widely on humour, media, cultural industries and cultural globalization, and is the author of *Good Humor, Bad Taste: A Sociology of the Joke* (Berlin/New York, 2006). Currently, she is working on a comparative study of the social shaping of beauty standards in the transnational modelling industry in six European countries, which is funded with an ERC starting grant.

**Tania Lewis** is Associate Professor and a Vice Chancellor's Senior Research Fellow in the School of Media & Communication at RMIT University, Melbourne. The author of *Smart Living: Lifestyle Media and Popular Expertise* (Lang, 2008), editor of *Television Transformations* (Routledge, 2009), and co-editor (with Emily Potter) of *Ethical Consumption: A Critical Introduction* (Routledge, 2011), she has published extensively on lifestyle and reality television. She is a chief investigator on two large Australian Research Council projects: a national study of ethical consumption in Australia; and a comparative project on lifestyle and reality television in India, China, Singapore and Taiwan.

**Julian Matthews** lectures in the Department of Media and Communication at the University of Leicester. His research interests include the cultural work of journalists. He is author of *Producing Serious News for Citizen Children: A Study of the BBC's Children's Programme, Newsround* (Edwin Mellen Press, 2010) and has published on news production and the professional mediation of social problems, including environmental issues. He also convenes the British Sociological Association Media Study Group and is Communication and Media Section Editor on the international journal *Sociology Compass*.

**Liz McFall** is Head of Sociology at the Open University. Her work explores how markets are made especially for 'low finance' products like insurance and credit. Her book *Devising Consumption: Cultural Economics of Insurance, Credit and Spending* (Routledge, 2014), argues that it takes all sorts of technical, material, artistic and metaphysical know-how to devise consumer markets. Liz is author of *Advertising: A Cultural Economy* (Sage, 2004), co-editor with Paul du Gay and Simon Carter of *Conduct: Sociology and Social Worlds* (Manchester University Press, 2008) and co-editor of the *Journal of Cultural Economy*.

**Toby Miller** is 20% Professor of Journalism, Media and Cultural Studies at Cardiff University/Prifysgol Caerdydd in Wales and 40% Sir Walter Murdoch Professor of Cultural Policy Studies at Murdoch University in Australia. The author and editor of over thirty books, his work has been translated into Spanish, Chinese, Portuguese, Japanese, Turkish, German, and Swedish. His two most recent volumes are *Greening the Media* (with Richard Maxwell) and *Blow Up the Humanities* (both 2012). His adventures can be scrutinized at www.tobymiller.org.

**Liz Moor** is a Senior Lecturer in Media and Communications at Goldsmiths, University of London. She is the author of *The Rise of Brands* (Berg, 2007) and co-editor with Guy Julier of *Design and Creativity: Policy, Management and Practice* (Berg, 2009).

**Sean Nixon** is Professor in the Department of Sociology at the University of Essex and is author of *Hard Looks: Masculinities, Spectatorship and Contemporary Consumption* (UCL Press, 1996), *Advertising Cultures: Gender, Commerce, Creativity* (Sage, 2003) and *Hard Sell: Advertising, Affluence and Trans-Atlantic Relations circa 1951–69* (Manchester

University Press, 2013). He is also co-editor with Stuart Hall and Jessica Evans of *Representation: Cultural Representation and Signifying Practices* (Sage, 2013, 2nd edn).

**Dave O'Brien** is a Lecturer in Cultural and Creative Industries at City University London, specialising in public administration, cultural value and urban cultural policy. His most recent book, *Cultural Policy: Value, Management and Modernity*, is published by Routledge.

**Richard E. Ocejo** is an Assistant Professor in the department of sociology at John Jay College of Criminal Justice, CUNY. In his research he has specifically used ethnographic and qualitative methods to examine gentrification as well as the meanings of work and craft among tradesmen. He is the editor of *Ethnography and the City: Readings on Doing Urban Fieldwork* (Routledge, 2012), and his book on community conflicts in gentrified downtown Manhattan neighbourhoods will be published by Princeton University Press in 2014.

**Lynne Pettinger** is Assistant Professor in the Department of Sociology, University of Warwick. Her research interests concern the relations between work and occupations and specific kinds of markets. She has explored this in projects about customer service work, sex work, music work and 'green collar' work. She co-edits http://nowaytomakealiving.net.

**Lise Skov** is a cultural sociologist, educated in Copenhagen and Hong Kong. Her PhD was about Hong Kong fashion designers between local and global fashion worlds. Since then, she has done extensive research on globalization and the culture and business of fashion, most recently a study of Danish fashion designers' careers. She was the editor of the West Europe volume of the *Oxford Encyclopedia of World Dress and Fashion*, published in 2010. She works as an associate professor at Copenhagen Business School.

**Jennifer Smith Maguire** is a sociologist of consumption, and a Senior Lecturer in the School of Management, University of Leicester. Her work on cultural intermediaries has had a specific focus on the cultural fields of fitness and wine. Her work has been published in such journals as *Consumption Markets & Culture*, *International Journal of Cultural Studies* and the *European Journal of Cultural Studies*, and she is the author of *Fit for Consumption: Sociology and the Business of Fitness* (Routledge, 2008).

**David Wright** teaches in the Centre for Cultural Policy Studies at the University of Warwick in the UK. He has research interests in the sociology of taste, popular culture and the cultural industries and is a co-author of *Culture, Class, Distinction* (Routledge, 2009).

# INTRODUCTION: THINKING WITH CULTURAL INTERMEDIARIES

## JULIAN MATTHEWS AND JENNIFER SMITH MAGUIRE

Cultural intermediaries are the taste makers defining what counts as good taste and cool culture in today's marketplace. Working at the intersection of culture and economy, they perform critical operations in the production and promotion of consumption, constructing legitimacy and adding value through the qualification of goods. Over the past twenty years, the body of research examining the operations of cultural intermediaries in commodity chains, urban spaces and cultural fields has gathered momentum. With Bourdieu's discussion (1984) of post-1960s 'new occupations' as a launch pad, early adopters of the concept argued for its significance in understanding the interconnections between the spheres of production and consumption (e.g. Featherstone, 1991; du Gay et al., 1997; Mora, 2000; Soar, 2000). Subsequently, themed journal issues confirmed and promoted the utility of the concept, and shifted the focus from the continuity between production and consumption to the dialectical relationship between culture and economy (e.g. Nixon and du Gay, 2002; du Gay 2004; Smith Maguire and Matthews 2012). With cultural economy – and the insights of actor network theory and new economic sociology – increasingly informing work on cultural intermediaries, scholars have explored the 'relational work' (Cochoy, 2003) of the professional qualifiers of goods (Callon et al., 2002: 206).

Whether following a Bourdieusian or cultural economy approach, or some combination thereof, scholars have produced a diverse collection of empirical accounts of the roles of cultural intermediaries in the production of meaning, which is understood both as a form of value for specific goods and practices, and as increasingly central to the generation of capital and the reproduction of markets. This research spans a range of cultural intermediary occupations involved in constructing meaning for such various goods as wine and spirits (Smith Maguire, 2010; Ocejo, 2012b), 'nerd culture' (Woo, 2012), and 'retro' furniture (Baker, 2012), with many studies clustering in particular fields, including advertising and branding (Cronin, 2004b; McFall, 2004; Moor, 2008, 2012; Nixon, 2003); media production and distribution (Childress, 2012; Crewe et al., 2003; Gough-Yates, 2003; Kuipers, 2012; Wright, 2005a); and fashion design and retail (Entwistle, 2006; Pettinger, 2004; Skov, 2002).

If such a list renders the fecundity of the concept of the cultural intermediary self-evident, it also highlights the relevance of a considerably larger group of occupations than Bourdieu initially discussed, and begs the question of conceptual parameters. For some, the expansion of the field suggests a too-loose analytic category (Hesmondhalgh, 2006b; Molloy and Larner, 2010); for others, it is a call to better specify cultural intermediaries' shared contexts and characteristics, and their points of differentiation (du Gay 2004; Nixon and du Gay, 2002; Smith Maguire and Matthews, 2012). As a starting point for this collection, then, let us offer a working definition of cultural intermediaries.

First, cultural intermediaries are market actors who construct value by mediating how goods (or services, practices, people) are perceived and engaged with by others (end consumers, and other market actors including other cultural intermediaries). However, this is a description of a power relationship that might be applied to any daily interaction in which we attempt to influence how the other regards something or someone: we are all implicated in the 'varied impulses and articulations through which value is formed, added and circulated' (Amin and Thrift, 2004: xv). As such, value formation through mediation is a necessary but not sufficient condition for identifying cultural intermediaries. Second, cultural intermediaries must also be defined by their expert orientation and market context. In the struggle to influence others' perceptions and attachments, cultural intermediaries are defined by their claims to professional expertise in taste and value within specific cultural fields (and the foundations on which such claims rest). And, they are differentiated by their locations within commodity chains (vis-à-vis the actors and stages of cultural production they negotiate with and between, and the goods that they mediate), and by the autonomy, authority and arsenal of devices and resources that they deploy in negotiating structural and subjective constraints to accomplishing their agendas.

Such an operational definition attempts to acknowledge the varied work that populates this field of research; implicit within it are nods to the occupational location of the work (Bourdieu, 1984), the devices and dispositions (du Gay, 2004) by which cultural intermediaries accomplish their work, and the regimes of mediation (Cronin, 2004b) within which they are located. The definition also reflects our interest in bridging these various legacies and contributions, which we regard as complementary. The definition – and by extension, *The Cultural Intermediaries Reader* – is intended as a broad church, through which to examine, in both empirical and theoretical terms, the continuities and discontinuities within and between cultural intermediaries.

The *Reader* offers a comprehensive introduction to the field of cultural intermediary research. The chapters in Part I introduce the field's key conceptual frameworks and methodological foundations; the case studies in Part II demonstrate the diversity of its empirical research. In bringing together such a collection, we hope to make the case that cultural intermediaries are good to think with, on (at least) three fronts: as a point of entry to think about *theory*, *creative work*, and *cultural production*. Let us spell each of these out in more detail.

# 1. THINKING ABOUT THEORY

Cultural intermediaries represent a shared empirical object of interest for different theoretical frameworks; thinking through the lens of the research object can assist in an assessment of the relative merits or complementarity of different theoretical frameworks. Most notably for this field of research, this involves thinking about the contributions of, on the one hand, Bourdieu and, on the other hand, cultural economy, new economic sociology and actor network theory.

Smith Maguire's chapter attempts to recover some of the inter- and intra-class dynamics at play in Bourdieu's treatment of cultural intermediaries, which have largely been absent in later, Bourdieusian research. This involves relocating cultural intermediaries within the cultural and economic context of the research that underpins *Distinction* (Bourdieu, 1984), including the implications of the expansion of higher education and the development of a consumer market, both of which contributed to new – and newly redefined – occupations. Through the lens of these new occupations, Smith Maguire provides an overview of Bourdieu's account of the new petite bourgeois and new bourgeois cultural intermediaries, and their work as taste makers. Both groups work on and through notions of cultural legitimacy, drawing upon their own cultural capital and dispositions in order to shape consumer perceptions of and preferences for goods, practices and styles of life. Bourdieu's focus with regard to the growth of these new occupations is largely on class dynamics; nevertheless, he locates them primarily in cultural and artistic production. These sectors – and their perceived mode of organizing economic activity – have come to dominate contemporary discussions of cultural work and economic development, as we note below with regard to thinking about creative work.

A brief glance through the case study chapters in Part II will make clear that there has been no wholesale shift from Bourdieu to new economic sociology in this field of research. Yet, the relationship between these two approaches might be better articulated and developed. To this end, Nixon's chapter discusses the insights that the two approaches offer to an understanding of advertising executives as cultural intermediaries, and the constraints they place on thinking about their activities. Reflecting on his research on this occupation, Nixon highlights the value of Bourdieu's account of the 'social construction of agents and their trajectories in their intermediary role' (this volume) and Callon et al.'s (2007) guiding insights into market devices. Nevertheless, accepting one account or combining them has consequences for understanding cultural intermediaries. Nixon suggests how including a more expansive view of human subjectivity would offer a step forward for grasping the complexities that surround the actions and thoughts of cultural intermediaries. However, that dimension remains relatively underdeveloped within the study of 'the social trajectories and social formation of individuals and socio-technical devices' (this volume).

Locating cultural intermediaries between the moments of production and consumption has been conceptually useful, but so too has new economic sociology's problematization of that location. McFall suggests in her chapter that the concept of the cultural intermediary raises as many questions about the relationship between production and consumption as it answers, and she highlights the shortcomings of conceiving cultural intermediaries' role primarily in symbolic terms. Considering the interdependence between the two spheres of production and consumption as conceptualized in the literatures on economization and the economy of qualities, McFall situates the intermediary as one actor among many involved in the qualification and requalification of goods. In calling attention to the ways in which product attributes – not simply product meanings – are the outcomes of material practices, McFall's chapter helps to situate cultural intermediaries as key market makers in contemporary consumer economies.

Overall, the collection makes the case for the continued relevance of Bourdieu's account, alongside the increasingly common focus on cultural intermediaries as the 'professionals of qualification' who operate on the supply side of the market to intervene in how consumers perceive and engage with goods (Callon et al., 2002: 206). In their cumulative – if not necessarily coordinated – impact, both streams of research offer an empirically grounded understanding of cultural intermediaries vis-à-vis their class and market positions (although not often at the same time). A grounded appraisal of such work is significant for offering insight into how culture and economy are interwoven in practice. It is also especially timely, in light of the claims made about creative work in the contemporary era.

## 2. THINKING ABOUT CREATIVE WORK

Cultural intermediaries perform creative work; thinking about their actual practices, experiences and impacts can assist in a critical assessment of the claims made about creative work in contemporary economies. The concept usefully foregrounds the material – and often mundane – work of market actors, casting light on the routinized aspects of creative work, the subjective dynamics of occupational conventions, and the contested nature of constructing value and legitimacy for cultural goods.

Along these lines, Miller's chapter provides a critical review of the claims made for creative work and creative industries. The chapter charts the prevalent discourses of creativity that exist within both enthusiastic retellings of individuals' skill in the use of new technology (i.e. the Internet) to produce culture, and wider views on the nature of cultural work, the operations of cultural organisations, and the emergence of a stratum of workers – the creative class. An assumption that creativity creates innovation underpins these claims: an outcome that Miller suggests is difficult to substantiate when assessing the actual operations of the cultural industries in terms of their ownership patterns and impacts, and practice of purchasing smaller competitors as part of their policy of vertical and horizontal integration.

Miller's critique is situated within a relatively recent history of wishful-thinking-led cultural policy in the UK and elsewhere (Belfiore, 2009). Studies of cultural policy chart the context of these developments and explain how local and national policy has embraced particular views of cultural industries and work when responding to shifts in labour and trade markets and a growth in conglomerates and competition on the global stage (Hesmondhalgh, 2002, 2006a). National policies, though inflected by the concerns specific to their national contexts (Newsinger, 2013; O'Connor, 2005), converge around a popular view that cultural institutions offer significant and valuable sources of 'creative work' that will provide growth for modern economies (see United Nations, 2010; Florida, 2002). This recurring, optimistic position on creative work, as Miller underlines, has been criticized for its questionable definition of the creative industries as a coherent sector and its claims as to their overall profitability (Belfiore, 2009; Garnham, 2005; Miller, 2009). The critics of this position are troubled also by the implicit view of a contented creative worker. Overused and loosely defined, the notion of 'creativity' in this discourse (Bilton, 2010) implies an 'empowered worker' (Schlesinger, 2007), but hides the negative effects that cultural workers experience, including precarious, poor-quality and poorly remunerated employment conditions (Cohen, 2012; Hesmondhalgh and Baker, 2011; McGuigan, 2010). While critics disavow optimism on these grounds, studies of cultural institutions provide further evidence for a tempered view of cultural work and its institutional conditions.

Studies in organizational sociology and political economy not only dispel the optimism surrounding 'creative work' but also problematize the notion of workers' creative 'authorship' of cultural products. They characterize the institutionalized cultural production process in which most workers are employed as operating according to tensions between 'creativity' and 'commerce' (Hesmondhalgh, 2005). In reality, cultural workers will often perform gatekeeping functions and other daily activities that are regulated according to wider bureaucratic structures of their institutions (Hirsch, 1972; Patterson, 1985). Within this institutional analysis, the loci of organizational control are the supervision of workers' creative activities (Di Maggio, 1977) and the circulation of their cultural products. Political economy and other critical theoretical approaches extend these concerns to those top-level institutional processes and structures geared to profit-making. Corporations in the cultural sector gain dominant market positions through mergers and acquisitions (Bagdikian, 2000); through their increasing ownership and control of cultural production, they regulate workers' activities, the manufacture of standardized products and the distribution of rewards (McChesney, 2004; Adorno and Horkheimer, 1979). Subsequently, it is claimed that this subaltern workforce experiences exploitation in the working environment – a process that critical theory links to the formation of cultural workers' subjectivities.

This change in perspective shifts the view of workers' conformity: it is the actualiza-tion of corporate discourses when workers actively create and follow regimes of dis-cipline and management (e.g. Ursell, 2000). Moreover, the contrasting theoretical lens of 'individualization' (Beck and Beck-Gernsheim, 2002) has helped to re-imagine the relationship between subjectivity and institutional structures. This brings into focus a contrasting image of institutional structures as less constraining and providing different outcomes including opportunities for authority and self-realization in the working environment (see Banks, 2007).

Notwithstanding the importance and popularity of these debates, the positions they introduce provide little guidance on what cultural workers actually think and do (Hesmondhalgh and Pratt, 2005). Their abstract theorizing, focused narrowly around workers' autonomy, obscures how workers' agency is bound up as part of the com-plexity of their work: dimensions of concern to those who approach the question of cultural work through the figure of the cultural intermediary. Thinking 'with' cultural intermediaries has the advantage of not reducing cultural work to an institutional basis; it avoids the narrowcasting effect of institution-based analysis and theorizing of cultural work by focusing on the subjective experience of work and accomplished negotiation of institutional parameters; and it assists in recognizing the myriad actors working within and across various locations, moments and connections between pro-duction and consumption. We regard the concept of cultural intermediaries as an invitation to think critically about the nature of work in the creative industries, in terms of its mundane, precarious and unappealing dimensions; and to think 'outside the box' of creative work (i.e. to recognize the cultural work of occupations more broadly, and the broader range of occupations involved in cultural production).

# 3. THINKING ABOUT CULTURAL PRODUCTION

Cultural intermediaries are among the market actors who perform the work of cultural production; cultural intermediaries serve as an empirically grounded point of entry to highly complex political, economic and cultural processes. As a comple-ment to the methodological suggestion to 'follow the things' (Appadurai, 1986: 5), the concept of cultural intermediaries encourages us to follow the people in order to capture the interactional dynamics – structural and interpersonal – that produce and animate the market for cultural goods, and the properties of those goods.

Notwithstanding the always, already intertwined nature of culture and economy (du Gay and Pryke, 2002a), the contemporary period has witnessed increasingly long and complex global commodity chains, alongside an increase of both personal con-sumption as a proportion of gross domestic products, and immaterial labour as a pro-portion of labour markets and as a source of value for institutions, companies, industries, nations and so forth. Within such massive complexity, cultural intermediaries are the 'street-level bureaucrats' (Lipsky, 1980) who actually implement abstract institutional policies and operationalize intangible cultural values; they thus offer one way in to studying the cultural production of objects and practices and their associated halos of legitimacy and desirability. Moreover, it is a way in that remains attentive to agency and affect as vital forces shaping markets (and thus to the possibility for affective agents to imagine and perform markets in other ways).

As such, it is little surprise that the dominant mode of research in this field of research is qualitative, drawing heavily on ethnographic-inspired methods. Kuipers' chapter considers the methodological challenges of observing and capturing the (often inconspicuous) work of cultural intermediaries. Reflecting on her experience of studying television buyers, Kuipers provides a richly detailed and practice-oriented survey of research approaches and empirical points of entry. Her chapter suggests several avenues of research, from gathering background information on the relevant market and products, to methods of investigating the subjective experiences of inter-mediaries. In-depth interviews and other ethnographic devices are discussed with regard to developing adequate knowledge of the attitudes and activities of intermedi-aries and the interactions and events in which they participate. Nevertheless, cultural intermediary research can be like a 'hermeneutic pinball machine' (this volume) due to the exigencies of 'multi-sited' fieldwork, and researchers must negotiate barriers to gaining access to those in positions of power (such as television buyers). Establishing and maintaining access through gatekeepers, including intermediaries themselves, demands the researcher be fully prepared on field-specific nomenclature, devices and practices. In this way, the researcher can hope to establish their credibility and success-fully frame research as a 'good thing' in the eyes of their research subjects.

Summarizing the contributions within this field of research (Smith Maguire and Matthews, 2010), we have previously suggested that three core themes characterize the trajectory of cultural intermediary research: (1) the historicizing of cultural intermediary occupations; (2) the conceptual and empirical specification of the material practices, generic devices and subjective dispositions involved in cultural intermediary work; and (3) the identification of the impacts (cultural, economic, political) of cultural intermediaries in the production and reproduction of consumer culture. While the case study authors in Part II vary in their conceptual approaches and empirical findings, each chapter follows this tripartite structure in order to facilitate a comparative reading of cultural intermediaries and what they have, and do not have, in common. In structuring the case studies in this way, we suggest that beyond being good to think with, the concept of cultural intermediaries is a research device that offers useful sensitizing research questions. It is not that these three are the only questions to ask; rather, that asking similar questions of multiple cultural intermediaries (in designing research, and in the meta analysis of previous research) assists in producing an empirical basis from which to accomplish the larger research aim of identifying the differences between cultural intermediaries, as well as their 'family resemblances' (Nixon and du Gay, 2002: 498).

Before turning to these three research themes, let us briefly note the variety of case studies in Part II. The first three chapters consider endeavours typically associated with the promotion of consumption: Kelly's chapter looks at advertising, Moor's at branding and Hodges and Edwards' at PR. As cultural intermediary research makes clear, however, the promotion of consumption far exceeds these disciplines, as is underlined in the remaining case study chapters. The diverse and diffuse character of the promotion of consumption is highlighted in the case studies by Durrer and O'Brien of arts promotion, Skov of fashion, Fairchild of popular music, Lewis of lifestyle media, and Matthews of journalism. The service-oriented (and sometimes menial) dimensions of the promotion of consumption are explored in case studies by Smith Maguire of physical fitness and personal trainers, Pettinger of clothing retail, Wright of book retail, and Ocejo of the food and drink industry, and bartenders in particular. These chapters introduce advances made in the study of different cultural intermediary occupations, with some authors discussing occupations long-established as intermediaries, and others making the case for analysing occupations afresh through this lens.

In general, the complex variations and interactional contingencies involved in the qualification of goods remain under-examined and under-theorized. While not intended as an exhaustive template of theoretically informed research questions, the structure of the case studies may alert researchers to useful points of enquiry and comparison along three lines – historically, materially and impact – as discussed below.

## Thinking historically: how did we get here?

The first front on which to consider cultural intermediaries is historical. Through situating cultural intermediaries historically, we can assess claims as to the 'newness' of cultural intermediaries, creative work and cultural production, and the specific context and conditions for the emergence and development of these occupations. Gathering this type of knowledge allows the researcher to locate the formation of occupations – and their occupants, objects, institutions and markets – in line with long-term, ongoing shifts in cultural, economic and political structures. When the historical perspective is trained on developments *within* the occupation, this can also reveal the pace and pathways of professionalization: how an occupation's knowledge and practices become formalized and routinized, legitimized and reproduced.

The case study chapters introduce the historical origins of a variety of cultural intermediary occupations and highlight the significance of their connections with wider institutional developments, including globalized trade, changing communications technologies, growth of multinational corporations, decline of protected markets and other conditions that require market actors to make goods (products, corporations, nations) intelligible beyond a local market and differentiable in a global market. Such broad changes – at local and global scales – are interwoven with other factors, including the reproduction of long-term gendered divisions of work, the development of new occupational and professional codes of conduct and institutionalized devices (through which inter-intermediary competition for authority is waged, their outputs legitimized, and their occupations expanded in scope, professionalized and made durable), and the emergence of new (and the reframing of old) cultural goods for circulation. The development of many of the occupations covered in the case studies are linked in particular to changes within the consumer market. The increasing emphasis in leisure and retail sectors on notions of service, appearance management and the selling of experiences are relevant for various cultural intermediary occupations, as are various state-led initiatives that lend weight and resources to the promotion of particular practices (or discouragement of others). It is no surprise that the functions and functionaries of advertising, branding and public relations crop up in various chapters beyond those chapters explicitly devoted to these fields.

Attention is thus required to the wider changes in cultural fields and industries, and transitions in cultural and political-economic contexts that serve as points of genesis and/or stimuli for the growth and professionalization of cultural intermediary occupations. With this historical context as a foundation, we can better articulate the material practices of cultural intermediaries.

## Thinking materially: what takes place and how?

The second front on which to consider cultural intermediaries concerns the everyday accomplishment of their work via particular material practices, generic devices and subjective dispositions. Consideration of material practices involves asking about practices: How and when and by whom the work of framing and qualifying goods is accomplished? How and where cultural intermediaries are located in relation to other human and non-human actors? What forms of professional knowledge, cultural capital and other resources are called upon, how, and by whom in the performance of expertise in framing or qualifying of goods? Such a practice-oriented approach entails attention to occupational tools, bodies of knowledge, techniques and criteria; to the articulation and standardization of such devices through training programmes and in textbooks; to the ways in which devices are made manifest (and modified) in their 'street-level' implementation; to the ways in which dispositions, rationalities, motivations and aspirations inform the implementation and modification of devices; and to how idealized dispositions are rendered as devices and codified through occupational training and (quasi)professional socialization.

Common to many of the *Reader's* case studies is a discussion of the devices by which cultural intermediaries construct legitimacy for something else (products, or product qualities), and for themselves. Much rests on knowledge of the consumer – be it the end consumer, or the market actor who is the intended receiver of the cultural intermediary's influence – in terms of having access to such knowledge, and to the means of putting it into practice. Related to this is an understanding of the goods in question and, in particular, a view of their potential economic viability in the marketplace. Be it for cocktails, clothing or a creative advertising strategy, cultural intermediaries must be able to translate their knowledge – of the product, the consumer, the market – into 'saleability' and desirability.

Material practices also involve the performance of expertise and accomplishment of influence. Cultural intermediaries must make credible to others their diagnoses of the marketplace, interpretations of intended consumers, and framing of product qualities. The bases for the performance of expertise are varied. Expertise may be substantiated through reputation, or more formal modes of accreditation; it may also be accomplished in situ, in the interactions that form part of their work, and the embodied capital (appearance, habitus) that lends authority to presence and pronouncements. From an understanding of these different material practices, we can start to identify the outcomes and impacts of these occupations.

## Thinking about impact: so what?

The final front on which to consider cultural intermediaries concerns the occupation's impact on processes of value formation. This involves examinations of the flows and effect of their recommendations and devices, to build up a tempered view of their real-world impact on tastes, value and markets. Impact provides a further basis – along with historical development and material practices – for the empirical investigation and comparison of cultural intermediaries. Certainly, there are mythologized views that occupations rehearse about their own impact on, and significance to, their respective fields or even social life (see Moor's work on branding, for example: 2008, 2012, this volume). Setting these aside, a case can be made for cultural intermediaries' significance on economic and cultural grounds.

Cultural intermediaries have an impact with regard to the production and reproduction of markets. They produce discrete and concrete engagements with and between goods and individuals, which figure in the governmental mobilization of their consumers. While the focus is often on the impact of cultural intermediaries in reproducing the cultural foundations for the consumer marketplace (e.g. a fashion-oriented mentality; a valuing of novelty and competitive consumption), they can also have the potential to contribute to new and perhaps radical definitions of products, consumers and consumption, and substantiate 'provocations to think differently about how to live' (Lewis, this volume).

Cultural intermediaries also impact on the production and reproduction of discourses, shaping perceptions of the social world on an interpersonal and/or much wider scale, relative to the cultural intermediary's market context. Their impact may be downstream (e.g. impacting on client or consumer perceptions) or upstream, making their market devices and decisions credible to those in elite positions in a chain, who control the allocation of resources or distribution of information.

Furthermore, cultural intermediaries produce and reproduce the hinges between culture and economy, as is evidenced in their impacts on others' perceptions of value. In concert with other market actors, including consumers, cultural intermediaries construct new meanings of goods/practices and their value – at times, as a challenge to the established power hierarchy in the cultural field. Elsewhere, customers' understandings of 'value' and their purchasing decisions materialize through their interactions with cultural intermediaries, such as frontline service intermediaries.

Most broadly, cultural intermediaries impact upon notions of *what*, and thereby *who*, is legitimate, desirable and worthy – and thus, by definition, what and who is not (Smith Maguire and Matthews, 2012: 552). Thinking about cultural intermediaries is therefore an opportunity to think about the contested construction of cultural legitimacy. Such a concern combines Bourdieu's (1996) interest in the socially constructed boundaries between legitimate and illegitimate culture with new economic sociology's interest in the pragmatic accomplishment of boundaries (Callon et al., 2007).

## (Not) the last word ...

For a final comment, let us take our lead from the case study authors, who conclude their chapters with suggestions for future research directions. Reading across the collection, we can identify empirical directions for future research, with regard to advancing the historical, material and impact-oriented assessment of cultural intermediaries. Generally speaking, more work is required on how cultural intermediary occupations, goods, devices and dispositions are made manifest and modified in particular cultural contexts, be that in terms of new occupations, new goods or new markets. For example, established intermediary roles are gaining hold in new, emerging consumer markets – as is the case of fine wine promoters in China (Smith Maguire, 2013). Similarly, new media has paved the way for new types of occupants for established intermediary roles – as is the case of amateur (consumer) intermediaries for media goods (Fletcher and Lobato, 2013; Lee, 2012).

Moreover, the various authors in the *Reader* offer an invitation to think about consumer markets, cultural work, creative industries and the promotion of consumption in ways that are sensitive to both structures and institutions, and actors and agency. While new economic sociology – and its relations – have provided a lens and a vocabulary for disentangling the role of devices in the enactment of economies, making of markets and qualification of goods, less attention has been paid to the narratives, identities and emotions of those who deploy and enliven those devices. Yet, this dimension is striking in so much cultural intermediary research: if there is a single recurrent finding that echoes across interviews, it is that cultural intermediaries often love (some of) what they do. That passion informs how they tell stories and construct frames for goods; it provides an embodied filter for identifying what is 'good' or at least saleable; it compensates for some of the disadvantages of their occupational position. A focus on cultural intermediaries thus offers a close reading of the affective and subjective dimensions (pleasure, passion, pride; anxiety, envy, fear) that mobilize actors and animate markets.

In closing, then, we suggest that thinking with cultural intermediaries is fruitful for investigating the present and future intersections between production and consumption, and economy and culture. Cultural intermediaries are involved in the production of value and desire; thinking through their practices, challenges and rivals offers the potential to think ahead and identify new directions in the production of value. This is not the final word on the conceptualization of cultural intermediaries; current and future work will continue to challenge and refine our understanding of what cultural intermediaries do, and why they matter.

# PART I

# CONCEPTUAL AND METHODOLOGICAL FOUNDATIONS

# 1

# BOURDIEU ON CULTURAL INTERMEDIARIES

## JENNIFER SMITH MAGUIRE

... these 'need merchants', sellers of symbolic goods and services who always sell themselves as models and as guarantors of the value of their products, who sell so well because they believe in what they sell ... (Bourdieu, 1984: 365)

A student of cultural intermediaries is likely to be familiar with Pierre Bourdieu and – by virtue of oft-quoted passages, such as that above – some of the content of *Distinction: A Social Critique of the Judgement of Taste* (1984), Bourdieu's mammoth contribution to the sociology of cultural consumption. First published in 1979, *Distinction* presents cultural intermediaries as a group of taste makers and need merchants, whose work is part and parcel of an economy that requires the production of consuming tastes and dispositions (101[1]). Although cultural intermediaries are not discussed in a level of detail commensurate with the scale of Bourdieu's study, the popularization of Bourdieu's concept as a focus of research owes much to academic taste makers, who framed it as one of value for scholars of cultural studies and sociology of consumption (e.g. du Gay et al., 1997; Featherstone, 1991). More recently, research on cultural intermediaries has been engaged to a greater extent with actor network theory, economic sociology and cultural economy (e.g. Callon et al., 2002, 2007; see Nixon, McFall and others in this volume). Such engagements have contributed conceptual clarity and empirical detail, but sometimes at the price of forgetting Bourdieu (cf. Hinde and Dixon, 2007).

The chapter begins with a brief discussion of Bourdieu's larger project, and then identifies five interrelated dimensions of his account that pertain to cultural intermediaries. These five points are not exhaustive; rather, they are intended as a set of sensitizing themes and signposts, offering an invitation to return to *Distinction*.

# *DISTINCTION*: A TASTE OF THE BIG PICTURE

Bourdieu's oeuvre was broadly concerned with the processes by which social strati-fication is reproduced, vis-à-vis forms of economic and cultural capital, and the pursuit of social prestige (e.g. Bourdieu and Passeron, 1977). In the case of *Distinction*, the specific focus of the research was on how social stratification is reproduced and legitimated through notions of taste, as they are expressed and enacted through consumption. The research

> sought to determine how the cultivated disposition and cultural competence that are revealed in the nature of the cultural goods consumed, and in the way they are consumed, vary according to the category of agents and the area to which they are applied. (13)

The findings regarding that variance established two relationships. On the one hand, there is a close link between cultural practices (e.g. what people like to do, and how they do it) and educational capital and social origin (i.e. the amount of formal education received, and social class of parents); on the other hand, people with similar amounts of education from different social origins may be similar in what they like and do in areas of 'legitimate' culture (e.g. their views of modern art or composers – knowledge that is more readily transmitted via education) but will differ most in areas of everyday life, such as clothing, furniture and food choices (13,78, passim).

Those specific findings sit within a bigger picture: Bourdieu's conceptualiza-tion of taste (56, passim). Tastes are social; they are acquired through conditioning relative to social origin and trajectory (e.g. class position, education and upward or downward mobility), and are experienced as if they are natural and personal. Notions of 'good taste' and definitions of 'good culture' are oriented around the dominant group, but – in being socially constructed rather than inherent – are subject to negotiation by groups seeking to improve or defend their social posi-tion. Both because they are experienced as natural and because they are stratified in legitimacy relative to the dominant group's 'good' taste, expressions of taste unite people (who do and like similar things and tend to come from similar ori-gins) but also separate them from others with unlike tastes and origins. This is true not only of the appreciation of and access to established or 'elite' culture, but also – as noted above – the quotidian culture of dressing, home decorating, cook-ing and so on. In sum, taste is a mechanism of social reproduction: it enables the continuation – and veils the arbitrariness – of hierarchies between and within class groups.[2]

With his broader argument in mind, we can make better sense of Bourdieu's interest in cultural intermediaries as those who 'perform the tasks of gentle manip-ulation' of tastes (365): they are both shaping tastes for particular goods and prac-tices, and defining and defending (new class) group positions within society. The remainder of the chapter offers a five-point primer to Bourdieu's discussion, with regard to understanding cultural intermediaries' context, location and defining attributes:

1 New economy, new class relations
2 New occupations
3 Taste makers
4 Expertise and legitimacy
5 Cultural capital and dispositions

As a precursor, we must bear in mind that *Distinction* was based primarily on French survey data collected in 1963 and 1967–68. The account of cultural intermediaries is thus located in a particular time and place (some of the economic and cultural parameters of which are highlighted in point one),[3] but it is also a prisoner of the research design. Built into the analysis of the survey data were existing measures used by the INSEE (Institut National de la Statistique et des Études Économiques) for socio-occupational groups: cultural intermediaries (already) existed as a petite bourgeois category of occupations (505). This creates confusion with regard to cultural intermediaries: are they (simply) an INSEE socio-occupational category? Or, should they be defined by their role as taste makers? A typical Bourdieusian approach to cultural intermediaries takes the former route, locating them specifically within the new petite bourgeoisie, which

> comes into its own in all the occupations involving presentation and representation (sales, marketing, advertising, public relations, fashion, decoration and so forth) and in all the institutions providing symbolic goods and services. (359)

Within that large and internally differentiated class group are cultural intermediaries, 'the most typical of whom are the producers of cultural programmes on TV and radio or the critics of "quality" newspapers and magazines and all the writer-journalists and journalist-writers' (325).

Such a definition is problematic. The work of mediating cultural forms is performed by a range of occupations, which are neither monopolized by petite bourgeois critics, nor confined to the realm of 'creative' work (e.g. Negus, 2002; Nixon and du Gay, 2002). However, if Bourdieu's use of the specific term 'cultural intermediaries' is locked to the INSEE category, his analysis of what they do – the mediation of cultural forms, the pedagogic work of shaping tastes – spans his discussion of the 'new occupations' of the new petite bourgeoisie *and* new bourgeoisie (as discussed in points two and three). This chapter adopts the wider angle lens of the 'new occupations' to read Bourdieu on cultural intermediaries, and, as such, endorses the latter route: a conceptual approach that defines cultural intermediaries by what they do (Smith Maguire and Matthews, 2010, 2012).

## 1. NEW ECONOMY, NEW CLASS RELATIONS

Bourdieu's analysis of cultural intermediary occupations is informed by what he regarded as a 'new economy … whose functioning depends as much on the production of needs and consumers as on the production of goods' (310). Bourdieu was not alone in noting the expansion of a consumer economy over the 20th century and considering its consequences for the rise of a consumer culture (e.g. Lash and Urry, 1994; Slater, 1997). In this new economy, 'changes in economic production … place ever greater emphasis on the production of needs and the artificial creation of scarcity' (369). Hence the need for needs merchants and taste makers.

Furthermore, cultural intermediaries cannot be understood outside of changes in class relations arising from the expansion of higher education. As sex- and class-based barriers to educational qualifications diminish, several things occur. There is an 'overproduction of qualifications, and [a] consequent devaluation' (147) – a process familiar to any university student today. At the same time, as access to bourgeois jobs is arguably more open (with points of entry structured through educational qualifications), competition for those jobs intensifies:

> The combined effect is to encourage the creation of a large number of *semi-bourgeois* positions, produced by redefining old positions or inventing new ones, and designed to save unqualified 'inheritors' from down-classing and to provide parvenus with an approximate pay-off for their devalued qualifications. (150; see also 357, passim)

These new occupations are the 'refuge' of the sons and daughters of the bourgeoisie who, failing to acquire appropriate educational capital, are in danger of *déclassement*, and the sons and daughters of the petite bourgeoisie (and working class) who have acquired appropriate educational capital, but find that their expectations of upward social mobility are not matched by objective opportunities (147).

Therefore, cultural intermediary occupations are, for Bourdieu, an effect both of an economy requiring the production of need, and of class anxiety about upward and downward social mobility. It is the latter factor that attracts most of Bourdieu's attention: this strengthens his understanding of the subjective dynamics at play for the new petite bourgeoisie; however, it is also a limitation, as noted by critics who complain that Bourdieu largely ignores the institutional, political-economic context of cultural industries and the division of labour that has developed therein (e.g. Garnham, 1986)[4]. With that in mind, let us now consider Bourdieu's view of these new occupations.

## 2. NEW OCCUPATIONS

Bourdieu's concern was with the new, or intensified, professionalization of existing occupations (as noted by his contemporaries; e.g. Wilensky, 1964), through which the new class fractions could distinguish themselves from their established counterparts (358). Critics have called into question the 'newness' of Bourdieu's economy (as one uniquely involved in the production of cultural tastes) and cultural intermediary occupations (e.g. Nixon and du Gay, 2002); nevertheless, what is of particular use in Bourdieu's account is the emphasis on the professionalization of occupations that mediate between the fields of production and consumption.

The redefinition of old, and invention of new, occupations is especially found in the 'most ill-defined and professionally unstructured occupations, and in the newest sectors of cultural and artistic production, such as … radio, TV, marketing, advertising, social science research and so on' (151). As noted above, most of the attention in Bourdieusian cultural intermediary research has been on the new petite bourgeois occupations involved with presentation, representation and the provision of symbolic goods and services (359). In moving into these new sectors of the economy, the new petite bourgeoisie could exploit the relative lack of bureaucratization in order to match the occupations to their ambitions (359).

However, Bourdieu also discusses the new bourgeoisie, who have adapted to 'the new mode of profit appropriation' (311) through new occupations – in particular, executives 'in marketing or management' (301), and

> the vendors of symbolic goods and services, the directors and executives of firms in tourism and journalism, publishing and the cinema, fashion and advertising, decoration and property development. (310–11)

These new 'masters of the economy' (315), in concert with the petite bourgeoisie, are the 'vanguard' of new tastes for goods, and a new 'art of living' (370–1). Yet, despite their obvious significance, there remains a lack of attention to the new bourgeois fraction of cultural intermediaries and their relationship to the new petite bourgeois occupations. While research might implicitly draw from across a class spectrum (in fashion, for example, studies of buyers as well as sales assistants: see Entwistle, 2006; Pettinger, this volume), the study of intermediaries reflects social scientists' difficulty in gaining access to the powerful as research subjects.[5]

Both class fractions of new occupations are involved in the creation of wants. The new bourgeois cultural intermediaries are the instigators of new tastes and practices, because their profits and power are reliant on the production of needs (310). The new petite bourgeois occupations are closely aligned with their new bourgeois counterparts: they accomplish the objective orchestration between production and consumption (230, passim) not only because it is their paid work to do so, but also because in so doing they assuage subjective anxieties about class mobility. Thus, the new occupations reproduce both the consumer economy and the class positions of their practitioners.

Bourdieu offers a number of partial catalogues of the new occupations (e.g. 220, 310, 359, 365; 1996: 229). For example, they include:

the aesthetic and semi-aesthetic, intellectual and semi-intellectual occupations, the various consultancy services (psychology, vocational guidance, speech therapy, beauty advice, marriage counselling, diet advice and so on), the educational and para-educational occupations ... and jobs involving presentation and representation (tour organizers, hostesses ... press attachés, public relations people and so on). (152)

Such diverse lists raise the question of what cultural intermediaries have in common that defines them, and differentiates them from other occupations. This brings us to the third point.

## 3. TASTE MAKERS

Cultural intermediaries are defined by their work as taste makers. This is intertwined with Bourdieu's understanding of how taste operates as 'a match-maker' between people and things (243). Cultural intermediaries cannot enforce desires or purchases; rather, they create the conditions for consumers to identify their tastes in goods. At a general level, this entails what Bourdieu calls the 'ethical retooling' of consumer culture: the new class fractions pursue – and encourage others to adopt – a 'hedonistic morality of consumption, credit, spending and enjoyment' in place of an 'ascetic ethic of ... abstinence, sobriety, saving and calculation' (310). By using that new style of life to set themselves apart from the established classes, the new groups act as a 'transmission belt', pulling others into the 'new morality of pleasure as a duty' by having made it the stakes in status competition (365, 367). Bourdieu saw the new bourgeoisie and new petite bourgeoisie working in tandem as taste makers in this ethical imposition: 'the new petite bourgeoisie ... is predisposed to collaborate with total conviction in imposing the life-style handed down by the new bourgeoisie' (365).

At the same time and more immediately, cultural intermediaries attempt to construct elective affinities between goods and tastes. This involves fitting goods to existing tastes and vice versa. For example, as a young advertising executive explains: 'In my business, we're constantly classifying people, there are social classes, castes, and it's a matter of fitting a product to the right caste' (299). Through their 'symbolic imposition' (362, passim) of meanings, cultural intermediaries frame goods and practices so that they appear to the consumer to 'go together' with his or her taste (232). In this, cultural intermediaries do not act alone; Bourdieu notes the role of retailers, popular media and other institutions (231–2; see also 1996: 229) in assisting or channelling the perceptions and choices of consumers.

In attempting to effect this ethical and symbolic imposition, cultural intermediaries require a degree of authority – their constructed meanings and personal lifestyles must carry credibility if they are to be taken up by others. We now turn to this issue of legitimacy, which was central to Bourdieu's account (see also 1990a, 1996).

# 4. EXPERTISE AND LEGITIMACY

Shaping tastes and matching things to people require that cultural intermediaries frame particular practices and products as worthy of their claimed value, involving them in constructing repertoires of cultural legitimacy. Consequently, cultural intermediaries are not simply taste makers; they are *professional* taste makers and 'authorities of legitimation' (1990a: 96). This role implicates cultural intermediaries in the long-term struggle for dominance between different groups, which is 'fought' in part through definitions of good taste and the appropriate relationship to legitimate culture – a struggle that Bourdieu dates back to the 17th century (2). In the context of mid-20th century France, Bourdieu understands this struggle in terms of the new class fractions' attempts to establish their (occupational and generational) distance from, and superiority to, their established bourgeois and petite bourgeois counterparts, via their 'casual' lifestyles and consuming habits (e.g. 311, 325, passim).

Broadly, cultural intermediaries are concerned with legitimacy on two, interrelated fronts – and in both respects, they operate within and between the sphere of the culturally legitimate (with its established norms of what is good) and the sphere of the legitimizable (1990a: 96). The first front concerns the social standing of their occupation (in relation to other more and less legitimate, competing authorities). As the new petite bourgeoisie lack an established position of authority, they pursue established channels of professionalization or 'symbolic rehabilitation strategies' through which, for example, the secretary is redubbed the 'personal assistant' (358) and the bartender the mixologist (Ocejo, this volume), whereas the new bourgeoisie derive authority from their established class position and their positions of dominance within their fields. Through professionalization strategies, 'new' cultural intermediary occupations will emerge, to compete over what counts as 'good' (or cool, prestigious, fashionable and so forth). Negotiating the precariousness of one's expertise is arguably more pertinent to the new petite bourgeois occupations; however, the professionalization of such fields as advertising, marketing and management will also serve to reinforce the authority of the new bourgeoisie within.

The second dimension of legitimacy concerns the field within which a cultural intermediary is located (and thus the goods, practices and forms of capital associated with that field). Drawing on their knowledge of the sphere of legitimacy (furnished via educational capital and – especially for those originating in the bourgeoisie – the family), cultural intermediaries work to canonize the 'not-yet-legitimate' (326). One way in which this occurs is through transposing the hallmarks of established authority (such as an emphasis on mastery of abstract knowledge, and theoretical criteria for assessments of quality) on to new cultural forms. As a result, there is a strategic migration of restricted culture into the field of large-scale production (583; 1996) and a transformation of legitimate culture into middle-brow taste (327, passim). In this way, new cultural forms are upgraded (and subject to a mode of 'poor man's' (220) connoisseurship, through which no object is seemingly too banal for aesthetic discernment); so too are the cultural intermediaries, as masters of new forms of good taste.

The ability of a cultural intermediary to undertake the construction of legitimacy thus hinges on particular forms of capital and subjective dispositions – the personal dimension of the work, which constitutes the final point.

# 5. CULTURAL CAPITAL AND DISPOSITIONS

Cultural intermediaries are more than simply their occupational category. They are taste makers and legitimation authorities *because* of their personal investment in the work. Bourdieu's account suggests that there is a strong link between cultural intermediary occupations and individual practitioners' habitus, and particularly their stocks of cultural capital and subjective dispositions. This dimension of Bourdieu's account offers useful insights into the subjective dynamics that underpin the reproduction of an economy of cultural goods: dynamics which often go missing when the focus is macro- and micro-scale conventions and structures, be they institutional arrangements or market devices.

Bourdieu calls attention to the importance of class position in providing cultural intermediaries with the cultural capital and dispositions necessary to accomplish their work. Cultural intermediaries rely on their 'good manners, good taste or physical charm' (152); 'familiarity with the culture of the dominant class and a mastery of the signs and emblems of distinction and taste' (141); and 'aesthetic dispositions' and appropriate forms of 'self-presentation' (362). Such capacities are supplied most assuredly through bourgeois origins and internalized as habitus. However, education and (now) over fifty years of middle-brow, popularized forms of bourgeois culture also transmit, if less securely, the resources required for the work of an arbiter of cultural legitimacy and taste.

Bourdieu's discussion of the new petite bourgeoisie is further developed with regard to the dispositions that channel them into such occupations and provide them with crucial occupational resources. In parallel with the class anxiety noted above, there is also a perceived harmony between personal tastes and professional function and position, which gives rise to a vocational mentality (110, 240, 362, passim). Using a literary critic as an example, Bourdieu notes the 'elective affinity between the journalist, his paper and his readers' (240): the cultural intermediary is also his/her own ideal consumer. In typifying their market, the cultural intermediary is thus also well-placed to understand and direct it – a crucial resource for a taste maker. As a result, the literary critic writes with 'a perfect sincerity which is essential in order to be believed and therefore effective' (578). The harmony between the personal and professional generates a sincere disposition, which is fundamental to the effectiveness of the new occupations' symbolic and ethical impositions. As a result, cultural intermediaries do not experience their work as instrumental calculation because it is an expression of their own tastes and dispositions. In short: they 'sell so well because they believe in what they sell' (365).

Bourdieu's cultural intermediary seemingly arrives at an occupation with a fully-formed arsenal of tastes and dispositions that suit the job. This is problematic in that it presents a static notion of the intermediary (whose tastes and capital surely develop over the course of their work; e.g. Entwistle, 2006). It nonetheless has the benefit of casting light on how individuals inhabit these occupations and embody their intended markets, and thus on how the reproduction of consumer economies rests on the personal, affective investments of its promoters. In addition, Bourdieu paints an ideal type of cultural intermediary – sincere, vocationally-oriented, motivated by inter- or intra-class dynamics to proselytize for new tastes and needs. While this does not capture the entire complex range of positions and negotiations adopted by cultural intermediaries, it offers a set of sensitizing questions to ask, for example, of those who do not like what they sell (e.g. Kuipers, 2012), or do not like the selling of what they believe (e.g. Smith Maguire, 2008b). What are the comparative experiences (of success or failure, career trajectories and burnout) for those cultural intermediaries whose habitus does not fit the job?

This chapter suggests that *Distinction* provides not a fully-formed account, but a provocation to further examine the objective relations and subjective dynamics of taste making in contemporary consumer cultures. In closing, it should be noted that the themes outlined above continue to inform more recent new economic sociology research, and highlight areas for future research. First, recent research has more fully developed the economic and longer-term historical context of cultural intermediaries (e.g. McFall, 2004); however, the changing class dynamics that generate cultural intermediary work, and the role of cultural intermediaries in generating and legitimating new taste regimes, remain underexplored. Second, there remains strong interest in cultural intermediaries as taste makers, and growing attention to the relations between them in processes of qualification of goods (e.g. Méadel and Rabeharisoa, 2001); and yet, the powerful remain under-represented in our understanding of these regimes of mediation. Third, as Bourdieu's 'transmission belt' of consumption has been replaced with more empirically grounded accounts of the governmental mobilization of consumers (e.g. Moor, 2012), the material practices through which product properties and consumer desires inform each other and give rise to conventionalized points of attachments remain an unexhausted area of research.

Fourth, professionalization strategies remain central to analysing cultural intermediary occupations and the strategies by which they accomplish and reinforce their intended impacts (e.g. Kuipers, 2012); nevertheless, further attention is required to identify the range of strategies by which cultural intermediaries delimit and defend their occupational position against the ongoing emergence of new taste makers. Fifth, the subjective dimensions of cultural intermediary work remain a focus for exploring the 'devices and dispositions' involved in the promotion of consumption (du Gay, 2004). However, the current emphasis on conventions and devices risks reducing the agency of market actors to routinized procedures and formulaic performances. Bourdieu's cultural intermediaries offer a point of entry to study how tastes are formed, legitimated and continue to develop. By locating market actors at the intersection of forms of economic organization, group status competition and individual mentalities, Bourdieu's account assists in keeping agency, passions, anxieties and habituations in the frame.

## NOTES

1   Page numbers refer to *Distinction* (Bourdieu, 1984) unless otherwise noted.
2   *Distinction* can thus be understood as Bourdieu's elaboration on the relationship between class and status as proposed by Weber (1946b), within the context of contemporary consumer culture and the economy of cultural goods (xii).
3   Some have questioned whether the case of France – with its particular relationship to 'elite' culture – maps on to other societies (e.g. Garnham, 1986; Jenkins, 1992). However, Bourdieu suggested that the issue isn't the *means and stakes* (e.g. elite culture) but the *game*; thus, the findings should be 'valid ... for every stratified society' (xii).
4   Bourdieu would likely have viewed a request for 'better specification of the division of labour involved in mediating production and consumption' (Hesmondhalgh, 2006b: 227) as falling into the tradition of Howard Becker (1982), against whose analysis Bourdieu frames his own as one of exploring the '*objective relations* which are constitutive of the structure of the field and which orient the struggles aiming to conserve or transform it' (1996: 205).
5   It is telling that the interview in *Distinction* with a new bourgeois advertising executive (who derived from a bourgeois family) was enabled by a personal connection (300). Kuipers (this volume) usefully reflects on gaining access to such respondents.

# 2

# CULTURAL WORK AND CREATIVE INDUSTRIES[1]

## TOBY MILLER

In a First Wave economy, land and farm labor are the main 'factors of production.'
In a Second Wave economy, the land remains valuable while the 'labor' becomes
massified around machines and larger industries. In a Third Wave economy, the
central resource – a single word broadly encompassing data, information, images,
symbols, culture, ideology, and values – is actionable knowledge – *A Magna Carta
for the Information Age*. (Dyson et al., 1994)

This chapter offers a *tour d'horizon* of macroeconomic and theoretical developments
in cultural labor and the rhetoric surrounding creative industries. It indicates the
ongoing importance of intermediaries in the area of culture and the media, *contra*
the beguiling idea that they are *passés*, and proposes that those who argue for
disintermediation through technology and creativity, such as signatories to the epi-
graph above, are themselves intermediaries.

Cultural work includes a wide array of occupations that generate and use the
'actionable knowledge' so prized in the *Magna Carta* of cybertarianism[2] quoted
above. Some cultural jobs directly create performances and texts, while others
involve intermediation. Consider this list:

- artists, comprising musicians, directors, writers and actors
- artisans, including sound engineers, editors, cinematographers, and graphic designers
- impresarios, proprietors, executives, promoters, advertisers, and curators
- regulators, censors, politicians, bureaucrats, and litigators
- lobby groups
- critics, audiences, journalists, and consumers.

The positions that undertake cultural intermediation come from the latter four groups. They operate as gatekeepers, determining who and what counts as cultural.
Cultural workers operate within institutional contexts:

- private bureaucracies – managing investment, production, and distribution across the media while relying on public agencies to aid accumulation
- public bureaucracies – offering what capitalism cannot, while comporting themselves in an ever more commercial manner
- small businesses – run by charismatic individuals
- networks – fluid associations formed to undertake specific projects
- families – shared homes, live-work spaces, pop-up galleries, bars, coffee shops, arenas, transport systems, and stadia.

A significant proportion of highly-qualified artists and intellectuals experience precarious employment, despite their generally middle-class origins. This situation is frequently in stark contrast to that of their parents, for whom schooling either solidified secure employment or provided a route to class transformation. The new precariousness is connected to the discourse of the creative industries.

That discourse began in the 1960s through somewhat improbable cultural intermediaries – Republican Party politicians. Barry Goldwater, Ronald Reagan, and their kind railed against 'Great Society' liberalism. Defeat at the 1964 Presidential election, seemingly their death rattle, was soon followed by Reagan's successful 1966 campaign for the governorship of California. He launched it with the words: 'I propose … "A Creative Society" … to discover, enlist and mobilize the incredibly rich human resources of California [through] innumerable people of creative talent.'[3]

Reagan's principal domestic legacy was, of course, to reverse the state's role in democratically redistributing wealth. Subsequent disciples of inequality – the various Bushes, William Jefferson Clinton, and Barack Hussein Obama II – carried on this work. But Reagan's proto-gubernatorial address also heralded neoliberal ideology, which was part of the Global North's economic shift from agriculture and manufacturing to services and culture via the creative industries and their labor force, the cognitariat.

## THE COGNITARIAT

In the 1970s, pundits saw that what we can now discern as the cognitariat would be vital to productivity gains (Bar with Simard, 2006). To Cold-War Yanqui futurists such as former National Security Advisor Zbigniew Brzezinski (1969), professional anti-Marxist Ithiel de Sola Pool (1983), and cultural conservative Daniel Bell (1977), converged communication technologies promised both the permanent removal of grubby manufacturing from the Global North to the South and continued US textual and technical power, provided that the blandishments of socialism and negativity towards global business did not create class struggle.

The rhetoric of these intermediaries and their neoliberal successors maintains that technology can unlock creativity, which is supposedly lurking unbidden in everyone, waiting to make us happy and productive. The hidden correlative of such transformations is that we become contingent labor, members of a precarious cognitariat. Antonio Negri (2007) redeployed the concept of the cognitariat from Reaganite futurist and digital *Magna Carta* signatory Alvin Toffler (1983). Negri defines the cognitariat as people undertaking casualized cultural work who have heady educational backgrounds yet live at the uncertain interstices of capital, qualifications, and government in a post-Fordist era of mass unemployment, limited-term work, and occupational insecurity. They are sometimes complicit with these circumstances because their identities are shrouded in autotelic modes of being. Work is pleasure and *vice versa*; labor becomes its own reward (Gorz, 2004).

These cognitarians putatively transcend the work of cultural intermediaries. The comparatively cheap and easy access to making and distributing meaning afforded by Internet media and genres is thought to have eroded the one-way hold on culture that saw a small segment of the world as producers and the larger segment as consumers. New technologies supposedly allow us all to become simultaneously cultural consumers and producers (prosumers) without the say-so of media gatekeepers. The result is said to be a democratized media, higher skill levels, and powerful challenges to old patterns of expertise and institutional authority – hence the term 'disintermediation' (Graham, 2008; Ritzer and Jurgenson, 2010).

In this cybertarian world free of intermediaries, fans write zines that become screenplays. Coca-Cola hires streetwise African Americans to drive through the inner city selling soda and playing hip-hop. AT&T pays San Francisco buskers to mention the company in their songs. Urban performance poets rhyme about Nissan cars for cash, simultaneously hawking, entertaining, and researching. Subway's sandwich commercials are marketed as made by teenagers. Cultural-studies majors become designers, and graduate students in New York and Los Angeles read scripts for producers then pronounce on whether they tap into audience interests. Precariously employed part-timers spy on fellow spectators in theaters to see how they respond to coming attractions. Opportunities to vote in the Eurovision Song Contest or a reality program determine both the success of contestants and the profile of active viewers, who can be monitored and wooed in the future. End-user licensing agreements ensure that players of corporate games online sign over their cultural moves and perspectives to the very companies whom they are paying in order to participate (Miller, 2007). This is the world of the prosumer, who breaks down the distinction separating making and receiving culture and rejects intermediaries (Ritzer and Jurgenson, 2010). But there is another side to it

for those who can keep a job in the post-Fordist labour market, decent and meaningful work opportunities are reducing at a phenomenal pace in the sense that, for a high proportion of low- and middle-skilled workers, full-time, lifelong employment is unlikely. (Orsi, 2009: 35)

Cultural work is subject to local, national, regional, and international fetishization of each component, matching the way that the labor undertaken is largely fetishized away from the texts and performances produced. Business leeches want flexibility in the numbers they employ, the technology they use, the place where they produce, and the amount they pay – and inflexibility of ownership and control. The orthodoxies that created this economy, the neoclassical *doxa* preached by neoliberal chorines, favor an economy where competition and opportunity cost are in the litany and dissent is unforgiveable, as crazed as collective industrial organization. Hence the success of Mindworks Global Media, a company outside New Delhi that provides Indian-based journalists and copyeditors who work long-distance for newspapers whose reporters are supposedly in the US and Europe. There are 35–40 percent cost savings (Lakshman, 2008). Or consider Poptent, an intermediary advertising firm that under-cuts big competitors who actually make commercials by exploiting prosumers' labor in the name of 'empowerment.' That empowerment takes the following form: the creators of the homemade commercials they distribute make US$7500; Poptent receives a management fee of US$40,000; and the buyer saves about US$300,000 on the usual price (Chmielewski, 2012).

Is this democratization, or exploitation?

Even reactionary bodies like the US National Governors Association recognize the eventual reality: 'routine tasks that once characterized middle class work have either been eliminated by technological change or are now conducted by low-wage but highly skilled workers' (Sparks and Watts, 2011: 6).

## CREATIVE SEDUCTION

As per Reagan's doctrine, many US municipal, regional, state, and national funding agencies (also intermediaries) have dropped venerable administrative categories like arts and crafts, replacing them with the discourse of the creative industries. The US President's Committee on Arts and the Humanities welcomes the 'Creative Economy' and

> focuses its leadership, with other agencies and the private sector, on the power of the arts and humanities as an economic driver, sustaining critical cultural resources and fostering civic investment in cultural assets and infrastructure. These efforts help speed innovation and expand markets and consumers, directly benefiting local economies. (www.pcah.gov/creative-economy – accessed December 2013)

Similar things have happened across the globe. In 2006, Rwanda convened a global conference on the 'Creative Economy' to take the social healing engendered by culture and commodify/govern it. Brazil houses the United Nations Conference on Trade and Development and the United Nations Development Program's International Forum for Creative Industries, which decrees that '[c]reativity, more than labor and capital, or even traditional technologies, is deeply embedded in every country's cultural context' (United Nations Conference on Trade and Development, 2004: 3). The United Nations Educational, Scientific and Cultural Organization's Global Alliance for Cultural Diversity (2002) heralds creative industries as a *portmanteau* term that covers the cultural sector and goes further, beyond output and into the favored neoliberal *canard* of process. Even India's venerable last gasp of Nehruvianism, its Planning Commission, has a committee for creative industries (Ramanathan, 2006). China has moved 'from an older, state-dominated focus on cultural industries … towards a more market-oriented pattern of creative industries' (Keane, 2006) and Singapore, Hong Kong, Japan, and South Korea follow similar strategies (Peichi, 2008; Cunningham, 2009c).

True believers argue for an efflorescence of creativity, cultural difference, import substitution, and national and regional pride and influence thanks to new technologies and innovative firms (Cunningham, 2009a). In the words of lapsed-leftist cultural theorist and inaugural President of the European Bank for Reconstruction and Development Jacques Attali, a new 'mercantile order forms wherever a creative class masters a key innovation from navigation to accounting or, in our own time, where services are most efficiently mass produced, thus generating enormous wealth' (2008: 31). This allegedly gives rise to an 'aristocracy of talent' (Kotkin, 2001: 22) where mercurial meritocrats luxuriate in ever changing techniques, technologies, and networks. Labor is acknowledged by its intermediaries in this brave newness, provided that it is abstracted from physical, dirty work (Mattelart, 2002), as per Toffler, Bell, de Sola Pool, and Brzezinski's prescriptions.

The high priest of creative-industries intermediation, business professor Richard Florida (2002), speaks of a 'creative class®' that is revitalizing post-industrial towns in the Global North devastated by the relocation of manufacturing to places with cheaper labor pools. He argues that the revival of such cities is driven by a magic elixir of tolerance, technology, and talent, as measured by same-sex households, broadband connections, and higher degrees respectively. Florida has even trademarked the concept: his claim to own the 'creative class®' is asserted with the US Patent and Trademark Office via registration number 3298801 (http://tess2.uspto.gov).[4]

Creative-industries discourse has become a grand passion of the age for intermediaries of many stripes. Urbanists, geographers, economists, planners, public intellectuals, think-tank inmates, and policy wonks have all been central to its development and dispersal via a blend of research, innovation, and inclusiveness (Brint et al., 2009). These intermediaries articulate research, the arts, public policy, and everyday life to capital. In order to transcend the intellectual's traditional status as 'the little match seller, nose pressed to the window, looking in on the grand life within' (Cunningham, 2006), many have shifted their discourse to focus on comparative advantage and competition rather than heritage and aesthetics, as neoliberal emphases on unlocking creativity succeed old-school protections of cultural patrimony. The alleged capacity of the market to govern everything opens up new life worlds. Pragmatic leftists no longer even speak of mixing socialist ideals with reformism. Former historian and poet Stuart Cunningham, for instance, favors an instrumental 'matching of curriculum to career' via 'practical business challenges' such that 'non-market disciplines' compete with colleagues in forging 'an alliance with the business sector' (2009b, 2007b, 2007a).

These newly powerful intermediaries, who were once free-floating but socially ineffectual humanities critics, are in thrall to the idea that culture is an endlessly growing resource capable of dynamizing society.

Peak bodies parrot their prayers. The Australian Academy of the Humanities calls for 'research in the humanities and creative arts' to be tax-exempt based on its contribution to research and development, and subject to the same surveys of 'employer demand' as the professions and sciences (Australian Academy of the Humanities, 2012; also see Cunningham, 2007a). The Australian Research Council's Centre of Excellence for Creative Industries and Innovation has solemnly announced an 'industryfacing [sic] spin-off from the centre's mapping work, Creative Business Benchmarker' (Cunningham, 2011b).

The British Academy seeks to understand and further the 'creative and cultural industries' (2004: viii). In partnership with the Arts and Humanities Research Council, the UK's National Endowment for Science, Technology & the Arts says '[t]he arts and humanities have a particularly strong affiliation with the creative industries' and provide research that 'helps to fuel' them, in turn boosting innovation more broadly (Bakhshi et al., 2008: 1). In Canada, the Presidents of the Universities of Toronto and British Columbia advise that:

> [I]ndependent-minded university and college graduates from diverse backgrounds are critical to building creative societies with innovative foundations.
>
> [A] culture of innovation and entrepreneurship should be promoted in all sectors of the economy, not least social agencies, non-profit enterprises, public administration, and postsecondary and health-care institutions. (Naylor and Toope, 2010)

Academic cultural intermediaries delivering the glad tidings descend on welcoming burghers eager to be made over by branded celebrities whose books appear on airport news stands rather than cloistered scholarly shelves (Gibson and Klocker, 2004). Prone to cybertarianism, these dutiful chorines of digital capitalism and the technological sublime pile out of business class and onto the jet way in three major groups. Richard Floridians hop a limousine from the airport then ride around town on bicycles to spy on ballet-loving, gay-friendly, multicultural computer geeks who have relocated to de-industrialized, freezing rustbelts. True-believer Australian creationists criticize cultural studies as residually socialistic and textual. And Brussels bureaucrats offer blueprints to cities eager for affluence and ready for reinvention via culture and tolerance. The promise on offer is a makeover 'from the rusty coinage of "cultural industries" to newly minted "creative industries"' (Ross, 2006–07: 1). For a date with Florida, visit http://creativeclass.com (accessed December 2013); if you'd prefer Attali, who also knows how to make use of public money, the Global

Speakers Bureau is your destination (http://speakers.co.uk/csaWeb/speaker. JAQATT (accessed December 2013); Stevenson, 1993). It's PowerPoint intellection and it's coming to a town near you.

The working assumption of these intermediaries is that the culture industries' intermediation between art and the public has been overrun by individual creativity. In this Marxist/Godardian fantasy, media technologies obliterate geography, sovereignty, ownership, and hierarchy, alchemizing truth and beauty. People fish, film, fornicate, and finance from morning to midnight, frolicking in a deregulated, individuated world that makes consumers into producers, frees the disabled from confinement, encourages new subjectivities, rewards intellect and competitiveness, links people across cultures, and allows billions of flowers to bloom in a post-political cornucopia. Consumption is privileged, production is discounted, and labor redefined (Dahlström and Hermelin, 2007). It becomes both a pleasure and a responsibility to invest in human capital – signs of a robust civil society and private self.

# THE MORNING AFTER

But after all that free-floating fornication and professorial promotion, one must awaken and ask 'Who *is* that person next to me?' Consider the artists who are invoked by creative-industry consultants in city regeneration proposals as attractions for accountants and lawyers to shift location. The artists blink, pay newly inflated rents, or move on.

And there are definitional and hence statistical problems with the very concept of creative industries. The assumption that what is made in a sector of the economy does not *characterize* it, that 'creativity' is not an input but an industry's defining quality, is misleading. A bizarre shift in adjectival meaning catalogues anything profitable under 'creative'. More precise efforts at definition have significantly diminished the claims made for the sector's economic contributions, unmasking the boosterist sleight of hand that places culture at the center of economic innovation by pretending that it encompasses corporate and governmental information technology (Miller, 2009; Garnham, 2005; Cunningham, 2011a). True believers have generated a revealing figure of speech designed to counter this critique. The metaphor of a 'creative trident' covers

> the total of creative occupations within the core creative industries (specialists), plus the creative occupations employed in other industries (embedded) plus the business and support occupations employed in creative industries who are often responsible for managing and technically supporting creative activity (support). (Cunningham, 2011b)

This concept adequately covers the occupations listed earlier, but fails to specify their place in culture or the economy or the transformations they embody.

There is also an issue with these intermediaries' Schumpeterian faith in small businesses and their role in cultural work. Giant corporations rarely innovate. But that does not represent a shift in the center of gravity. The culture industries are still largely controlled by media and communications conglomerates. They gobble up smaller companies that invent products and services, 'recycling audio-visual cultural material created by the grassroots genius, exploiting their intellectual property and generating a standardized business sector that excludes, and even distorts, its very source of business,' to quote *The Hindu* (Ramanathan, 2006). The beneficiaries of innovations by 'talented amateurs' are corporations (Ross, 2006–07; Marcus, 2005). In other words, the cognitariat creates 'cool stuff' that others exploit.

There is minimal proof that a creative class® exists or 'creative cities' outperform their drab brethren economically. There is no evidence that the tastes, values, life-styles, and locations of artists and accountants match, despite their being bundled together in the creative concept. The centrality of gay culture in the Floridian cal-culus derives from assuming same-sex households are queer (but university dorms and sorority/fraternity houses are not quite there). Even if this were accurate, many wealthy cities in the US roll with reaction (consider Orlando and Phoenix) (Nathan, 2005; Hoggart, 2004: 168; Linklater, 2006; Ross, 2011).

The idea of urbanism incipient in US demographic statistics includes the sub-urbs (which now hold more residents than do cities), so that, too, is suspect in terms of the importance of downtown lofts to economies; nor is it sensible to assume other countries replicate the massive internal mobility of the US population. Numerous surveys pour scorn on the claim that quality of life is central to select-ing business campuses as opposed to low cost, good communications technology, proximity to markets, and adequate transport. Companies seek skills when deciding where to locate their businesses – but skills also seek work. City centers largely attract the young who are not yet breeding. And a European Commission evalua-tion of 29 Cities of Culture disclosed that their principal goal – economic growth stimulated by the public subvention of culture to renew failed cities – has failed. Glasgow, for instance, was initially hailed as a success of the program; but many years down the line, it has not seen sustained growth (Oakley, 2004, 2006, 2010; Bell, 2007; Freeman, 2007; Huijgh, 2007; Peck, 2007; Ross, 2006–07).

And today's discourse of the creative industries ignores some critical issues. For instance, the Australian Council for the Humanities, Arts and Social Sciences' submis-sion to its national Productivity Commission refers to a 'post-smokestack era' (CHASS, 2006) – a utopia for workers, consumers, and residents, with residues of code rather than carbon. Yet the Political Economy Research Institute's 2004 *Misfortune 100: Top Corporate Air Polluters in the United States* placed media owners at numbers 1, 3, 16, 22, and 39. Media production relies on the exorbitant water-use of computer technology, while making semi-conductors requires hazardous chemicals, including carcinogens. Waste from discarded electronics is one of the biggest sources of heavy metals and toxic pollutants in the world's trash piles. The accumulation of electronic hardware causes grave environmental and health harm as noxious chemicals, gases, and metals seep into landfills and water sources from the Global North to Malaysia, Brazil, South Korea, China, Mexico, Viet Nam, Nigeria, and India. Pre-teen girls pick away without protection at discarded televisions and computers, looking for precious metals to sell. The remains are burned or left in landfills (Maxwell and Miller, 2012).

## CONCLUSION

At best, creative-industries discourse offers 'an industry training program' (Turner, 2012). At worst, it stratifies cultural labor markets and generates unsafe environmental detritus. And the intermediation it announces as outmoded continues to matter, arching all the way from Cold War futurism to creative-industry divination, via academia, bureaucracy, and journalism. Cybertarian fantasies birth new cognitarian and ecological inequalities. Intermediation continues its work.

## NOTES

1   Segments of this chapter draw on work I have done over three decades, some of which has appeared in various forms elsewhere, but not as assembled, added to, and subtracted from here.
2   Cybertarianism is a fantasy mixture of libertarianism and faith in new technology. It assumes that individualism is the core of innovation.
3   Reagan was not original. In 1848, Ralph Waldo Emerson wrote that a 'creative economy is the fuel of magnificence' (1909–14).
4   Thanks to Bill Grantham for directing me to the Office's Trademark Electronic Search System.

# 3

# CULTURAL INTERMEDIARIES OR MARKET DEVICE? THE CASE OF ADVERTISING

## SEAN NIXON

Towards the end of the first series of the Emmy-award-winning US drama *Mad Men*, set in the fictional world of the New York advertising agency Stirling Cooper in the early 1960s, there is a scene which offers a seductive vision of advertising practitioners and their role in the weaving of commercial fables. The scene features the drama's central protagonist – and central enigma – Don Draper. Draper is Stirling Cooper's key creative asset and their top 'creative man'. Not only is he viewed within the agency as the source of some of the most innovative and inventive advertising ideas, but also as something of a star performer when it comes to selling these ideas to clients. The scene shows Draper pitching his ideas for a campaign to representatives from Kodak, the makers of cameras, film and photographic equipment. Kodak have asked the agency to help them market a new piece of domestic technology – a device that allows a smoother and more convenient showing of photographic slides. Kodak calls the device the 'donut' or 'the wheel' because of its circular shape. This is how the scene unfolds:

> Kodak Man 1: So have you figured out a way to work the wheel in?
>
> Kodak Man 2: We know it's hard, because wheels aren't really seen as exciting technology, even though they are the original.
>
> Don Draper: Well, technology is a glittering lure, but there's the rare occasion when the public can be engaged on a level beyond flash. If they have a sentimental bond with the

product. My first job, I was in-house at a fur company. This old-pro copywriter, Greek, named Teddy. And Teddy told me the most important idea in advertising is 'new'. Creates an itch. Put your product in there as a kind of calamine lotion. We also talked about a deeper bond with the product. Nostalgia. It's delicate, but potent.

[*Projects slides of his children, his wife and himself eating on holiday, a shot of his wife pregnant.*]

Teddy told me that in Greek, 'nostalgia' literally means the pain from an old wound. It's a twinge in your heart far more powerful than memory alone. This device isn't a space ship, it's a time machine. It goes backwards and forwards. It takes us to a place where we ache to go again. It's not called the wheel. It's called the carousel. It lets us travel the way a child travels. Round and round and back home again. To a place where we know we are loved.

'The carousel, a time machine, something that takes us to a place where we know we are loved.' These are evocative themes. And Draper's is a beguiling, seductive performance designed to play on the emotions, the private memories and desires, of the client. There is more to say about the scene. It conforms to a particular idea of the creative process in advertising as resting on the insights of unique, gifted indi-viduals and also sets into play the idea of the 'creative pitch' as a drama of revelation and the sanctifying of a selling idea. It also suggests that what ad men and their agen-cies do is to forge connections between material objects and cultural values and ideals. In Draper's pitch, he is not selling the product per se, but what it can contrib-ute to – in this case, the generation of memories. And he uses a powerful fantasy of private life, of family life, to invoke a set of tender feelings. In doing so, Draper draws upon his own biography and literally the raw material of his own life – the pictures of his wife and family. What is so telling about these images – and this is evident from their context in the wider series narrative – is that they represent a powerful form of wish-fulfilment and evasion on Draper's part. This is, after all, the man who is a serial adulterer, seeking to relocate himself in the mythology of the 'happy family', to use the power of fantasy to negate the more messy reality of his private life and sexual adventures. Because there is no easily available, positive public narrative for the complexities of his life, he falls back upon the allure of idealized, conjugal matrimony.

Draper's subjectivity, and the drama of the advertising pitch, offers some broader clues as to the commercial role played by advertising agencies. I want to use the scene to draw out further insights into the conceptualizing of advertising. In par-ticular, I want to use the scene to test the value of two ways of understanding advertising. The first of these is the idea of advertising people as cultural intermedi-aries derived from the work of the French sociologist Pierre Bourdieu. The second is the idea of advertising as a 'market device' associated with the work of another

French sociologist, Michel Callon. Both approaches offer suggestive ways of thinking about advertising. My aim is not to force us to choose between them. I will, however, highlight their relative strengths before returning to a dimension of advertising as a practice that both models are weak on theorizing but which is central to the *Mad Men* scene: this is the question of subjectivity and desire.

# ADVERTISING PRACTITIONERS AS CULTURAL INTERMEDIARIES

Pierre Bourdieu's conception of the 'new cultural intermediaries' developed in his book *Distinction* (1984) is instructive for thinking about the economic and cultural role played by advertising practitioners. It helps us to do this by drawing attention to the bridging role that these actors play in linking production with consumption. This bridging role involves helping manufacturers and service providers to manage their relations with consumers and to generate an identification between the client's goods and those consumers at whom they are targeted. We can see these processes at work in the scene from *Mad Men*. The pitch is the moment when the advertising agency makes its claim to be able to understand how to promote the client's goods, where it reveals its authority as a cultural broker in the field of mass consumption, where it seeks to tell a compelling story about the product to the client. Much of this hangs on the ability of advertising people – especially art directors and copywriters – to mobilize specific forms of cultural capital to persuade the client that they have the ideas to successfully promote the client's goods (that they have the unique cultural resources and know-how to do the job) and that they really understand the consumer and know how to reach them.

Bourdieu's idea of 'new cultural intermediaries' additionally offers some clues as to why advertising people might be good at mobilizing this cultural capital and adding cultural values to the product. It comes from Bourdieu's comments on the dispositions and capacities of the individuals who occupy key positions in 'new professions' like advertising. Bourdieu sees these new occupations as part of an emergent class fraction within the middle class – what he calls the 'new petite bourgeoisie'. This class fraction is defined by Bourdieu as possessing very different class-cultural dispositions from the older, more established fractions of the petite bourgeoisie – the shopkeepers, clerks and master artisans. Whereas the established petite bourgeoisie are associated with a cultural conservatism in their tastes and dispositions (being drawn in particular towards a desire to ape middle-class ease with legitimate culture and seeking out popularizations of legitimate forms of culture) the new petite bourgeoisie are open to a different set of cultural preferences and tastes. As Bourdieu suggests, they are drawn to 'forms of culture on the lower boundaries of legitimate culture – jazz, cinema, strip cartoons, science fiction – and to flaunt American fashion and models as a challenge to legitimate culture' (1984: 359).

These elements manifest themselves in a preference for both high and popular cultural forms – and for strategies of cultural rehabilitation, such as an embrace of retro-imagery.

To put it another way, this class fraction, in its own lifestyles and patterns of cultural consumption, is both very attuned to established forms of legitimate cultural knowledge, but also to new cultural currents on the fringes of popular culture – in music, fashion and style. This gives them the ability to draw upon and mix both 'high' and 'low' culture – and to use this capacity to shape the tastes of others.

The cultural dispositions of the new cultural intermediaries are closely related in Bourdieu's account of the social make-up of these jobs. He notes the diverse social backgrounds and social trajectories of individuals within these occupations, suggesting that they are the natural refuge for both déclassé individuals (i.e. socially downwardly mobile middle-class individuals) and parvenus from the working class and lower middle class – socially aspirational individuals from these subaltern classes (Bourdieu, 1984: 358). This gives these occupations a distinctive social profile for Bourdieu. Don Draper fits into this picture of the social make-up of cultural intermediary occupations. In the drama he is depicted as a social parvenu, a man from humble origins with limited formal education who through his own auto-didactism pieced together a role for himself within the advertising industry. The relative openness of the industry, at least in terms of the formal educational qualifications required to enter the industry, allowed this socially mobile subaltern to establish a place for himself in the industry. Draper's ability to invent himself – he has literally taken on the name and identity of a dead man – is paradigmatic of the chameleon-like qualities of the 'ad man' and their openness to presentation and masquerade, attributes that we can see in Bourdieu's conception of the new cultural intermediaries.

Does this way of thinking about advertising practitioners as cultural intermediaries informed by Bourdieu's work, however, fully capture the role that they perform? A different way of understanding advertising is offered by the idea of 'market device' derived, in particular, from the work of French sociologist Michel Callon and his co-authors. This places more emphasis on the technical and material elements or devices of advertising, rather than the social composition and class-cultural dispositions of its practitioners.

# ADVERTISING AS A MARKET DEVICE

Michael Callon is associated with the 'performativity programme' within economic sociology and focuses upon the role of economic knowledges in the formatting and framing of economic activity (Callon, 1998; du Gay, 2010). In doing so, this approach takes issue with established sociological accounts of economic life which seek to embed economic processes – like markets and market relations – within social life. This includes the move (evident from Durkheim's work to the writings of Karl Polanyi) that the abstract idea of economic man needed to be socialized.

Against this, Callon proposes that economic discourses and devices help to produce forms of economic action, especially forms of market calculation and cognition. In short, they work to format and frame economic behaviour (Callon, 1998; Callon and Muniesa, 2005). One key strand of Callon's work has been to elaborate upon the ways in which markets make certain kinds of calculation possible, and it is the practical, technical organization of calculation that he explores at length. At the heart of this argument is the claim that 'market devices' or socio-technical devices shape calculation, and it is the role of these devices in staging or framing the encounter between supply and demand that figures in his writings (Callon et al., 2002).

Callon's account of the socio-technical devices that constitute choice and calculation is closely related to his interest in the process of making goods calculable; that is, as objects that can be chosen or about which calculations can be made. Callon suggests that in order to be exchanged, and chosen, the qualities and characteristics of goods need to be defined. He explores this process principally through the attention to what he calls the 'qualification of goods' (Callon et al., 2002). At the heart of this process of qualification is the establishment of the characteristics and properties of goods so that they can be detached from the seller's world and can in turn enter into the buyer's world. Callon sees a distinctive dynamic of market exchange involving the disentanglement and re-entanglement of goods. It is the socio-technical devices of the market that enable this to happen. Callon and colleagues like Frank Cochoy have shown how retailing spaces like supermarkets can be seen as 'market devices' that work to frame a set of choices for consumers: separating goods from the world of producers, staging these objects so that they can be chosen and seeking to entangle them in the world of the consumer (Callon et al., 2007; Cochoy, 2007).

The market devices of supermarkets, then, work to position goods within a frame of calculation. But they also do something more than that. Callon makes much of the idea that agency is not a capacity contained in human beings, but is rather the product of hybrid collectivities comprising both human and non-human elements. This combination constitutes what Callon calls an 'agencement' (Callon et al., 2002: 200). 'Agency' is the product of this hybrid entity and produced in the combination of human and non-human elements. In the case of mass retail, the organization of retail space, shelving, trolleys and so on constitute market devices that enable certain kinds of agency from buyers. Callon also talks about the way 'shopping lists' constitute 'cognitive protheses' that shape shoppers' agency and choices. Capturing this range of market devices – generated from both the supply and demand sides of the market – is central to Callon's project to produce 'ethnographies of socio-technical devices'.

What are the implications of these arguments for understanding advertising? I think we can draw on Callon's work in a number of ways. First, his account of the 'qualification of goods', the process that helps to establish and fix the characteristics of goods so that they can circulate, gives a large role to what Callon calls the 'professionals of qualification'. Advertising practitioners fit squarely into this category, along with designers and other market professionals. They are certainly involved, in Callon's terms, in the associated process of disentangling goods from the world of producers and attempting to entangle them in the world of consumers. In the scene from *Mad Men*, Draper effectively helps to 'qualify' Kodak's new piece of technology, shifting it from its representation as 'the wheel' to the 'carousel'. This shifts its meaning and helps to fix a new set of associations around the product. And there are innumerable examples from the history of advertising that one could cite. To give just one example from my own recent research, Oxo cubes, a processed meat supplement used for making drinks and gravy, was remarketed in the UK in the late 1950s. The aim was to shift the characteristic and associations of the product from a food supplement for the poor with strong associations of wartime austerity to an integral feature of making gravy and as something that modern, affluent and 'nice' people used (Nixon, 2012).

Developing this argument about qualification and entanglement further, we can see that advertising agencies use a number of different forms of expertise and technologies to perform this role. One device is market research. Market research enables agencies to generate knowledge of the world of consumers: to produce what Miller and Rose call an immense 'cartography of consumption' (1997), that is, a map of consumer habits, rituals and subjective investments in the world of goods. The knowledge of consumers generated by market research enables agencies to find ways of forging connections between the goods which they are advertising and the practices of consumers. It helps agencies to 'make-up' or 'mobilize' consumers – to use Miller and Rose's evocative terminology. In the 1950s and 1960s, advertising agencies were drawn to deploy a set of psychological knowledges to understand consumer motivations. This knowledge offered new and inventive ways of forging connections between consumers and goods. One of the most celebrated practitioners of this new kind of market research was Ernest Ditcher. Dichter conducted in-depth interviews with consumers in order to understand the symbolic meaning of goods and the deeper psychological needs they might serve. His Freudian approach not only introduced a thicker idea of human subjectivity into market research: it also worked to segment consumers less by social class or sex or age (though these categories were often still part of his consumer research) than by psychological disposition. Thus, in early research conducted in the late 1940s into the consumption of home appliances, Dichter developed a three-fold classification of women: the 'career woman', who disliked domesticity and hated housework; the 'pure housewife', who identified so strongly with her role as guardian of the home that she was anxious about the role played by home appliances and expressed hostility towards them because they undermined her role; and the 'balanced woman', who was the most fulfilled emotionally because she knew she was capable of both housework and career (Horowitz, 2004: 57). Later, Dichter recast his conception of the 'balanced woman' as the kind of woman who could be encouraged to see housework as an arena of creativity in which she could 'use at home all the faculties she would display in an outside career' (2004: 57).

Ditcher's conception of these psychological categories was informed by his own highly positive view of consumer society. He saw the whole process of market research as therapeutic for the consumer and not only useful for the selling of goods. In fact, Dichter was driven by a wholly positive conception of the private pleasures of consumption and saw his work as contributing to the unblocking of feelings of guilt about consumption within the population that derived from the puritan culture of self-restraint (2004: 56). Dichter argued that the central aim of advertising was to give the customer the permission to 'enjoy his life freely' and 'to demonstrate that he is right in surrounding himself with products that enrich his life and give him pleasure' (Dichter, 1957: 24).

This process of mobilizing the consumer, however, also involves other technologies: specifically, the technologies of print culture, posters, television, cinema and (more recently) online media to reach consumers. It is evident that these are historically specific and contingent means for entangling consumers – with their own histories and genres of representation – and they seek to engage consumers and enter their worlds in different ways. In the 1950s and 1960s, learning how to use television preoccupied agencies in both the US and the UK. In the UK, agencies adapted to television by, in the first instance, reworking elements of the older established advertising media. The first commercials used the animation of press and poster advertising. One early commercial even depicted an advertising poster being pasted up (Nixon, 2012). Others drew on the traditions of sponsored documentary film. What constitutes advertising as a particular kind of market device or assemblage of devices, then, will vary with the media technologies, bodies of expertise and styles of representation that are deployed. These market devices, however, are designed both to shape the 'qualification' of goods and to mobilise or entangle the consumer.

There is a final theme in Callon's work which we can usefully draw on to understand the practices of advertising. This is the broad notion of 'agencement' which Callon takes from actor network theory. As I noted earlier, an 'agencement' is a hybrid device combining human and non-human elements. This means that agency within the business of advertising – such as that pursued by Don Draper in the 'creative pitch' with Kodak – depends upon a set of material and technical supports. As Liz McFall has put it in describing the development and presentation of advertising ideas, the genesis of a campaign depends upon 'materials, tools, equipment and organizational settings' (2011: 196). In Draper's case, it is the office space of Stirling Cooper and the slide projector itself that enable him to realize the communication of his ideas. Draper's brilliant pitch is not, from this perspective, simply the product of a gifted individual, but reliant upon these technical elements.

# CONCLUSION

And yet, who Don Draper is, what he brings to the workplace, does matter. Bourdieu's account of the social construction of agents and their trajectories helps to fill out the account of the intermediary role performed by advertising practitioners. The assemblage of Draper and a set of technical devices should not blind us to the fact that Draper the man – his capacities and social formation – makes a difference. But who Draper is, is not sufficiently well caught by Bourdieu's approach either. Despite their differences, in important ways both Bourdieu and Callon deploy a technical and limited view of human subjectivity. Both posit a minimalist conception of the human material upon which social processes work. Both resist the idea that there might be deeper subjective processes at work. And yet surely, as the fictional instance of Don Draper illustrates, subjective process and desires animate and inform social practice. Human beings project a set of feelings onto the objective world – including the world of goods – and these material objects in turn are set in a realm of human relationships with all their complex psychological dynamics. It is not that an attention to these deeper subjective processes can fully account for the work of cultural production that goes on in advertising. Nor should we reduce the study of advertising to the subjectivity of its key practitioners. Rather, it is to argue that the articulation between subjectivity, the social trajectories and social formation of individuals and socio-technical devices needs to grasped – rather than seeking to privilege one conception or approach to advertising over another. Understanding these linkages means moving beyond the technical devices of the market and into the inner world of practitioners. Such an endeavour is difficult to pull off. However, it is worth trying. What might the desire for social recognition, adventure and the lure of an image of America fuelled by the stories of Huckleberry Finn and the books of Edith Wharton tell us about the status-striving advertising produced by David Ogilvy (1997), the British ad man who made it big in the US in the 1950s and 1960s? How much did Ogilvy's address to the 'snob in you' owe to his own inner dramas? Sociologists and historians of advertising and consumer society need to know more about these subjective aspects of the 'professionals of qualification'.

# 4

# THE PROBLEM OF CULTURAL INTERMEDIARIES IN THE ECONOMY OF QUALITIES

## LIZ McFALL

Production is ... at the same time consumption, and consumption is at the same time production. Each is directly its own counterpart. But at the same time an intermediary movement goes on between the two. Production furthers consumption by creating the material for the latter which otherwise would lack its object. But consumption in its turn furthers production, by providing for the products the individual for whom they are products. The product receives its last finishing touches in consumption. (Marx, 1980/1857–8: 24)

This passage in Marx's outline for his critique of political economy is famous for its provocative framing of the systemic, contingent links between production and consumption. It rather neatly introduces intermediation without labouring the theoretical problem raised by its status as a necessary movement between spheres that are simultaneous, unified and identical. The idea that some form of mediation between production and consumption has to take place for either to exist has a long history but interest in modelling how this mediation works in practice has been uneven. Bourdieu's (1984) formulation of the cultural intermediary occupations of the new petite bourgeoisie has acted as probably the single biggest impetus to research exploring the practical mediating function of work in professions like advertising, design, retailing, branding and marketing.[1] This research *almost* endorses Bourdieu's concept while making it clear that the idea raises as many problems as it solves. These problems are already looming in Marx's framing of the production–consumption relation and they continue to resist neat resolution. As I'll try to indicate in this short chapter, the attempt to understand better how the connection between production and consumption is realized in concrete market settings through the idea of cultural intermediaries has had some success, but of a limited kind.

This is not an indictment of cultural intermediaries research so much as a consequence of the magnitude of the rational and empirical challenges presented by the idea of a simultaneous, identical relation. If there were anything profoundly or conceptually wrong with Marx's characterization, things would be much simpler. But, while the habit of thought in which consumption is separated from production, often as its passive follower, has been pronounced in subsequent political economy – arguably including Bourdieu's – there isn't anything that is clearly just wrong. Production is only production when it is completed in consumption. This simultaneity makes the notion of intermediaries fraught because a process of intermediation inevitably introduces variables of distance and time that are hard to reconcile with simultaneity and identity. It is partly for this reason that an alternative, still largely Francophone, direction to that taken by those working to enlarge on Bourdieu's formulation has been pursued in economic sociology. In this work questions about production, consumption and their mediation certainly remain, but they are couched in rather different terms. Here the emphasis is on the processes, practices, relations and contexts involved in 'qualifying' (i.e. defining, or more precisely *equipping*) objects to function as fully-fledged products in the 'economy of qualities' (Musselin and Paradeise, 2005). This places the contextual interdependencies between products, producers and consumers as the central problem and spreads the task of intermediation across a crowd of actors including – but not restricted to – those in occupations tagged as 'cultural intermediary'. In what follows I outline briefly two of the biggest obstacles the notion of cultural intermediaries stumbles over before going on to discuss how intermediation fares in work addressing the processes of economic qualification.

# THE TROUBLE WITH CULTURAL INTERMEDIARIES, OR WHY YOU MAYBE SHOULDN'T USE A BRIDGE TO GET FROM PRODUCTION TO CONSUMPTION

The concept of cultural intermediaries has been introduced in a way that privileges a particular cluster of occupations. It accords certain workers a pivotal role in these processes of symbolic mediation, prioritizing a narrow and reductionist aesthetic definition of culture … Hence, representation, 'meaning' and the symbolic are treated as 'cultural', whereas the notion of culture as a 'whole way of life' seems to be rather marginalized or forgotten – or applied only to the selected workers engaged in 'symbolic' activities. So, advertising executives, designers and magazine journalists are cultural intermediaries, whereas it seems that biologists, physicists, accountants, priests and trade union leaders are not. Yet there are many other occupational groupings that are crucial to processes of cultural mediation or the linkages which might connect consumption with production. Indeed, a consideration of who might bridge this space, or who might be involved in 'articulating' production with consumption, raises some significant questions about the enduring distance between production and consumption. (Negus, 2002: 504)

In this extract, Keith Negus pins down two of the biggest problems with cultural intermediaries. First, there is the restriction of intermediary function to occupations identified as cultural or symbolic. Second, there is the related but still more perplexing problem of distancing that arises because intermediary functions enact a pairing and separation of parts which function nevertheless as a whole. As Marx highlights, the traffic between production and consumption defines them as each other. In this section, I will try to explain how closely, and stubbornly, connected these two problems are. It is the distinctions and oppositions that these problems introduce that the literature on qualification strives to avoid.

Cultural intermediary research has, since at least the early 1990s, played a significant role in offering a practical description of how the links between production and consumption are mediated. Bourdieu's (1984) remarks on intermediaries were famously sketchy but they nevertheless prompted a number of authors, many of whom are featured in this collection, to fill out the details of the working practices comprising key intermediary occupations. As Negus points out, these occupations – initially at least – tended to be those where the work of adding value and meaning to products is at its most overt, as in the case of advertising, journalism, design, fashion and so on. These are occupations explicitly charged with promoting consumption by 'mobilizing and motivating consumers to connect specific aspirations, fears and desires to particular product qualities' (Smith Maguire, 2008b: 212). This research has led to a much better informed understanding of what goes into such work and the conditions, constraints, compromises and contexts that shape it. In so doing, it has offered important correctives to the neglect of economic activity in culturally informed analyses and to the presumption that commercial signification involves only limitless meaning games. The trouble is that in the course of the investigation, problems with the concept itself just get clearer.

For one thing, as soon as cultural intermediary work is described, the list of occupations that can reasonably claim to be engaged in it grows. Thus the initial list of professional groups suggested has now expanded to include workers in retailing, branding, public relations, web and new media design, fitness, lifestyle and sports occupations, wine promotion and so on, and a widening range of historical and geographical settings invoked in which intermediary work seems to have taken place. This is hardly surprising since, when you think about it, the work to connect production and consumption in some way concerns almost everyone, almost all the time. It might be objected that although, say, textile machinists bring production closer to consumption, they are not engaged in processes of symbolic mediation. This neat solution only works, as Negus and others have observed (Nixon and du Gay, 2002; McFall, 2002), when culture is reduced to a strict, aesthetic definition with boundaries that are difficult to draw in practice and even harder to square with the current preference for more encompassing definitions that place culture in all meaningful practices or 'whole ways of life'.

Echoing John Law's insistence that if culture is to be a useful analytical category at all, it must be 'located and performed in human and non-human material practices' implicating 'technical, architectural, geographical and corporeal arrangements' (2002: 24), Negus outlines the way the cultural intermediary designation obscures the role played by other occupations, including record company 'suits', the senior managers, analysts and accountants, as well as factory and shop workers, in the commercial mediation of culture. While Negus concludes – as he has to really in order to hang on to the concept, albeit with reservations – that extending its embrace to include such workers would be unhelpful, other authors have sought to push the boundaries a little further. Moor (2008), for instance, makes the case for including branding consultants because their work too imbues goods and services and an ever-widening range of spaces, organizations and institutions with meanings and values. This, as her analysis reveals, is activity that implicates not just the traditional territory of symbolic meditation, but also an array of materials, buildings, layouts, fixtures, furniture and fittings that are enlisted to express and communicate. In different ways, Pettinger's (2004) account of fashion and Wright's (2005a) of book retail also push the boundaries of mediating work further into retail spaces, the branding of shops and shop-workers.

This expansion of the category, however, can't solve the boundary problem by repositioning it. The problem remains because it is always possible to make a case for the mediating, taste, symbol and meaning-making function of any group of workers. For Cronin (2004b) the concept struggles to capture the range and diversity of mediating functions even within the emblematic intermediary occupation of advertising. Advertising practitioners are not just channelling meanings to consumers but, she remarks, in a move towards the process of qualification, are 'trying to establish frame-works for defining or "qualifying" products and consumers in relation to specific forms of marketized exchange' (2004b: 365).

This is a substantial move, not just a shift of terminology. The emphasis on product qualities rather than meanings, symbols or brands might at a glance seem like just a substitution of terms, but it is underpinned by a quite different way of imagining relations between production and consumption. Those authors who have sought to expand the intermediary category to encompass a greater range of occupations and a greater diversity of materials, spaces, arrangements and bodies have, in so doing, drawn attention to the limits of thinking about the mediating role primarily in symbolic terms. Establishing a connection is not just a matter of adding meaning, whether through advertising campaigns, packaging or brand identities. Rather, production and consumption have to be always already, dynamically connected to continue at all. This involves a whole host of actors, intermediaries and followers being active throughout the process that Caliskan and Callon (2009, 2010) have labelled 'economization'. Economization involves the work of 'qualifying' behaviours, organizations and institutions *as* economic. This is positioned in contrast to the idea that there is some kind of mystery 'x-factor' which defines things as inherently economic. Instead, things are *rendered* (i.e. they become) economic through the actions of producers, governments, research organizations, media, consumers and so forth. Economization allows for the way things may, throughout their life-cycle, move in and then out of being economic. A tree growing wild, for instance, may not be an economic thing but it may become one if parcelled as real estate or cut as timber; similarly, in the burgeoning biotechnology market things like sperm and eggs which have not generally been understood as tradeable products may become so in certain circumstances.

As Cronin (2004) points out, the practitioners' enterprise of persuading clients that they alone have the special skills required to 'reach' consumers has the effect of reinforcing the division and increasing the distance between production and consumption. This is equally true of the intermediary category itself in both restricting the field of special mediating practices and ignoring the multitude and diversity of actors and objects that have to be in play for an economy to function. The effect is close to what Marx might have called the 'reification' of production and consumption as stable, concrete, self-contained island entities when they are dynamic processes: the outcomes of a chain of actions. If cultural intermediaries are the only group that can reach consumers, they are in the peculiar position of having to be in possession of a unique mix of engineering skills to bridge a gap that only appears through the constant articulation of the necessity of intermediation.

This is a problem that is avoided in Latour's (1991) approach to technological innovation. Here innovations achieve market success not through the special efforts of promoters, but through the sheer length of the chain of associations between human and objects. Forging more and more relationships in an expanding network is what secures the continued existence of an innovation. The domination or wide-scale adoption of any innovation is never assured, never guaranteed in advance no matter what technical accomplishments it can boast of. Innovations have to be 'deployed, black-boxed, repaired, maintained' (1991: 118) by all sorts of actors to ensure that what is produced is consumed. This means that innovations have to be constantly connected and reconnected to more and more humans and more and more objects to be securely adopted. An iPod, for instance, owes its vast adoption to its expanding, dynamic fit with enough computers, iTunes software, in-car stereos, domestic speakers, bicycle mounts, hipsters, teenagers, cyclists, software updates, designers, engineers, journalists, bloggers, legislators and so on. In order to understand, in this case, *market*, success or failure

the idea that an object is only taken up if it manages to interest more and more actors must be accepted. To consider that the socio-economic context was known once and for all, as if it were possible to define the product outside of all interaction with it, is contrary to all that we know about innovation. Innovation is perpetually in search of allies. (Akrich et al., 2002: 203)

This insistence that it is possible to define a product only in terms of all these interactions that surround it, as I'll explain in the next section, is central to the qualities debate.

## SIMULTANEITY AND IDENTITY IN THE ECONOMY OF QUALITIES

They have to fall in love with Standard Oil ... Our great secret you see is the secret we like to tell everybody: the constancy of the specifications for each different kind of oil. Now, for example, take our unbeatable Transformer Oil B, Grade 11 extra ... Absolutely waterless: this is the most basic essential; yes, the sine qua non: freezing point ... extremely low: viscosity ... 2.4 Wayne, at the outside: acid value, negligible: dielectric strength, amazing: flash point ... the highest of all American industrial oils. (Gadda, 2000 [1957]: 106)

The claim that a product is only defined dynamically through interactions with it is a significant departure from the cultural intermediaries framework. While authors have varied over precisely how they understand the character and aims of intermediary work, there is some agreement that the task centres on shaping the use and exchange values of products in order to better link them into the lives of potential consumers. By shifting the focus on to the role of *all* surrounding interactions, the location of the product moves out of the seemingly stable 'sphere' of production and into a location within a network of interactions. The product is held together, contained and defined by interactions – including those with consumers – that combine to establish its qualities. This, however, says little about what these interactions are and how exactly they work to define or 'qualify' products. In the space remaining, I elaborate a little on how the sheer variety of processes involved in product qualification have been characterized in the literature and point out some of the implications this has for understanding the location and role of cultural intermediaries.

As a conceptual term, 'economy of qualities' began to circulate in Anglophone contexts after the 2002 publication of Callon et al.'s article of the same name. The term, however, references a debate that can be traced back to Chamberlin's theories of monopolistic competition in the 1930s through to Ackerlof's work on uncertainties in the 1970s and through the more recent work of economists Francois Eymard-Duvernay and Jean Gadrey. In sociology, Michel Callon and Lucien Karpik have made the best known contributions to developing the concepts of quality, qualification and singularization, and it is their work that has the greatest bearing on the formulation of the cultural intermediary role. As Musselin and Paradeise (2005: 92) point out, while a shared interest in establishing contextualized product definitions that specify the characteristics of exchange only through the way products are related to producers and clients is to be found in all this work, there is not so much a unified approach in this literature as a 'swarm of correspondences'. It is impossible to do justice to all the distinctions within this long-running debate, so the focus here is only on identifying a few points salient to rethinking the role of intermediation.

Callon et al.'s (2002) account locates processes of qualification as working at both supply and demand sides to 'singularize' the attributes *of*, and in doing so create attachments *to*, particular products. Qualification processes combine consumers' social networks with business and marketing strategies in 'socio-technical devices' that aim to produce, and sustain, product attachment in dynamic market settings where competitors are always trying to prompt 're-qualification'. More colloquially, competitors are always trying to break into consumers' established patterns of market loyalty and trigger a re-evaluation, a reconsideration, of their alternative products. To illustrate, Callon et al. offer the example of the strategy adopted by an orange juice manufacturer facing declining sales:

> The origin of the oranges, the taste of the juice and its packaging (among other things) were changed. But customers still had to be informed of these changes. The strategy chosen, both simple and common, clearly illustrates the nature of the mechanisms at play in this switch. To the questions: 'How to break the consumers' attachment to their favourite brands? How to extract them from the routines they follow with a certain delight, and get them to grasp the bottle without thinking?' the solution devised by (re)qualification professionals offered an exemplary answer. The strategy consisted of reactivating the network in which customers were immersed by focusing, for example, initially on those consumers who were accompanied by their children. The idea was to attract the children's attention by means of a prominent feature, for example a bottle offering a free Pokemon. The child would predictably detach herself from her father, pull him by the arm, force him to leave the routine he automatically followed, and put him in front of a product which, strictly speaking, he had not seen. A discussion between father and child would follow, which was likely to end in a purchase and, eventually, in attachment to a new brand. (2002: 206)

Since the publication of the economy of qualities a substantial literature has emerged that attempts to pin down the definition of the socio-technical devices involved in these processes more precisely.[2] This task has been hampered a little by the simultaneous use of the term 'agencement' to describe basically the same phenomena, but as Muniesa et al. explain, 'market device' is intended as 'a simple way of referring to the material and discursive assemblages that intervene in the construction of markets' (2007: 2). The important thing to grasp of both terms is the emphasis given to the interconnections between agencies and arrangements with the capacity to *act*. Agencies in this literature consist of human bodies together with prostheses, tools, equipment, technical devices, algorithms and so on which when taken together make up 'agencements'. Market devices, also sometimes referred to as 'market agencements' (Caliskan and Callon, 2009, 2010), are particular instances of the broader category of agencements and share the same hybrid, collective character. Devices *do* things, 'they act or make others act' (Muniesa et al., 2007: 2). This approach shifts the emphasis away from intermediaries with an explicit function to act as symbolic mediators and instead emphasizes the actions of a much broader group of agencies:

> Instead of starting the analysis with agents who calculate their utility with regard to a set of given goods, the analysis starts with goods and follows their metamorphoses, careers, qualifications and re-qualifications, from laboratories to marketing departments, to the consumer. The consumer himself becomes increasingly less the endpoint of the analysis, as the process of re-qualification of goods now more and more entails the recycling of goods, which hence change hands many times during their social lifetimes. (Callon, 2005: 97)

Thus a whole 'crowd' of intermediaries are involved, many of whom may be engaged in activities that are not easily designated production or consumption, but might be anywhere within the surrounding space. Alongside the group Callon (2005) labels 'professional qualifiers', those involved in the conception, production, marketing and distribution of goods, there are other groups whose nature and composition varies in different market settings. In the case of innovations, there may be academic or semi-private research laboratories, clients and users implicated in innovation conception and financial intermediaries, while in pharmaceutical markets there may be patient advocacy groups, test subjects, doctors, scientists and so forth. The point is that the function of intermediation is spread across a network, not situated in the middle of a line connecting production and consumption.

Qualification-requalification works to make product attributes identifiable, a process termed 'singularization' since it refers to singling out the defining attributes that are judged the best way of qualifying the product to fit in with consumers. It does not, Musselin and Paradeise (2005) point out, explain how consumers are to *evaluate* these defining attributes. It is how people are to evaluate qualities that prompts the strongest disagreement between Callon and Karpik. For Karpik, evaluation is the function of judgement devices that help 'dissipate the opacity of the market' by offering buyers the information and knowledge to allow them to make reasonable choices (2010: 44; 2005). In what he terms the 'market for singularities', which he defines as goods and services with multidimensional, uncertain and incommensurable qualities, judgement devices are essential for the market to function. Using examples ranging from psychotherapy, fine wines, restaurants and classical music, Karpik explains how guides and rankings, personal trust, critics' reviews and brands all work as judgement devices that furnish consumers with the credible knowledge essential for them to make anything other than random choices.

In taking this stance on the necessity of specific devices to enable judgement only in *particular* (i.e. 'singular' markets), Karpik expressly counters the version of qualification offered by Callon and his various co-authors. Famously, Callon concluded that 'framed, formatted and equipped' humans calculate (1998: 51), and in his account the socio-technical devices employed in product qualification are geared to enable this. Here, devices are involved in equipping all forms of market action, in sharp contrast to Karpik's invocation of devices that aid judgement only for products like luxury brands and psychotherapists that are too singular to be judged on price alone. Callon et al. insist the 'dynamic of reflexive attachment implies consumers who are calculating, that is, capable of perceiving differences and grading them, and who are accompanied and supported in this evaluation and judgement by suppliers and their intermediaries' (2002: 213). Judgement for Callon is not set apart from but incorporated within calculation in a move to avoid what he and Muniesa describe as a 'conventional but too sharp' (2005: 1231) distinction in economies made up of calculative devices. Eymard-Duvernay (2005) and Karpik (2010) regard Callon's solution of expanding calculation to include judgement as a capitulation too far to neo-classical economics.[3]

The disagreement on how qualification works runs all the way through the notion of singularization. Callon et al.'s (2002) singularization is the process whereby products become singular by taking on particular attributes. For Karpik, singularities are very particular kinds of products, products that have to be judged differently from 'standard' products. This idea is beautifully elaborated in Karpik (2010), but it stumbles nevertheless on the dichotomy it sets up, between singularities markets, which require qualification and re-qualification, and standard abstract markets, which don't, since they can be regulated by price adjustment alone. This, Callon argues, isolates 'calculation and economic rationality on one side, judgment and social mechanisms on the other' and reinforces the vision of the market in line with economists' models (2005: 98). Given Karpik's rejection of Callon and his co-authors' expanded definition of economic calculation to incorporate judgement on the grounds that it gives insufficient space to the role of human judgement in market action, this leaves them both in the interesting position of accusing each other of the same failing: that of being too close to standard economic models of how markets work.

The qualification literature, then, is far from a unified approach but it nevertheless prompts a very different way of *seeing* the relation between production and consumption and the role of intermediaries. What emerges is a distributed, crowded network of intermediaries who, in different ways, contribute to the qualification of products. This is a very different account from that of symbolic mediators because it draws attention to the variety of tasks involved. The problem with cultural intermediary accounts, as with the sociology of consumption more generally, has been a tendency to get carried away with all that symbolism, signification and taste-making at the expense of the more mundane work involved in market-making. It is the significance and variety of this mundane work that the product qualification literature exposes. As Gadda's description of the reliable qualities of Standard Oil at the start of this section implies, this work is sometimes about defining, maintaining and stabilizing product attributes; a process far removed from the meaning games associated with advertising practitioners. In concrete market settings, intermediary work can take many different forms in the service of keeping production and consumption simultaneous and identical.

The purpose of cultural intermediaries remains absolutely central: the work carries on and clearly matters in the vast economies of qualities that make up contemporary global product markets. What the qualities literature does is not so much dispense with the role but call timely attention to the diversity of forms it can take and its distribution across a much broader range of actors than those concerned with making overtly symbolic interventions. Even those professional qualifiers of goods, the narrower set of actors directly tasked with *cultural* intermediation, are a fluid category, at one moment copywriters, at the next art directors and at the next the digital orchestrators of flash mobs, crowds and social media. These cultural intermediaries have to take their place amongst the many product qualifiers whose significance in sustaining production-consumption cycles varies from market to market, device to device.

## NOTES

1   See discussions of the intermediary role of branding in Moor (2008); retailing in Wright (2005a); the music industry in Negus (2002); and advertising in Cronin (2004a) and McFall (2002).
2   See Callon and Muniesa (2005) and Callon et al. (2007) in particular.
3   Karpik (2010) elaborates on his express disagreement with Callon and Muniesa on this move in the 'Interlude' section of his book.

# 5

# ETHNOGRAPHIC RESEARCH AND CULTURAL INTERMEDIARIES

## GISELINDE KUIPERS

When I first encountered cultural intermediaries during my research – television buyers, in my case – I felt I was discovering a whole new world. I had no idea there was so much work involved in getting television programmes to local audiences. I was not even interested in television executives, imagining them to be a rather insignificant step in the process I was trying to study: how audiences come to know and (dis) like imported television programmes (cf. Kuipers, 2011). Insofar as I had an image of what television buyers would do, it was quite different from what I found – and much more work than I had imagined.

Cultural intermediaries are easily overlooked. In part, this is because many of them work behind the screens of (cultural) production. Traditional gatekeepers, like television buyers, literary editors, scouts, agents or A&R managers in the music industry mediate between producers and other producers, making them invisible to the public. The expanding class of 'new cultural intermediaries' – sellers and peddlers of cultural goods and meanings in the service economy (Bourdieu, 1984; Hesmondhalgh, 2006a) – often operate more publicly. But their professional contribution, too, is often overlooked.

Cultural mediation is always most effective when it looks artless and natural, thus escaping attention. When the editor, PR person, personal trainer, journalist or spokesperson seems to be nothing more than a window through which obvious, self-evident messages and meanings flow, their intermediary work has most impact. The mediations, translations, interventions and subtle shifts of meaning they provide escape the audience's notice; thus, the message arrives all the more convincingly.

This relative invisibility of cultural intermediaries has implications for empirical research on cultural mediation. First, as my own experience highlights: researchers often do not set out to study cultural intermediaries. Rather, they encounter them in the course of a research project that is about something else – a field or a process in which cultural intermediaries turn out to be central, like food culture (Johnston and Baumann, 2010) or urban regeneration (Bovone, 2005; Lloyd, 2006). Alternatively, researchers gradually come to understand the group they study as cultural intermediaries. What starts out as a study of fitness trainers (Smith Maguire, 2008b), advertising (Moor, 2008) or booksellers (Wright, 2005a) increasingly focuses on the cultural mediation that is part of – or central to – their professional skill.

Second, the 'inconspicuousness' of cultural intermediaries makes them challenging research subjects. Cultural intermediaries bring their skill in making things seem artless and self-evident to every professional encounter, including meetings with researchers. It may be difficult to penetrate the smooth talk of these professional meaning-makers and image-builders. At times, I realized after an interview that seemed pleasant and cooperative enough, that hardly any of my questions were answered.

Finally, the actual work of intermediaries often is hard to observe, let alone 'measure'. It typically consists of long hours spent behind computers, emailing, browsing, twittering and writing, interspersed with meetings that are often off limits to researchers. Moreover, much of the work done by cultural intermediaries does not look like work. Their professional encounters and activities look deceivingly casual: sipping lattes in Starbucks, having lunch in hip venues, flipping through magazines, browsing stands at festivals and fairs, and most of all: talking to people.

This chapter discusses the possibilities and pitfalls of researching cultural intermediaries. While I discuss various research strategies, I focus on ethnographic research, arguing that this approach – a combination of methods rather than a method per se – is the best way to study the many professions that can be described as 'cultural mediation'. This article then has a dual aim: it is both a plea for ethnography and a how-to guide for doing ethnographic research on cultural intermediaries. Drawing on various examples from my own (or jointly conducted) research in television, publishing and the beauty industry, as well as other people's studies of cultural mediation, I describe the research process step by step, from locating and getting access to the field, to strategies for collecting, triangulating and interpreting research findings.

# CULTURAL INTERMEDIARIES IN EMPIRICAL RESEARCH

Cultural intermediaries here are defined broadly as professionals engaged in the framing, dissemination and qualification of meanings and commodities in processes of symbolic (cultural) production. As Smith Maguire and Matthews put it:

They construct value, by framing how others (end consumers, as well as other market actors including other cultural intermediaries) engage with goods, affecting and effecting others' orientations towards those goods as legitimate – with 'goods' understood to include material products as well as services, ideas and behaviours. (2012: 552)

This description encompasses some of the oldest professions in the world, like preachers and teachers. However, in today's advanced service economies, a larger proportion of the labour force than ever before falls into this category. This includes traditional mediators and gatekeepers in the cultural industry. Many other service jobs increasingly revolve around the construction of cultural value. For instance, work in restaurants, bars or cafes today is as much about the creation of symbolic value – status, experience, meaning, identity – as it is about providing customers with a meal or a drink (Lloyd, 2006; Johnston and Baumann, 2010; Ocejo, 2012b).

How to study cultural intermediaries? A useful first step in any study of cultural intermediaries is the analysis of existing quantitative data: audience or sales figures and ratings, labour market surveys, annual reports of companies, policy reports, and output, trade and production figures. Policy and government data are easily accessible, and often provide a rich source. The 'creative industry' policy fad of the early 21st century has led to the setting up of many databases, research and policy centres that can be used to great advantage for academic research. Commercially produced data are not always freely available and sometimes quite expensive – the production of such figures is an industry itself, employing many cultural intermediaries. However, summaries usually are available from professional publications, like trade journals, specialized websites or newsletters.

Figures and numbers are central to the life-worlds of many cultural intermediaries, who consult such figures avidly as part of their work. The construction of cultural value is a most uncertain business. It is not defined by use value, but lies in experiences, meanings and symbolic significance. These are socially constructed, and cannot be predicted or foreseen (Bielby and Bielby, 1994; Hesmondhalgh, 2007). Numbers and rankings play an important role in the management and reduction of this uncertainty because they give clues about cultural value. For instance, no television buyer would buy a show without looking at ratings and reviews from other 'markets'. Moreover, figures, ratings and reviews function as quick indicators of success. Many cultural intermediaries start their working day by looking at yesterday's ratings, sales or box office figures and so on. Consulting such quantitative data therefore helps to understand intermediaries' everyday life. Moreover, when informants realize that a researcher is familiar with such information, it helps to establish rapport and create credibility (cf. Ostrander, 1993).

Researchers studying cultural intermediaries may also collect their own quantitative data, using survey methods or standardized interviews. Given the ample supply of high-quality data and the difficulties involved in getting access and securing satisfactory response rates, I would not recommend this unless the research is very generously funded. Commercial research organizations are much better equipped to conduct large-scale surveys than academics or students. It is more worthwhile to spend one's energy trying to get face-to-face meetings.

A second way to study cultural intermediaries is by looking at their products: the texts and images they produce. For instance, there is a considerable body of literature on arts criticism (Janssen et al., 2011) and advertising (Moor, 2008), analysing how critics or advertising professionals frame, evaluate and legitimate cultural goods. However, cultural intermediaries overwhelmingly produce symbolic goods that have no such clear material 'form' as the review or the advertisement.

The obvious method for studying cultural intermediaries is the interview. Most studies of cultural intermediaries rely (at least partly) on interviews (e.g. the various case studies in this volume). Interviews allow for a more open-ended approach and richer data than surveys. It allows informants to give their own account of their lives and their activities – and researchers can gauge from this account meanings and valuations. Moreover, it is a genre that cultural intermediaries understand: a conversation in which meanings and values are discussed, dissected and co-produced. That the genre is so close to their habitus has a downside: it is not always easy to penetrate cultural intermediaries' professional presentation. Whereas interviews often are a good way to get confidential information or to uncover previously unarticulated meanings, interviews with cultural intermediaries often are very 'frontstage' affairs. It is difficult to get respondents away from the polished accounts they feel comfortable telling, and they are skilled at avoiding unwanted questions.

Therefore, formal interviews are ideally complemented with ethnographical methods: observation of and participation in the interactions and events in which cultural intermediaries take part. Thus, researchers can see informants in their natural habitat, in interactions with others rather than in the somewhat forced interview setting. Ethnographers can also observe the unsaid and the everyday: the things that are so self-evident that interviewees neglect to tell researchers, as well as things interviewees prefer not to divulge. Finally, ethnography enables the researcher to triangulate: to test conclusions based on one type of data (interviews, quantitative data) with ethnographic data. So ethnography can remedy distortions and blind spots inherent in interviews or other methods.

In contemporary societies, the in-depth and long-term immersion of classical fieldwork is difficult to achieve. Ethnography in present-day social science research typically is a more fragmented practice: observation and participation in scattered settings and locations, supplemented with interviews, secondary materials and – as media form an important part of people's everyday environment – online research. The first step in ethnographic research therefore is to locate the field(s): where are the informants, and more importantly, where can they be observed?

# FINDING THE FIELD

Ethnographic research needs a research locale: the 'field' where 'fieldwork' can be done. Studies of cultural intermediaries usually start with interviews in workplaces: offices, studios, shops and so on. The workplace, then, is the first research site. Even brief visits in the context of an interview provide opportunities for ethnography. In advanced services, presentation is crucially important, so locations, buildings and furnishings are often carefully chosen and arranged, questions about this generously answered, and tours easily given. The same attention to self-presentation may show in personal workspaces and personal presentation (Kuipers, 2012). Thus, even a single interview visit may lead to a wealth of information.

Ideally, however, workplace ethnography goes further than observations around interview meetings. Some cultural intermediaries do work that can easily be observed or participated in: in semi-public places like shops, clubs or restaurants. Intermediary work can also be part of a collaborative process. For instance, during fashion photo shoots several cultural producers and intermediaries work together to create an image: a model, photographers, make-up artists, stylists, fashion editors. Such processes of collective production are rich sites for ethnography because they show how cultural value is constructed in practice.[1] Many cultural intermediaries, however, spend most of their working hours in offices. While 'office ethnography' (Markowitz, 2001) may sound like the dullest subcategory of workplace ethnography, much more happens in offices than solitary computer gazing. Office workers have meetings, work discussions and more informal social gatherings. While it is not always easy to get access to such meetings (a matter discussed below), it is certainly not impossible and one can always ask.

Much of the work of cultural intermediaries happens outside formal workspaces, and researchers should be prepared to follow their informants to other locales. Marcus (1995) distinguished various strategies for 'multi-sited fieldwork'. One can 'follow the person', a strategy adopted in an ongoing study by Ashley Mears who literally follows around modelling scouts looking for new models.[2] Since in advanced services, work and leisure are rarely strictly separated, researchers may join intermediaries in their wider life-worlds, including the public and semi-public places and 'scenes' where they hang out (Negus, 1992). Another relevant strategy is 'follow the thing'. For instance, a book manuscript moves from agents or scouts to editors at publishing houses, then on to the financial branch and subsequently the production department of the publisher, then to marketing people, and finally to booksellers and consumers. In this process, the manuscript is handled by different types of intermediaries who mediate between different regimes: between author and the field; national and transnational; financial and literary; and producers and consumers (Franssen and Kuipers, 2013). As a product moves from one setting to another, it also moves from one 'regime of mediation' to another (Cronin, 2004b).

Finally, researchers can go to where 'the field' materializes. Today's scattered, multi-sited fields of symbolic production often have get-togethers where producers, intermediaries and clients meet. Academics and other professional groups have conferences, the fashion world has fashion weeks (Entwistle and Rocamora, 2006), the publishing and media industries have fairs (Bielby and Harrington, 2008) and festivals (de Valck, 2008). At such events ephemeral cultural fields, held together by mediated interaction most of the time, suddenly come to life. During such meetings, standards are negotiated, made and put in practice; relations are forged; hierarchies performed and challenged; 'buzz' is created; and knowledge is disseminated and transferred. Such materializations of the field are ideal fieldwork sites: it is easy to blend in, people are at their most accessible, and one can observe intermediaries in their natural habitat. However, these are primarily business events, and people may have better things to do than talking to researchers. Such events are therefore more suited for ethnographic observation and establishing contacts than for interviewing or long conversations.

# GETTING ACCESS: STUDYING (RELATIVE) ELITES AND THEIR BACKSTAGE LIVES

Getting access is the most dreaded part of fieldwork. It takes patience and per-severance, and researchers must be prepared to deal with rejections that, despite the professional context, may feel remarkably personal. Cultural intermediaries in many respects are easier to approach than other people. They are generally reflexive about their work and can be convinced of the relevance of academic research. On the other hand, cultural intermediaries often are busy professionals with (relatively) high-status jobs who deal with confidential information or transactions involving serious money. While cultural intermediaries may consent to being interviewed, ethnography may be more difficult to negotiate.

However, getting access is often less problematic than researchers fear. Ethnographers have been allowed access to the most unlikely and seemingly inac-cessible work settings: government meetings (Gains, 2011), NGO offices and board meetings (Markowitz, 2001), architectural firms (Ewenstein and Whyte, 2007), auditions for fashion models (Godart and Mears, 2009). I have been allowed into programming meetings at television broadcasters – a very closed world indeed.

Careful preparation significantly improves chances of getting access. Often, requests to participate mainly reflect the interests and motivations of the researcher. Having a good 'pitch' is crucial. Researchers should carefully think through what they have to offer. Information, feedback or (media) attention is valuable to many cultural intermediaries. Good self-presentation extends to the person of the researchers: physical presentation (clothing, cards) as well as presentation on the phone, in writing or online. Assume that people will look you up on the Internet, and try to tweak your own online presence. I have benefited greatly from my personal and project websites. Since a personal website is usually the first hit in a Google search, a personal website gives you control over your Internet 'persona'. Moreover, websites can provide potential research participants with information about the research, and former participants information on findings and publications.

Access is greatly facilitated through good introductions, especially with elite informants – and cultural intermediaries often are. Never be afraid to ask informants to introduce you (but accept graciously if they refuse – after all, it's their professional life). Think carefully about where in the hierarchy you start approaching people. In case of doubt, I recommend starting high up. Make sure to have a specific name of the person you want to approach: never simply move upward from the person at the counter, the phone or the reception desk. Instead, find out beforehand the name of the person you need. Always be prepared to name others with whom you have spoken: this is a common test of 'insiderness'. If the list is long or impressive, people more easily cooperate because they are afraid to miss out.

Participating in research comes with risks, in particular the exposure of confidential or sensitive information. It is essential to give guarantees about confidentiality and anonymity in the published results. Often, it helps to agree upon themes that will not be discussed or reported. Money or relations with competitors are sensitive issues to informants, but often are quite irrelevant to theoretically informed research questions. Personal or project websites are good places to provide general information about ethical codes and informant confidentiality. When discussing confidentiality, I have found it helpful to make agreements concerning timing, rather than content, of publication. Academic publishing trajectories are so slow by the standards of the real world, that many concerns about confidentiality vanished once I had explained my project's timeline.

Getting access is a constant negotiation, especially in multi-sited fieldwork. There are always new people who need to be asked and informed. In negotiating access, researchers should keep in mind the reasons for doing ethnography: why isn't it enough simply to interview people? Ethnographers should be able to explain this to themselves and to their informants. Common reasons for doing ethnography are the observation of naturalistic, 'real' interactions in everyday settings, in particular interactions in the 'backstage' areas of people's lives. However, a researcher's presence in such settings may be awkward and confusing: if you want to understand our work, why do you want to join us for lunch in the cafeteria? Why is hanging around in our lobby 'research'? What is the point of attending introduction meetings for new colleagues, or confidential boardroom meetings? Access requires trust and habituation. In 'old-fashioned' ethnography, this was gradually built up. However, the ethnography of cultural intermediaries and their fleeting social worlds requires a convincing and reassuring story for each new informant and setting. This story should highlight what can be found and learned in the everyday routines and the backstage areas – and nowhere else.

Studying cultural intermediaries means 'studying up': they are people with a good position and often considerable status and power.[3] Ethnographers typically study 'down': blue-collar rather than white-collar workers, simple services rather than advanced, in the global South rather than 'at home'. Access is easier when the researcher more or less automatically has the upper hand. Moreover, lower-status people and professions traditionally have been conveniently less mobile (although this is changing fast), and their social settings are less enclosed by formal barriers.

Studying elites calls for specific research strategies (Gains, 2011; Markowitz, 2001; Ostrander, 1993). High-status informants often have the power to block a researcher's entry into the field, and may be quite unimpressed with university qualifications. Ostrander (1993) gives a useful overview of tactics and strategies for elite ethnography. She stresses that elite ethnography is not as difficult as many people believe. However, it requires a firm and clear presentation, and a more goal-oriented and business-like approach than is common in qualitative research. Elite ethnographers should expect to be tested repeatedly before getting access. This confirms my experiences with intermediaries in the cultural field: they usually took me seriously, and opened up, when they saw I took the lead and could speak knowledgeably about the field. Thus, the open-ended, expectant, wide-eyed attitude that works so well in many research situations is likely to backfire when studying 'up'.

# WHAT'S TO SEE? STUDYING IMMATERIAL LABOUR

Workplace ethnographies often focus on places and professions where work is observable and tangible: kitchens, factories, shops, bars, police stations, schools, the military. However, cultural intermediaries perform 'immaterial labor' (Hardt and Negri, 2000): the product of their work often is intangible and mostly symbolic. Moreover, the labour process often is quite immaterial as well. Often, studying immaterial labour looks like this:

> I sit uncomfortably eying to open space in the first-floor offices of Boom Cubed, a Wicker Park design and marketing firm, listening to the drone of techno music coming from oversized speakers. My perch is the makeshift reception area. [...] Often the employees – six are active as I sit here – cluster around a terminal, commenting on a work in process: 'That's radical,' 'that jams', 'that's dope', or perhaps offering creative input. Then they zip back to their own projects. I write things down, trying to be invisible. With embarrassing frequency someone asks if I need anything. They are clearly unsure of what to make of a sociologist in their midst. (Lloyd, 2006: 212)

This sums up the challenges of participant observation in advanced services: the bemused response of research subjects, the awkward position of the ethnographer, and most importantly, the question of the research object: how to study this? What is there to see?

In research locales like the office described by Lloyd, there is little to see unless one knows what one is looking for. As methodology textbooks never fail to note: empirical observations never appear spontaneously, but need to be guided by research questions. Studies of immaterial labour underscore this point rather vividly: the setting itself often does not provide many clues. There are, of course, many questions one could ask about cultural intermediaries. How to find and formulate a research question falls outside the scope of this chapter (but other chapters may offer inspiration). Roughly speaking, I see four types of broad questions one could ask about intermediaries that can be answered using ethnographic methods, and that provide pointers on how to conceptualize and grasp immaterial labour.

Traditionally, ethnographic research is employed to study culture: what are the meanings, symbols and beliefs central to informants' lives? How are such meanings produced in everyday practices, and how do everyday practices produce them? Such broad questions need to be specified (on the basis of theoretical considerations) into more focused research questions, such as: What is the role of embodied and implicit knowledge in cultural intermediary work? (Entwistle, 2009; Ewenstein and Whyte, 2007). What arguments, criteria and justifications do cultural intermediaries use when making creative decisions? (Godart and Mears, 2009). How are explicit criteria, like those voiced in interviews, related to decisions made in practice?

Second, ethnographies are guided by questions about social structures and relations: what are the hierarchical relations and sources of authority? When, how and between whom do conflicts happen? What are the networks in the field? This broad focus translates into concrete questions like: When and how do cultural intermediaries (and producers) disagree or argue about quality standards, and how are such conflicts resolved? (Negus, 1992). What are the sources of capital in cultural mediation? (Kuipers, 2012). Or even more concretely: with whom do cultural intermediaries socialize when the field materializes, what do they talk about, and how does this affect their work or their professional status?

Two types of questions are more specific to cultural mediation. A growing number of studies look at the 'material' aspect of social relations, often inspired by actor network theory (cf. Moor, 2012). This is a particularly fruitful approach to grasp and 'unpack' immaterial labour: how are places, products, technologies and physical settings involved in creating symbolic value? Childress (2012) showed how a new computer system transformed the work of literary agents. In my own research I found that in screen translation, the technologies of screen translation – dubbing, subtitling or voiceover – guide and shape intermediaries' work. While subtitling is a solitary process, dubbing is a complex enterprise involving many professionals who all depend on each other's work. Moreover, material surroundings produce institutional 'closure': routines and technologies become physically embedded into computer systems or workspaces (large dubbing studios vs. solitary workspaces for subtitlers) that further shape and constrain intermediaries' working practices.

Finally, research questions could focus specifically on the *process* of cultural mediation. In this approach, the concept of the cultural intermediary functions as a 'lens' or 'prism'. By understanding specific types of activities as cultural mediation, it becomes possible to ask new questions that are simultaneously social and cultural: between which 'regimes of mediation' do intermediaries mediate? How is value created and framed in this process? When is cultural mediation successful, and for whom? (cf. Smith Maguire and Matthews, 2012). Thus, the focus shifts from cultural intermediaries as research topic to cultural mediation as a framework for research: many (professional) activities can be seen as the translation and production of cultural messages for specific social groups. Studying this process then allows ethnographers to investigate the intersections between the social and cultural, the material and immaterial.

## MEDIATING THE INTERMEDIARIES: HOW TO DO THINGS WITH ETHNOGRAPHIC DATA

After the field has been located, accessed and investigated with appropriate questions, the ethnographer finds herself facing a growing, often bewildering amount of information. The final, and crucial, research phase therefore is mediation on the part of the researcher: how to make a coherent, plausible and theoretically relevant story out of the data?

This question is not specific to studying cultural intermediaries. Rather, it is typical for ethnography, with its extremely open-ended and diverse data. Ethnography handbooks devote considerable attention to this problem (Atkinson et al., 2001; Van Maanen, 2011), as do many monographs.

Ethnography (and most mixed-methods and qualitative research) requires a balance between a continued focus on the research aim and questions, and openness to new discoveries. As I argued above, when the research aim is not clear, the field may seem nothing but a chaotic jumble of information, or even worse: a place where nothing ever happens. However, the strength of ethnography is that it can yield unexpected results, leading to new empirical and theoretical insights. Ideally, ethnographic research is a constant back-and-forth between empirical exploration and theoretical reflection, each building on the other to create further insight: this process is called the 'hermeneutic circle' (cf. Geertz, 1973).

However, fieldwork among cultural intermediaries is more like a 'hermeneutic pinball machine'. The researcher moves from observations in public places to backstage conversations, from online to offline interactions, from statistics to interviews, from trade press to reception chatter – and from all these data to theoretical reflection and theory construction. Creating a story, or a theory, out of this process requires both disciplined data administration and a clear theoretical focus. Moreover, it requires a solid theoretical basis to rely upon to 'catch' unexpected but theoretically relevant findings.

On a practical note: there are now several computer programs that allow qualitative researchers to store, sort and analyse data. Such programs are quite useful to ensure self-discipline in the recording of findings (quite an issue for many researchers, including myself). Moreover, the structured (but open) coding these programs make possible can be used to share data analysis procedures with outsiders. The process of analysis, or 'writing up', often is presented as a solitary and rather intuitive affair. Thus, new software may lead to much-needed transparency and intersubjectivity in ethnographic analysis – and put an end to unnecessary solitary suffering. More generally, the heroism of the solitary fieldworker is often not conducive to good analysis. For most people, the 'hermeneutic' process is much helped by discussion with other researchers.

The use of various methods and materials typical of (multi-sited) fieldwork is often referred to as 'triangulation'. However, in my view the pinball machine is a more fitting metaphor. Triangulation suggests that one should use several rather than one measuring point to better catch sight of the object under observation. While I agree with the multiple methods, I am not so sure that the object under observations stays put. With cultural intermediaries, the target moves. And it talks back.

Cultural intermediaries are typically reflexive about their work, which requires them to move back and forth between various contexts and frames, often leading to a certain distance vis-à-vis their surroundings. In this respect, they are not unlike researchers. This affects the relation with informants in all phases of the research, including the analysis and writing up. Cultural intermediaries may want to see the publications – and unlike many other informants, they are quite likely to understand what you have written. It is important to clearly agree on what you can and cannot write down, but it is still possible that they will not like what they see. However, rather than seeing this as a nuisance or a threat, the input of informants can also be quite useful. Especially in fieldwork involving many settings and types of data, it can be very helpful to sit down and share and compare interpretations.

## CONCLUSION: SLIPPERY PEOPLE

This chapter had a double aim: it was both a plea for ethnography in the study of cultural intermediaries, and a (succinct) how-to guide for doing ethnographic research of cultural intermediaries. As I have argued, ethnographic research can pose, and answer, questions that other methods cannot. The method – or combination of methods – is particularly useful for cultural intermediaries because so much of what they do is intangible, and because they themselves, as professional meaning-makers and image-builders, can be rather hard to grasp. Studying cultural intermediaries is not necessarily more difficult or challenging than studying other groups, but like all fieldwork it does require careful preparation as well as some specific precautions. What sets them apart most from other types of informants is their extreme reflexivity about their work. This directly affects the relation between informant and researcher: cultural intermediaries likely have considered most of the questions you ask, and they may not agree with the researchers' interpretations. Cultural intermediaries will always have things to add to what a researcher has to say about them. Adding to other people's work, after all, is what they do for a living.

## NOTES

1   This ethnography of photo shoots is part of an ongoing, as-yet-unpublished study I am conducting jointly with Elise van der Laan.
2   This is part of an ongoing study. Preliminary results are currently only available as conference paper (Mears, 2012).
3   This characterization of cultural intermediaries as (relative) elites diverges from Bourdieu classification as (petty) bourgeois. Despite considerable variations in this rather fuzzy group, many of them have considerable status, power and (cultural) capital, and are probably best described as 'upper middle class'. On a practical note: most cultural intermediaries are powerful enough to ward off researchers if they want to.

# PART II

# CULTURAL INTERMEDIARY CASE STUDIES

# 6

# ADVERTISING

## AIDAN KELLY

The activities of cultural intermediaries are of particular interest to a diverse range of fields including media, marketing, entertainment and the arts. They are critical to the production and mediation of meaning within society and are specialists in the shaping of symbolic goods and services. This chapter contextualizes the theory of cultural intermediaries within advertising production and reports the findings of a study of Irish advertising practice. The findings reveal the various social, cultural and economic mediations performed by advertising agencies, and I argue that a wider conception of advertising practitioners as 'ideological intermediaries' (O'Reilly, 2006: 267) would be a more appropriate theorization of advertising work. Suggestions for future research on cultural intermediaries are also provided to develop this theoretical concept in advertising, marketing and related organizational contexts.

## HISTORICIZING CULTURAL INTERMEDIARIES

Advertising practitioners as cultural intermediaries have a key role in constructing the commercial mythology of the corporate world and uniting the cycle of production and consumption (Leiss et al., 2005). According to Olsen, 'advertising practitioners, in multiple capacities, participate as cultural intermediaries in the production of meaning for consumers who are often co-creators in this process' (2009: 59). Scott notes how 'ads are crafted by people who share a social milieu with the audience and thus reflect collective cultural knowledge and imply the probability of response' (1994: 468). For this process to take place, 'advertising agencies must tap into the cultural knowledge of consumers in order to design advertising that has the potential to resonate with meaning for potential consumer communities' (Hackley,

2002: 211). McCracken (1986) illustrates how advertising works by framing elements of the culturally constituted world within the context of an advertisement, a process which 'contributes to the organization of experience through the shaping and reflecting of our sense of reality' (Sherry, 1987: 441). These meanings are extremely relevant to consumer life themes and life projects (Mick and Buhl, 1992), and Elliott argues that 'advertising as a cultural product provides the individual with the opportunity to construct, maintain and communicate identity and social meanings' (1997: 285). A key aspect of the advertising practitioner role is the extraction and manipulation of cultural meaning for advertisements that resonates with socially and historically situated audiences. For critics of advertising, this process is inherently ideological as it infuses commodities with cultural and psychological appeal (Wernick, 1991), and disrupts flows of meaning to create false relationships that are interpreted by consumers as somehow natural and self-evident (Williamson, 1978).

Advertising practice is essentially a hybrid activity that fuses elements of the cultural and economic (McFall, 2004; Slater, 2010), and advertising agencies have been portrayed as cultural enclaves within business that have atmospheres of informality and subversiveness (Hackley, 2000; Nixon, 2006). The process of advertising development is socially constructed through the interactions and negotiations of clients and account team personnel (creatives, account managers, account planners, etc.) (Hackley, 1999; Moeran, 2005a; Malefyt, 2003). Advertising is produced on behalf of a corporate client, and conflicts between the artistic ambitions of creatives and the commercial imperatives of clients are a prominent feature of the industry (Lien, 1997). As clients are often larger organizations, they enjoy an asymmetry of power in their relationship with agencies (Lury and Warde, 1997). Creative personnel can feel insecure as a result of this commercial imperative (Hackley and Kover, 2007), and conflicts over the ownership and control of creative work are common in advertising agencies (Hackley, 2003; Hirschman, 1989). This is particularly prevalent in the application of market research techniques to evaluate the output of creative work (Kelly et al., 2008), and the division between aesthetic and scientific philosophies has been an historical feature of advertising agency practice (Fox, 1997).

The conceptualization of advertising practitioners as cultural intermediaries finds much support in both sociology and marketing literature (Featherstone, 1991; Hackley and Kover, 2007; McFall, 2004; Soar, 2000). Indeed, Bourdieu (1984: 359) identified a 'new petite bourgeoisie' of practitioner, specifically those engaged in marketing, advertising or public relations, who had a significant influence on the production of symbolic goods and services. McFall's (2004) work provides an historical perspective on the evolution of cultural intermediaries in advertising agencies and demonstrates how the hybridization of culture and economy and providing a bridge between production and consumption has always been a central feature of advertising work. The intersection between art and commerce has often been quite difficult to negotiate for artists who worked in advertising agencies in the 20th century as they tended to find the atmosphere oppressive and creatively restrained (Bogart, 1995).

Advertising practitioners are immersed within various forms of creative culture, and are what Featherstone describes as 'the new tastemakers, constantly on the lookout for new cultural goods and experiences' (1991: 35). As the critical link between the corporate and culturally constituted world (McCracken, 1986), advertising agencies mediate between economic and cultural meaning systems and develop relationships between organizations and consumers through the production of advertisements that have social, cultural and historical significance for consumers. Cultural intermediaries such as advertising practitioners are the vital interpersonal connection between the cultural and corporate spheres in this context.

Holt (2004) and Frank (1997) detail how advertising practitioners have historically co-opted mass cultural, social and political meanings and channelled them to brands to create ideologically potent market myths (also, see Thompson, 2004). As cultural intermediaries, advertising practitioners have been positioned as 'bourgeois bohemian' (Holt, 2004), and through their informal cultural knowledge develop symbolic associations for advertisements (Nixon, 2003; Cronin, 2004b). Jackall and Hirota note how 'creatives … [are] endlessly searching for fresh ways to take the raw stuff of their culture and society and organize it into internally coherent messages, little stories in which "products are heroes"' (2000: 101), while Soar (2000) sees advertising practitioners as occupying 'front row seats' in both the encoding and decoding of advertising meaning through their dual situated positioning as producers and consumers.

Cronin (2004a) envisages a wider role for advertising practitioners as not solely cultural intermediaries between producers and consumers but also as negotiating multiple 'regimes of mediation' that flow between clients, agencies, regulators, academics and consumers. This more expansive theorizing of agency is particularly useful as it considers the range of mediations advertising agencies engage in within their work practices. Advertising practitioners as cultural intermediaries have a crucial role in synthesizing and ascribing meaning for commodities and advertisements, and it is investigating this process to which our attention will now turn.

# MATERIAL PRACTICES

This chapter reports the findings of an ethnographic study into Irish advertising practice and investigates how advertising agencies encode ideological meaning into commercials. It builds upon sociological, anthropological and business literatures that explore advertising agency processes and practices from an interpretive perspective (Hackley, 2000; Lien, 1997; Malefyt and Moeran, 2003; Moeran, 2005a; Nixon, 1997; O'Boyle, 2011; Soar, 2000). The advertising agency was based in Dublin, Ireland, and like many Irish agencies it was a subsidiary branch of a major international advertising group. In this respect, many of the institutional agency practices were informed by the parent group; however, the approach to advertising development retained a distinctively Irish flavour.

Access was negotiated to observe advertising agency work as a non-participant (Arnould and Wallendorf, 1994), as my specific interest was to examine the advertising process from a discursive perspective. Discourse analysis draws from social psychology to explore how people use language to construct and make sense of their social world (Elliott, 1996). As a non-participant, I was invited to internal agency meetings and account team briefings, and I was permitted to record these interactions. While my presence was noted at meetings, after a while I was treated as a member of the team and even asked for input into certain campaign interactions. I also interviewed several members of the account team, which included account planners, copywriters and art directors within the agency. These interviews discussed the nature of their role, how they approached their work and the tensions and conflicts associated with contemporary advertising work. The analysis in this chapter presents key themes and devices of the study which were draw upon in interviews generated during the inquiry. These are categorized from the key findings of the study (Spiggle, 1994), which provide insights into the social process of Irish advertising development. The key themes here are compared with cognate theoretical perspectives to evaluate how we can conceptualize advertising work from a cultural intermediary perspective (Nixon, 2003).

Advertising practitioners mediate the social world and recontextualize lived experience within advertisements (Goldman and Papson, 1998). The role of this cultural knowledge is often understated in managerial treatments of advertising (Pickton and Broderick, 2005), and the ways in which informal knowledge is incorporated into the advertising development process is crucial to understanding how practitioners develop commercial linkages for goods and services (Nixon, 1997). The practitioners interviewed recognized the role of social experiences and how these were incorporated into advertising narratives:

| | |
|---|---|
| *Raymond (Copywriter):* | It's all the stuff you bring to it about whether from your, like, I was about to say childhood experiences but I didn't really mean that but from like whatever you ate for breakfast that morning or whoever you were talking to last night or whatever, you use all that stuff as fuel to what you're trying to think of but yeah you try to process all these thoughts through a brief, maybe that isn't the way you are supposed to do it you probably should just start with the brief but a lot of the time you bring quite a lot of baggage to it. |

David Ogilvy once remarked how 'I have a theory that the best ads come from personal experience. Some of the good ones I have done have really come out of the real experience of my life, and somehow this has come over as true and valid and persuasive' (Higgins, 2003: 85). These experiences were drawn upon in response to the creative briefs developed by account planners for particular clients. Both account planners and creative personnel sought to empathetically see the world the way consumers do by using a combination of market research and social observations, and they did not exhibit the narcissism sometimes associated with advertising practitioners who base creative ideas only on their own personal frame of reference (Soar, 2000).

What qualifies as research knowledge was often quite informal as the agency did not have enormous resources to spend on commissioned consumer research. One account planner explained how consumer-based insights would be developed when working on accounts for fast-moving consumer goods (FMCGs) by standing by a fixture in a supermarket to watch how people behaved in situ. This sort of 'panoptic' observation allowed advertising practitioners to mediate the social world and channel these insights and experiences for the production of ideologically infused advertising (Hackley, 2002). Both account planning and creative team members engaged in this 'informal' knowledge collection, and it often was more valued than formal market research findings. Where copywriters and art directors could not directly observe or experience something, they often relied upon conversations with friends or mass-media texts for insight and understanding, as one art director explained:

*Paul (Art Director)*:     The beer, I mean the beer thing is kind of nice in that we're big beer drinkers. I suppose we've all worked on products, I mean I've worked on products for period pains and stuff in the past and, you know (*laughs*), you're never going to experience that, so you do have to sort of, you know you either talk to people, read up on the target market and the audience and stuff like that and you, you try as much as possible to see if you can get your head into their body a little bit as much as you can, especially when it comes to advertising products where maybe you don't have a huge amount of experience in.

Cultural intermediaries such as advertising practitioners observe and interpret the social world and embed these insights and experiences within the commercial texts they create. They perform a role of amateur commercial ethnographers in this practice (Jackall and Hirota, 2000), and these observations are implicit yet vital to develop commercials that will resonate with consumers within a social and cultural milieu (Mick and Buhl, 1992). The mediating effects of this informal knowledge and the ways in which it is acquired and drawn upon requires close attention to understand the social practice of advertising production.

Advertising practitioners weave various elements of other cultural text into the commercials they create, and intertextuality is a key feature of advertising discourse (O'Donohoe, 1997). Therefore, as cultural intermediaries knowledge and understanding of different aspects of creativity was vital to how they performed their role, and cultural capital was a key resource of agency practitioners (McFall, 2004). The creative practitioners in particular had a particular interest in the consumption of a vast array of cultural forms, as one describes:

*Aine (Art Director):*    Movies and music and you name it, that's the nice thing about this job is that it is so broad and you can just get inspiration from absolutely anything and everything, and the more you're exposed to the better, you know what I mean? You actually do need to watch quite a bit of TV and you do need to watch movies and you do need to listen to music, it all enriches the pool from which you can which you can draw, not that you're going along cogging stuff, but that you're just aware of what's out there and you know, I suppose it's a meeting of creativity from all other areas basically.

Advertising draws symbolic and ideological resonance from the various sources of culture, and advertising creatives are intermediaries who keenly follow cultural trends and developments (Soar, 2000). According to Clarkin, advertising practitioners are akin to 'cultural synthesizers more than cultural innovators, magpies searching the popular undergrowth for raw material with which to support the brands they seek to promote' (2005: 70). As Holt (2006: 374) argues, only in rare cases do advertisements or brands ever lead cultural movements; more often they are 'ideological parasites' that draw from existing myths, and tend to 'ride the coattails' of other more potent cultural movements. It is through the work of advertising agency creative departments, and their knowledge of such cultural and social movements, that companies are able to tap into and exploit these myths to develop associations with the advertised product. This embedded cultural knowledge is pivotal to creating a shared repertoire between producers and consumers to co-create advertising meaning (Lien, 1997; Ritson and Elliott, 1999), and as cultural intermediaries advertising practitioners have a critical role in embedding cultural discourses into brand narratives (Frank, 1997; Holt, 2004).

The nexus of the agency–client relationship within the creative development process was a particularly striking aspect of the study. Clients held the economic capital in their relationship with the agency and Turnstall has noted historically how 'the client pays and thus calls the tune' (1964: 50). Client ideologies and processes seemed to direct the majority of creative work for larger clients in particular and there were often conflicts and antipathy directed toward certain clients in negotiations of the creative process. According to one account planner:

*Edward (Account Planner):*    Clients pay the bills, this is not an art. It's not an art in the sense that it's commercially directed, it's a commercial activity. Clients get what clients want and we work to the ends that the clients determine.

Advertising agencies have historically had an ambivalent relationship with their clients and the division between agency and client representatives is well established within advertising history (Frank, 1997). There were various incidents within the ethnographic study which displayed evidence of this conflict, such as client representatives changing executional and creative elements of advertising sets and creative directors resigning in protest. The advertising process for one particular client was referred to as the 'Client X Way',[1] and the agency had to develop advertising ideas which conformed to this internal evaluation process. While this created some frustration amongst creative practitioners, they did not appear to harbour the ambitions of independent artists as some studies have portrayed (Van Wijk, 2006), and accepted this as a commercial reality of the industry they worked within. However, the nature of the process meant that the advertising produced became very inwardly focused purely upon client expectations rather than consumer insight, as one copywriter explained:

> Raymond (Copywriter): The reality is that it really doesn't matter if it gets made or not because you know it won't get made the way you want it to get made, but then again we are not paid to be a writer or an artist or anything else. We just get paid to write stuff and I'm writing stuff. Unfortunately I'm writing stuff for the client rather than for the consumer, and maybe that's the frustrating bit. It's like making a chair for the chair salesman rather than for the person who is going to sit in it, and that never really works.

In his exploration of Japanese advertising production, Moeran noted instances of what he terms 'impression management', where the work of an agency 'has virtually nothing to do with the customers at which the client's advertising campaign will be directed, and everything to do with the client company itself, and its representatives' (2005b: 921). This seems to resonate with Raymond's description here, and the level of antipathy in certain practitioner accounts seemed particularly palpable. Alvesson's (1994) research into advertising agency practice in Sweden revealed similar tensions, with the agency happy to 'get rid' of clients who were difficult for the agency to handle. David Ogilvy once famously said that 'clients get the advertising they deserve' (2004: 100), a phrase repeated several times during my interviews, and the agency seemed to retain some symbolic power in the relationship in terms of how they delivered creativity to certain accounts. There was also a clear distinction made between large and small clients, and creative team members in particular felt that smaller clients offered more potential for creativity owing to their flat organization and less bureaucratic structure, a theme which has been prominent within the history of advertising production (Fox, 1997; Frank, 1997).

Thompson and Haytko (1997) argue that the discursive relationship between cultural intermediaries and institutional forces needs to be considered by critics who present advertising as a uniform oppressive ideology. It was clear from the study that there was an imbalanced power relationship between the client and the agency, and the agency had to respond to the commercial imperatives of the client. It was somewhat surprising to witness how controlling this relationship with the client could be; however, in an Irish context the agency was very much dependent upon client revenue and had to stringently adhere to client processes. In this sense, the advertising agency mediated the dominant commercial imperative of its client, and these interactions and exchanges had a significant impact upon the texts they produced (Moeran, 2005a).

A central feature of the history of advertising agencies has been the attempt to make advertising more 'scientific' (Hopkins, 1998), and the incorporation of market research techniques into advertising practice has been a contentious issue, particularly with copywriters and art directors in agencies who have resisted its use (Fox, 1997). Lury and Warde note how 'advertising is a function of producer anxiety or uncertainty' (1997: 89), and clients have traditionally used market research techniques such as copytesting to evaluate the outcome of creative work and reduce risk. According to Hackley, 'the use and interpretation of research in advertising development is a major site of intra-account team conflict' (2003: 318), and there was evidence of division around the incorporation of market research in the evaluation stage of the creative process. While creative practitioners distinguished themselves from independent artists within their accounts and did see themselves as accountable to clients, they largely saw research as detrimental to creativity and at odds with how aesthetic products should be evaluated (Hirschman, 1983). Although market research in the creative briefing stage was considered helpful, advertising copytesting research which evaluated creative work was discussed particularly negatively. For Raymond (copywriter), this form of research reduced advertising to a diluted form of communication:

*Raymond (Copywriter):*　　　　I think that copytesting is the worst thing in the world. I don't like research and I don't like copytesting just because it creates nothing and nothing will ever come out of it that's any good … You'll never come out with anything that's worth anything because it just gets eaten away at and eaten away at and eaten away at, and eventually everything's the lowest common denominator.

The issue of ownership of the advertisement was also particularly prevalent (Hirschman, 1989), and creative teams continually referred to the commercial as 'their ad' which they sought to protect from what they saw as the maligning influence of copytesting research. The creative teams wanted to keep the integrity of the work they developed, and the achievement of peer recognition through the winning of creative awards was a key career strategy that helped them build their career portfolio. This obviously had the potential to create a conflict of interest between creative and commercial ambitions, which is often a feature of the work in advertising agencies (Hackley and Kover, 2007).

The art–science divide was closely related to the agency–client relationship, and decisions to test advertisements were often client-directed. In his ethnographic study of advertising production in Trinidad, Miller (1997) found that advertising research was a comfort mechanism for client representatives in making managerial decisions. Tasgal has been particularly critical of how research is used in creative and cultural industries, describing it as 'essentially a back-covering exercise, steeped in fear of failure and a need to justify/explain why such an ad or such a strategy was pursued' (2003: 145). The tensions over the incorporation of market research techniques in advertising production are well established and their manifestation was evident in the everyday work of advertising practitioners. This conflict between aesthetics and scientific approaches is a wider extension of the art and commerce divide in advertising agencies, which is also a prominent feature of the history of the industry (Lears, 1994). In order to develop creative work, agency practitioners had to negotiate this process and engage with client evaluation systems that caused much friction between practitioners in both organizations. The work of advertising practitioners as cultural intermediaries is itself mediated through ideologies that have significant consequences for how work is produced within an agency.

# ASSESSING IMPACT

This chapter has highlighted the role of cultural intermediaries in the context of advertising production. Advertising agencies are central to the development of commercial narratives and myths that build iconic status for brands within consumer culture (Holt, 2004; Randazzo, 1993; Twitchell, 2004). The work practices of advertising agency workers have been characterized by McFall (2004) as a 'constituent practice' which blends the cultural and economic together. This chapter has emphasized how advertising agencies mediate between cultural, social and economic meaning systems and develop their work through these multiple 'regimes of mediation' (Cronin, 2004b). It could therefore be concluded that a slightly wider conception of advertising agencies as 'ideological intermediaries' involved in the production, manipulation and mediation of multiple meaning systems seems a more robust description of the activities of advertising practitioners (O'Reilly, 2006: 267). This is not to suggest that the category of cultural intermediary as applied to advertising agency practice is not a useful conceptualization, but the range of mediations involved seem to be more expansive in practice than solely the cultural.

A key focus of this chapter is on the nature of the work practices of cultural intermediaries in a commercial organizational context. It was clear that the artistic and creative work they engaged in did not sit easily within the commercial environment within which they practised it. Many felt that their creativity was undervalued as a result of this commercial imperative, and while they understood the nature of the industry they still found the advertising development process frustrating and difficult to negotiate. The environment in which cultural intermediaries work and the conflicted nature of the work they do highlight the clash of art and commerce in the creative industries and the impact this has upon the identity construction of practitioners in the advertising field. The documenting of these organizational creative processes and the ways in which practitioners engage with them is of pivotal importance to understanding the role and work of cultural intermediaries in the contemporary world.

## FUTURE DIRECTIONS

There are clearly fruitful research avenues to be investigated in relation to cultural intermediaries and their workplace processes and practices. The relationship between cultural intermediaries and institutional stakeholders seems a particularly ripe topic for future research; the agency–client interface portrayed in this chapter demonstrates how these power relations can be manifested in material practice, and investigating such commercial relationships in other fields (e.g. commercial stakeholders and their relationship with cultural intermediaries) could be interesting. An investigation of agency–client relationships from a client perspective is also an area which deserves attention in future studies of advertising practice.

The ways in which cultural intermediaries engage with consumers to co-create products and services may also be a worthwhile pursuit, as evidenced in the recent work of Hatch and Shultz (2010), and theorizing these interactions could lead to a richer understanding of the role of consumers as co-producers of marketing products and experiences (Vargo and Lusch, 2004). Investigating the activities of cultural intermediaries historically, as McFall's (2004) work has illustrated, could help to explain how these roles have emerged and evolved through time, and the use of historical methodologies could produce new archival-based understandings of the work of cultural intermediaries. The identity construction of cultural intermediaries is still very much underexplored, and work that adapts the approach of Nixon (2003) to other industry contexts such as product design, marketing or media would be a welcome contribution. Finally, investigating the life trajectories of cultural intermediaries and how they develop their career paths may produce more insight into industry access and progression opportunities in the creative industries (McLeod et al., 2011). It is hoped that this chapter has provided some insight into the nature of advertising work and the ideological mediation performed by advertising agencies within consumer culture.

## NOTE

1    The name of the client has been protected for confidentiality purposes.

# 7

# BRANDING[1]

## LIZ MOOR

Commercial brands have existed since the late 18th century, but it is only in the last twenty years that a distinct branding industry has emerged. During this period, branding and corporate identity have gone from being relatively obscure subfields of the design industry to commonly used terms and, in some cases, matters of political debate (e.g. Klein, 1999). There is a growing social scientific literature on branding (e.g. Lury, 2004; Arvidsson, 2006; Moor, 2007; Kornberger 2010; Aronczyk and Powers, 2010) but it is small in comparison to the much larger literature on advertising, and there remains much work to be done in tracking the distinctive viewpoints and practices associated with branding. This is especially so since both the practice of branding and the broader logic of 'brand thinking' have rapidly expanded beyond the business world and into a range of public or non-profit institutions, including charities, local government departments and public education providers. Most obviously discernible in the reworking of an organization's visual and material culture, but often also involving changes to the substance of business practice, branding is used in these sites for the purposes of differentiation, to delineate and animate core values and beliefs, and to galvanize staff and other stakeholders. Understanding the work of branding is therefore part of a broader project of tracking the ways in which specific techniques of presentation and promotion are deployed to support forms of social and institutional organization and governance. It is also important in clarifying changes in the types of work conducted by cultural intermediaries.

Information about the size of the branding industry is difficult to track because branding work gets done in many organizations that do not define themselves as branding consultancies. Many businesses have in-house brand managers, as well as communication and/or design teams responsible for the coordination of company materials, and make only occasional use of independent branding consultancies.

Furthermore, many agencies that do branding work also provide other services and therefore do not define themselves *primarily* as branding agencies. Finally, because many contemporary branding consultancies have emerged from other design disciplines, or have absorbed smaller specialist studios into larger multi-disciplinary agencies, it is hard to find comparative data to track changes in the industry over time. Nonetheless, a number of observations can be made. First, the turnover of the design industry as a whole was estimated to be £11.6 billion in 2004–05 (Design Council, 2005; Work Foundation, 2007), compared with a turnover of £18.3 billion in the advertising industry in 2004 (IPA, 2007). Communications design, which includes 'graphics, brand, print, information design, corporate identity', represents the largest single category of all design work conducted in the UK (Design Council, 2005), and the number of agencies offering branding and graphics work rose from 48 per cent in 2000–01 to 65 per cent in 2003–04 (British Design Innovation, 2003, 2004), while the number of agencies offering events and exhibition design (another important component of branding activity) rose from 17 per cent of agencies to 48 per cent during the same period. Perhaps more significantly, it has recently been estimated that more than a million people are employed in the UK in 'the creation and building of brands' (IPO, 2009: 6). Although this figure includes those involved in the design, manufacturing, advertising and legal protection of new branded goods and services, it reflects the broader point that brands are now seen as central to development and growth across various sectors of the economy. This wider field of brand creation is, however, beyond the scope of the present chapter, and in what follows I therefore focus on the historical development and current practices of dedicated branding and brand-led design agencies, before making a provisional assessment of their impact and significance and suggesting avenues for future research.

## HISTORICIZING CULTURAL INTERMEDIARIES

Branding has its roots in the discipline of industrial design, which has a long history but became more obviously important to capitalist accumulation from the mid-20th century onwards (Woodham, 1997). More recently, branding emerged from the various corporate identity consultancies that began to emerge in the UK and the US during the 1980s (Olins, 1978; Julier, 2000). The increasing 'design intensivity' of capitalist production since the 1970s has been noted by a number of authors (e.g. Lash and Urry, 1994), but the emergence of a distinct industrial design profession can be traced to the US in the 1930s. The discipline was consolidated during the Second World War through a transfer of knowledge and personnel from Europe to the US, and after the war through the diffusion of knowledge, skills and techniques from the US back to Europe and also to Japan (Woodham, 1997).

The mutation of some commercial design consultancies into corporate identity and branding consultancies depended on the confluence of a range of factors that were largely external to the design profession. By the 1960s, the increasing globalization of trade, the growing number and power of multinational corporations and, in many European countries, the decline of Empire and therefore of protected markets, were all argued by early proponents of corporate identity work to necessitate new ways of making corporations 'intelligible' abroad (e.g. Olins, 1978). Some writers (e.g. Pilditch, 1970) claimed that the social changes of the 1960s were likely to make corporations and businesses new focal points for self-identification, while others saw the shifting economic situation and worker unrest of the 1970s as cause for the creation of new unified group (i.e. corporate) identities to counter worker alienation (Olins, 1978). Almost all writers in this area demonstrated an awareness of the extended range of *audiences* for corporate activity (e.g. Henrion and Parkin, 1967) and, in some cases, the necessity of a new media strategy with which to communicate with these audiences. James Pilditch, drawing explicitly on the work of Marshall McLuhan, argued that it was not the content, but the 'total effect' of corporate messages that would be important in the future, and that 'far from being an adjunct of advertising, corporate communications have become the new total' (1970: 9).

The election of conservative governments in Britain and America in the late 1970s and early 1980s led to an economic context that was conducive to the further growth of corporate identity consultancies. Both pursued policies of deregulation and privatization that led to a rise in the number of mergers and takeovers, and to the creation of new forms of competition in sectors where none had existed before (Julier, 2000). These in turn provided a greater volume of clients for design agencies specializing in corporate identity, while the relative decline of manufacturing industries at this time, and the growth in the service sector, also boosted the area of corporate identity by providing more clients for agencies specializing in retail design, packaging, events and exhibition design and annual report design (Julier, 2000). These shifts also led to new developments in the training of workers to embody and communicate corporate and brand values (Lury, 2004: 29; Pettinger, 2004).

These developments led to a new visibility for brands as distinct types of assets. At the beginning of the 1980s tangible assets, such as a company's equipment or factories, represented the greatest proportion of the amount bid for companies, but by the end of the 1980s this had dropped to 30 per cent (Batchelor, 1998), suggesting that intangible assets – usually the brand name and its associated reputation in the minds of consumers and the public – had become a more important part of a company's overall economic worth. Brands were seen as unique types of assets because their value did not necessarily decrease over time. They could also provide the basis for successful line extensions into new areas and reduce the risk for shareholders by transferring some of the 'goodwill' from the original product into new ventures (Murphy, 1998; see also Murdock, 2003: 28). Such risks were particularly pronounced in industries with high initial production costs, which partly explains the emergence of brand names, and 'brands' of content, within the cultural industries (Lash and Urry, 1994; Hesmondhalgh, 2002).

The subsequent emphasis on nurturing brand identities as assets was one of the factors behind the boom period, or 'second wave', of advertising during the 1980s (Lash and Urry, 1994), characterized by the development of more abstract and creative representations of brand 'personality' rather than distinct product attributes. By the early 1990s, however, an economic recession had placed new pressures on the advertising industries in Britain and America, as potential clients began to question the cost and effectiveness of conventional 'above the line' advertising campaigns (Nixon, 2002). These pressures were compounded by developments in national media policies leading to a proliferation of television channels and corresponding decline in the size of audiences for specific programmes or broadcasters. Such shifts, along with the emergence of new technologies that rivalled television for audience share, have been responsible for many of the ongoing problems of the advertising industry, which was initially slow to shift from its traditional role in providing 30- or 60-second advertisements for television and the cinema. In the design industry, by contrast, companies expanded the range of services they offered to include more strategic auditing services to clients (Julier, 2000) and, in time, by consolidating into larger organizations offering a wider range of services and competing for international clients. In this way, corporate identity and branding consultancies were able to compete with advertising agencies for the (sometimes significantly reduced) marketing budgets of major corporations. By positioning themselves as offering a more 'complete' communications package, corporate identity and branding consultancies moved closer to realizing James Pilditch's aspiration of becoming not simply an adjunct of advertising, but rather 'the new total'.

## MATERIAL PRACTICES

Part of what distinguishes the practice of branding from that of advertising is its extended spatial scope and broad conception of the potential *media* for commercial communication. Although advertising agencies began to engage with the communicative possibilities offered by 'ambient' media and digital technologies from the late 1990s onwards, branding consultancies take this logic much further, and began to do so earlier. Indeed, designers Henrion and Parkin noted as early as 1967 that corporations have numerous points of contact with their audiences, including 'premises, works, products, packaging, stationery, forms, vehicles, publications and uniforms, as well as the usual kind of promotional activities' (Henrion and Parkin, 1967: 7). Whereas advertising agencies almost never have any responsibility for such matters, all are included within the remit of the branding consultancy, which very often is responsible both for designing these materials and for coordinating them with the 'usual kind of promotional activities' to which Henrion and Parkin refer. This role is formalized within the routines of branding and design agencies as part of the 'design audit' stage of a project, in which all possible 'touchpoints' (points of contact between an organization or brand and its various audiences) are assessed.

Such interventions are premised on the idea of an entire environment of coordinated brand elements, and on a model of influence that emphasizes spatial immersion and experience, and engagement with concrete objects and sites, rather than simply the reception of, and response to, images and representations. The economic rationale for such efforts to consider all aspects of a company's material culture as forms of 'media', and to thereby extend the brand's spatial scope, is linked to the growing trend towards using brand-name assets as the basis for expansion into new product and service areas. Working upon brand image and design across a range of sites is part of a strategic effort to extend the range of sites at which the brand can be used to create new opportunities for sales. It has been estimated that up to 95 per cent of the new products launched each year in the US are brand extensions (Murphy, 1998). In this context, branding is used not only to market specific products (by providing images, experiences and feelings designed to attract consumers) but also to reshape the structure of markets themselves by consolidating the image, reputation and experience of the brand across multiple sites through repetition, and attempting to transfer it into new domains (Slater, 2002; Murdock, 2003).

The work of branding is, of course, a thoroughly 'material' matter at many levels and in many senses. For an understanding of cultural intermediaries, however, what makes the work of branding distinctive (and distinct from advertising in particular) is its use of trained designers (in areas like graphics, product design and interior design) to work on the material culture of a brand and to translate brand values from one space or material to another. Unlike advertising agencies, branding consultancies are often used to suggest and implement changes to products, and also to retail environments, company headquarters, stationery, uniforms, websites, trade stands and databases in order to achieve a greater 'design coherence' and to make these spaces more communicative. The physical and geographical scope of their influence is therefore potentially much greater than that of advertising practitioners, especially in a context in which the driver of future commercial activity and revenue is held to be the expansion of the brand.

But how exactly do these acts of translation and extension take place? As I have noted above, branding and re-branding projects often begin with consultancies conducting a 'design audit', in which the entire range of a client's branded materials and sites are evaluated. The subsequent focus lies with the *values* that the brand is intended to communicate, and the need to produce design solutions that align these values with their material extensions and embodiments so that they become mutually reinforcing. Sometimes clients come to branding consultancies with a clear idea of the values they want their brand to embody, while in other cases the consultancy itself is charged with undertaking research to assess such matters; this is particularly common for larger branding consultancies, who often function like strategic or management consultancies, and who may conduct substantial consumer research on behalf of their clients.

What gets changed as a result of a branding or re-branding exercise depends upon the branding consultancy's understanding of the communicative potential of different aspects of the brand's visual and material output. In the example below, a freelance branding consultant describes her work on a re-branding project for a luxury car brand. The company had come to the branding consultancy with the hope that a redesign of branded materials would make it more competitive with other brands in its sector. The consultancy interpreted this as a need to make the brand appear more 'classy':

> [T]he brand, as it was, was very sort of *nouveau riche* appeal, very glitzy ... a bit of a gangster car as well ... they are positioned price-wise in with Mercedes, but *obviously Mercedes has got a much more classy feel about it*, and they wanted to move that way. So basically we took all the gold out and toned it all down ... And looked at the badgeing in the cars and everything. (Sutton, 2002, my emphasis)

This process of 'toning down' was also extended to other areas:

> We looked at their trade stand and changed that. But then we had to look at what the girls on the trade stand were wearing. So I went around the Paris Motor Show taking notes about what everyone was wearing on all the different stands. The Lexus ones were looking very glitzy, little black dresses with gold, they looked, oh they looked quite cheap and tarty ... So we recommended some more modern, modern outfits ... very stylish, very sort of, sort of Prada Sport type thing. You know ... very clean lines and in certain colours that went with the colours that we were using as the colour palette as well. (Sutton, 2002)

This process of applying and extending a colour palette is central to the middle stages of a branding project and, crucially, involves acts of translation from one material to another. In the example above, the colour palette is translated into fabrics and the design of clothing for the trade show stand; in the example below, the colour palette is translated into furniture and materials for car showrooms:

> You've got your basic brand guidelines, you'll have a colour palette that goes with that, and when you get into doing interiors you'll take the basic colour for the corporate identity and you'll *move that into an environmental setting*. So say you've got a silver, you'll maybe use brushed steel ... *because the brand personality is set, you can translate that into certain types of material*. (Sutton, 2002, my emphasis)

These interventions are premised upon the assumption that abstract values can be expressed through particular materials, and that these material expressions of brand personality are not arbitrary, but rather reflect established conventional – or indeed for some designers 'natural' – associations between certain colours or materials and particular ideas and values. In the case above, for example, brushed steel is chosen not only because the colour corresponds with other colours in the brand 'palette', but also, implicitly, because the material itself is held to in some way reflect the brand 'personality' (more accurately, presumably, than other silver-coloured materials). This principle has been formalized within the design world since the 1980s with the idea of 'product semantics' (see Julier, 2000), which has involved a concerted effort to correlate the various formal features of products and materials with their known associations and emotional resonances. For some brand consultancies, such research techniques have become an integral part of the services offered to clients; one informant, the director of a company providing 'sonic branding' solutions for blue-chip clients and for other branding consultancies, argued that music could 'change people's whole perception of a brand' (Jackson, 2001) and that his company's research process enabled clients to shape consumers' perceptions in line with their strategic aims:

LM: Can you really kind of control those feelings? Is it that scientific?

DJ: Mm, yes and no ... There are some things that are absolutely a hundred per cent, we can always predict what people will think. Like if you use a French horn, it's very English corporate. It sounds like a bank ...

LM: How do you know that?

DJ: Because that's how, *that's our creative process*. We play people mood chords, different kinds of music, and we get feedback on what different kinds of music mean to them ... with every single client we go through that workshop process ... So we may do five or six different workshops, we may expose probably fifty, sixty people to maybe ten tracks of music, and ask them about the sounds, ask them about the use of strings or that melody or that rhythm. What does it make them feel? And is it consistent with the brand that we're trying to work on? And just by getting enough of that feedback we know, you know what it means. (Jackson, 2001, my emphasis)

Not all branding projects involve this degree of research and experimentation, however, and much of the work undertaken in-house, or by smaller consultancies or freelancers, may proceed with very little information about the target audience or its perception of the brand (Ennis, 2005). In the case of another informant, the publications officer for a London university, the effort to shift perceptions of the university from a more tradi-tional institution with a specialism in fine art to a more dynamic and creative centre of 'innovation' rested almost entirely with him and the university's in-house graphic designer. Together, they experimented with various modifications to the language and fonts of prospectuses and other printed materials to try to achieve this perceptual shift:

TL: ... that's our house font, which is ... Optima and Garamond, which are both quite traditional. But inside you see here we've used this one,

> Citizen font, which is trying to give a bit more of a creative and informal element ... as is the hung text, if you can see that.

LM: Yes.

TL: This the 1996 prospectus, when we had the creeper. Other people call it ivy [*laughs*]. It's sort of like, very traditional, looks like Oxbridge or something ... Whereas in this we have ... much more modern stuff. And you see in the writing ... it says, 'ideas, imagination, innovation, creativity', which are the words we use everywhere. (Lawson, 2001)

Yet even when substantial research has been conducted, applying this information in the preparation of design solutions depends upon the interpretation of findings by key personnel, as well as decisions about appropriate ways of implementing them in design form. In this respect, branding and design projects rely to a high degree upon the capacity of personnel within the consultancy first to identify various qualities, values and ideas that will be meaningful and recognizable to a specified target audience, and then to find or create a series of replicable design features that will reliably convey these preferred ideas and associations in visual and material form. This project of giving material form to ideas and values, which Grant McCracken terms the 'substantiation of cultural categories in goods' (1988: 75), is likely to be a contingent and unstable process, creating a situation in which 'imprecision and error ... are not only possible but legion' (1988: 78). In fact, the uncertainty and unpredictability of consumers' responses to new products and services has been a large part of the reason for the rise of branding, since 'brands' of goods (whether novelists or washing powder) that have proved successful with consumers in the past are increasingly regarded as the best (i.e. least risky) basis for the launch of new products and services in the future. This is particularly true of industries with high production costs or those that require high levels of initial investment, but is becoming more common across all industries.

At the same time, however, the likelihood of imprecision and error to which McCracken refers reflects a more general feature of industrial design since the mid-20th century, namely the absence of any *necessary* connection between the function of a commodity and the form it takes (Hebdige, 1988). The implications of this must be endlessly grappled with by branding consultants when deciding how to extend existing brand materials into new areas. To explore the implications of this a little further, I want to turn now to a consideration of the forms of knowledge, and general dispositions, upon which branding consultants draw in the course of their work.

## ASSESSING IMPACT

There is a pervasive assumption that cultural intermediaries 'are able to exert, from their position within cultural institutions, a certain amount of cultural authority as shapers of taste and the inculcators of new consumerist dispositions' (Nixon and Du Gay, 2002: 497). This assumption is strengthened by a degree of self-mythologizing by those working in these industries, who tend to assume 'that cultural work is special and mysterious and can only be undertaken by special and mysterious people' (Beck cited in Wright, 2005a: 112). Yet precisely how much authority they might be able to enjoy, or the form that this might take, is hard to gauge. The empirical material presented above suggests that there are reasons to be cautious in assuming that cultural intermediaries are able to shape tastes and influence consumer dispositions; even when engaged in an explicit effort to interpret or influence consumer behaviour through the selective appropriation of 'legitimate' culture, branding consultants often overestimate their capacity to understand the tastes and preferences of a target audience, and base their decisions on personal experience, speculation or stereotype, which in turn may lead to pronounced and expensive failures. Indeed, it may be the case that such workers are simply unable to see beyond their own habitus; in so far as branding consultants are able to 'connect' with consumers, this may be limited to consumers who share their demographic characteristics.

Yet while it is difficult to validate the typical claims made about cultural intermediaries' power, the evidence presented above suggests that branding consultants *do* exert considerable influence in specific domains. To a much greater degree than other cultural intermediaries, they are able to shape the physical spaces and materials of consumer culture, as well as the range of goods and services that large companies produce. In this respect branding consultancies, and the personnel working within them, are important parts of a production system in which 'the cultural sites, experiences, and meanings offered to the public are shaped in decisive ways' (Murdock, 2003: 17). By advising on programmes of innovation (Lury, 2004) and new areas of expansion, branding consultants are also frequently able to influence the sectors in which companies operate and thus the nature of competition within those sectors. In some cases they contribute to the design of company databases, customer service manuals and hiring policies, which have a direct impact upon workplace culture as well as services offered to consumers. It may be, in other words, that certain types of cultural intermediaries exert a far wider influence than has previously been claimed, but in different areas. This is precisely the claim I want to make for branding consultants.

There are, however, some notable differences among those working in branding, both in terms of what they are able to do and how they see their role – a fact that ought to bear upon any assessment of their influence. Branding work gets done in a wide range of institutional sites, very many of which do not see themselves or promote themselves as branding agencies at all. Being a brand manager or communications officer in a small or medium-sized organization means one is constrained in a range of ways that make it difficult to implement some 'pure' version of what branding is about. Furthermore, of those agencies that do define themselves as branding specialists, many are very small and lack the resources or reach of larger institutions. This often limits the types of work that can be taken on in the first place. It also operates as a considerable constraint on the amount of research and strategic planning that can be conducted beforehand, which, as I have indicated above, may make it harder to straddle the differences between the dispositions and assumptions of the producers of branded materials and those of consumers. Many of these smaller agencies are essentially graphic design agencies which specialize in branding and subsist almost entirely on publications design and periodic 'brand refreshes' for a limited number of clients. This kind of branding work is therefore predominantly visual and has little bearing upon, for example, corporate strategy or recruitment policies.

There are also differences in orientation and belief among those working inside branding. Some demonstrate a greater reflexive awareness than others, and some are more critical than others of the way in which branding and related marketing interventions work out in practice. When conducting research with branding consultants, as with those working in other cultural intermediary occupations, there may be a particularly 'evangelical' or promotional tone to people's accounts of their work because of a perceived need to persuade others of the value of their work. It is also important to consider the wider sectoral and/or organizational factors at play: branding consultancies, despite their growing influence, are less well established than advertising agencies, and may still have to persuade clients of the value of their services; similarly, 'promotional' talk about one's work may be more of a habit for those working in agencies who are constantly pitching for client work than for those working in in-house positions. Both of these factors may feed into the way that people account for themselves and their roles in research interviews.

Yet the emergence of larger and more strategically oriented branding consultants, and their role in guiding corporate expansion into new sectors, suggest that branding is an increasingly important driver of economic decision making, and consolidates the 'flow' logic of cultural production by which continuous sequences of goods and services are presented to the public (Murdock, 2003). At the same time, the use of branding to restructure materials (even if, as is often the case, this operates at a fairly low level of delivery vans, uniforms, store design etc.) is a significant contributor to the process by which goods are imbued with symbolic content, and therefore by which even relatively mundane consumption decisions become opened up to considerations based on taste or personal expression rather than simple functionality or cost. This in turn puts branding, as much as advertising, at the heart of processes of aestheticization (Featherstone, 1991), processes which may, in turn, contribute to increased institutional consumption and to a rise in the cost of basic goods (Lodziak, 2002). Taken together, such developments suggest that branding consultancies should be taken seriously by contemporary studies of the cultural intermediaries – not, contrary to some accounts, because they are necessarily instruments of consumerism but because they play an increasingly important role in structuring markets and institutions, and serve to intensify the informational and communicative properties of a wider material culture.

# FUTURE DIRECTIONS

How might the study of brands and branding be developed further? There remains a paucity of empirical studies of the work that goes on inside branding consultancies, and scholarship on cultural intermediaries would therefore benefit from more detailed observation in these sites, particularly in agencies of different types and sizes. On the other hand, the discourse of branding has extended so rapidly in recent years that it is no longer sufficient to study branding within branding agencies alone. Concepts of brand identity, brand equity and brand values have become central concerns within many, if not most, commercial organizations. They are also pivotal in the work of more established types of cultural intermediary, such as advertising agencies, and in newer organizations such as social media and digital communications agencies. One possibility for scholarship in this area is therefore to embed a concern with brands and branding within the studies of *all* types of intermediaries – and in commercial practices more generally – assessing its relative significance in different contexts.

A more focused set of research questions arises in relation to the introduction of discourses and practices of branding within primarily non-profit institutions such as charities, universities and local government agencies. Specialist agencies now cater to each of these, and each could be studied in more depth. One of the richest seams of current research is in the branding of cities and nations – an area in which public institutions take responsibility for the development of places as brands, in a way that usually draws together, and often blurs or conflates, public and private interests (see Mattern, 2008; Greenberg, 2008; Kaneva, 2011; Aronczyk 2013). One of the key concerns in this strand of research – and one that could profitably be studied further – is about the democratic or anti-democratic impulses at work in these initiatives, and the relationship between city or nation branding and earlier forms of national propaganda and public relations.

Another potentially fruitful line of future enquiry concerns the relationship between branding theory and practice. Nigel Thrift (2005) has written about the role of business magazines and management training programmes in formatting the subjectivities of those employed in the 'new economy'. The proliferation of 'how to' books about branding, not to mention the development of courses in brand management in business schools, marketing departments and elsewhere, provide further sites for examining the ways in which devices might (re)shape dispositions. This research agenda in turn might feed into a wider discussion of the ways in which the notion of 'brand values' is affecting business practice. In recent years, an understanding of brands as objects made up of 'values', 'identity' or 'personality' (rather than simply a name, logo and visual palette) has been used to propose brands as guides for business decision making, particularly in areas such as hiring and employment practice, and fairtrade policies and standards. A key question here therefore concerns the extent to which the brand is becoming a surrogate for the kinds of ethical decision making that might once have been guided by the state or by regulation.

A final area for future research is the issue of how brands are valued, ranked and measured. A number of authors (e.g. Arvidsson, 2006; Willmott, 2010) have pointed out that the existence of agreed-upon measures of brand value and brand equity has been essential for the expansion of branding, since these allow the relatively abstract entity of the brand to be quantified and financially valued, and thus considered in mergers, acquisitions, licensing and so on. But other researchers (e.g. Lury and Moor, 2010) have noted that ways of valuing, measuring and comparing brands are constantly evolving: measures of brand equity, in particular, are developing in multiple directions, and rankings and evaluations of brands (e.g. those conducted by *Ethical Consumer* magazine) are increasingly made by organizations that do not share – indeed may be hostile to – a brand's primary interests. The issue of brand valuation and rankings is thus one of the ways in which cultural intermediaries scholarship can pursue its interest in devices and material practices, but also extend into a consideration of what happens when those practices are opened up to scrutiny by a wider public, and begin to circulate and mutate within a wider media and information environment.

## NOTE

1   The author, the editors and the publishers would like to express their thanks to John Wiley & Sons Inc. for granting permission to reproduce parts of the article 'Branding Consultants as Cultural Intermediaries', *The Sociological Review*, 56 (3) © 2008 in this chapter.

# 8

# PUBLIC RELATIONS PRACTITIONERS

## CAROLINE E.M. HODGES AND LEE EDWARDS

This chapter will combine literature from Public Relations (PR) and Cultural Studies to outline so-far-underexplored ways of thinking about PR practitioners (PRPs) as cultural intermediaries. Our purpose in this chapter is to consider something of the breadth of PR practice and its centrality to 'everyday life'. We begin our discussion by establishing what we mean when we use the terms 'public relations' and 'culture'. The Chartered Institute of Public Relations defines PR as involving the communication and exchange of information and ideas through negotiation, attempting to 'maintain goodwill and mutual understanding between an organization and its publics'. Taking an interpretivist position, we suggest that culture emerges from the experiences of individuals and how they make sense of them (Geertz, 1973: 145). The role of public relations within culture then is to create and communicate shared meanings (Curtin and Gaither, 2007), and PRPs are deeply embedded in culture, an occupational group specializing in the production and dissemination of symbolic goods and commodities (L'Etang, 2006: 388).

The connection between culture and public relations becomes even clearer when we see that PR is itself meaning production, negotiation and relationship management for organizations. PRPs manage reputation as well as a range of external and internal relationships on behalf of organizations by constructing and deploying discourses within a range of contexts (social, political, economic, organizational, professional) and cultures (national, international, lifestyle etc.). Part of PRPs' remit as guardians of reputation is to develop corporate identities and to communicate these via logos, exhibitions, events, branding, all of which are cultural artefacts. PRPs can also have a social impact, for example by prompting the formation of communities of interest (Banks, 2000; Hodges, 2012). PRP work can, therefore, be described as a cultural activity which 'forms part of the communicative process by which society constructs its social reality' (Daymon and Hodges, 2009: 430). Practitioners' cultural role lies in helping to promote meanings associated with particular products, services, ideas or people.

Whilst PR has been examined through a cultural studies lens (Curtin and Gaither, 2005, 2007; Hodges, 2006, 2011, 2012; Pieczka, 2006; Edwards, 2012), these works are limited in their discussion. In this chapter, the field of PR as 'a social space of relations of dominance, subordinance, or equivalence, rooted in the types and amounts of resources that actors possess' (Ihlen, 2009: 62) will be considered within the context of the 'circuit of culture', the heuristic first developed by Stuart Hall and his colleagues (du Gay et al., 1997) to explore the processes by which communicative meaning is produced, circulated, consumed, commodified and endlessly reproduced and renegotiated in society (Curtin and Gaither, 2007: 35).

We will consider ways in which PR practitioners as cultural intermediaries negotiate the competing discourses surrounding culture, identity and power within the fields with which they interact: the occupational (or professional) field, the organizational field and the industry field (Edwards, 2012). The circuit of culture is a useful framework for analysing PR because whilst providing a structure within which to explore cultural practice, it also emphasizes that cultural meaning is always subject to change (Curtin and Gaither, 2007). Our discussion of PRP work as a cultural practice supports the argument proposed by Jacquie L'Etang (2008) that it is open to various possible meanings. Drawing on a new (radical) socio-cultural turn (Edwards and Hodges, 2011) which has emerged within PR scholarship in recent years, we will explore what being a PRP means in the context of the circuit of culture, opening up the links between societal culture, economy, production and consumption and the communication activities PRPs engage in.

## HISTORICIZING CULTURAL INTERMEDIARIES

The UK provides a useful illustration of the evolution of western approaches to PR practice that are typically based in neoliberal political–economic thought and shaped by new forms of mass media and communication. PR is a significant industry in the UK. Figures from a 2011 Public Relations Consultants' Association report estimated there were 61,600 PRPs in an industry with a turnover of £7.5 billion across the private, not-for-profit and public sectors (Bussey, 2011a). The roots of PR in the UK go back to the era of the British Empire during the 19th and early 20th centuries when it was used as part of efforts to expand and promote British interests overseas. The Empire Marketing Board, for example, was responsible for producing documentary-style films that explored particular facets of the British way of life and promoted British commercial interests (L'Etang, 2004). PR has remained tightly linked to the political Establishment and the development of a neoliberal commercial environment (L'Etang, 2004; Edwards and Pieczka, 2013; Miller and Dinan, 2000, 2007; Moloney, 2006). In the early part of the 20th century it was primarily used as an important tool of public information for national and local government authorities. Following the Second World War, PR expanded within the commercial sector also, as practitioners working in-house within commercial organizations became more common (L'Etang, 2004). The development of PR at this time went hand in hand with growth in the media and cultural industries more broadly, particularly advertising and design, as a consequence of wider political, economic and socio-cultural trends. These trends led to a boom economy in the 1980s which further fuelled PR's growth and expansion alongside consequent 'lifestylization' (L'Etang, 2007: 220) efforts associated with the cultural intermediary occupations which have continued until the present day. Technological changes, particularly the rise of social media in the early 21st century, opened up increasing opportunity for PR and 'PR-type' activities to be used by organizations, informal groups and individuals.

The development of PR in the UK has followed a similar trajectory to that of the US, which is regarded by many as the birthplace of modern western professional PR. During the boom of the early 20th century, Ivy Ledbetter Lee and Edward Bernays, to whom many have given the title the 'fathers of public relations', were the first to engage in organized media relations activities and, in Bernays' case in particular, draw on social psychology to inform, persuade and encourage consumption. The crises of the Great Depression and both the First and Second World Wars brought further need for PRPs to counsel US government on how to ease the growing tension and communicate their programmes and policies to the public. According to the Public Relations Society of America (PRSA), PRPs in the US today serve a wide variety of institutions such as businesses, trade unions, government agencies, voluntary organizations, hospitals, schools, colleges and religious institutions. Spending on PR services is recorded to have grown by 4.9 per cent during 2005–10, to $3.7 billion (Public Relations Society of America, 2012), and figures from 2010 suggest that the industry employs 320,000 people and has a faster-than-average projected growth rate (2010–20) of 21 per cent (Bureau of Labor Statistics, 2012).

In contrast, in contexts where free-market forces were not the primary drivers of PR, the practice developed in a different way. Under socialist governments such as the German Democratic Republic (the former East Germany), for example, the term 'PR' was rejected because of its associations with the West (Bentele and Wehmeier, 2003). Instead, in the GDR the term *Öffentlichkeitsarbeit* (publicity work) was used to define PRPs' primary role of disseminating public information on behalf of state institutions and state-sponsored economic entities. Such close links with the promotion of the socialist state both domestically and internationally meant that PRPs were engaged in profoundly and transparently ideological work, with the primary aim of fostering a socialist consciousness amongst citizens (Wehmeier, 2004).

The Latin American School of PR (Molleda, 2001; Molleda and Ferguson, 2004) tells a different story. Whilst PR emerged here in an era of political and economic transformation and was influenced by privatization, deregulation, market integration and the established power of the traditional mass media, the social and economic imbalances within the region have prompted PRPs to take on a more social orientation. The 1978 Mexican Accord of Inter-American Federation of Public Relations, for example, stated that the professional practice of PR should operate within a socially precarious environment to 'elevate the level of understanding, solidarity and collaboration between a public or private organization and the social groups linked to [it]' (Molleda, 2001: 516). PRPs in this region of the world have, therefore, focused on the interests of the community.

These brief summaries demonstrate how PRPs respond to the political, historical and socio-economic reality of the environment in which they practise. The examples emphasize how PRP work is shaped by different cultural, economic and political dynamics. In this sense, PRPs act as cultural intermediaries by addressing the social and cultural norms associated with particular areas of activity, as well as influencing different ways of thinking and being in society as a whole.


# MATERIAL PRACTICES

PRPs are cultural intermediaries whose practice is closely linked to other cultural intermediary occupations such as advertising, marketing and journalism, through the promotion of discourses about products, services, organizations, brands, people and policies in order to encourage material changes in audience values, attitudes or behaviours (Edwards, 2012; Mickey, 2008; L'Etang, 2006; L'Etang et al., 2007).

What creates the greatest power for PR is belief in the legitimacy of words and those who utter them (Mickey, 2008: 20). PRPs operate as 'discourse workers' or contemporary storytellers combining material objects with words, symbols, technologies and behaviours to construct particular, specialized identities (Gee, 2005: 7) and, to some degree, fantasy worlds that have resonance with the 'lifeworlds' of consumers to get their client (a brand/celebrity/political organization/place etc.) known and accepted (L'Etang et al., 2007; Elmer, 2011; Mickey, 2008). Anthropologists have thought of storytellers as reinforcing and revitalising the ways of thinking and/or behaving of a distinctive culture such as a tribe or a village. In today's society the same might be said about PRPs revitalizing the ways of thinking and/or behaving of consumer tribes or brand communities towards organizations. When we understand PRPs in this way, the focus of interest becomes PR as a form of expression and sharing information, as a tool of education concerned with persuasion and interaction, which places culture (i.e. the rituals, habits, beliefs and norms that bind a group of individuals together) at the heart of every PR story. Importantly, when PR practitioners engage with storytelling they are looking to engage with audiences on an emotional level, using symbolic representations that are both socially and historically determined and communicating extraordinary experiences and bringing those experiences to life. Such approaches are particularly effective in crowded communications environments, for example, when introducing a new and complex product or service to market; when a sustainable behavioural change is required such as in health promotion campaigns; or when (long-term) emotional buy-in is required, as might be found in political communications or not-for-profit/charity PR. The aim of an organization's PR activity in each of these contexts will be to stand out by engaging with people's everyday lives and their frustrations and aspirations.

The circuit of culture provides an important framework within which to make sense of the role of public relations practitioners as cultural intermediaries. By adapting the circuit of culture to PR, Curtin and Gaither (2005, 2007) captured the processes of meaning-making that involve PRPs and the ways in which these are shaped by a variety of actors and other influencing factors. These factors include the organization and its PR practitioners, publics that interact with the organization, and the environment in which interactions between the organization and publics take place. As we have seen elsewhere in this reader, the circuit of culture consists of five moments – production, representation, consumption, identity, regulation – that collectively provide a shared cultural space (Curtin and Gaither, 2007: 38). Below we summarize how PRPs are implicated in each moment:

- *Production:* The moment of production offers PRPs the power to attach specific cultural meanings to a product or idea through the use of language. They develop messages by deliberately choosing words and images that will resonate with the cultural context and experiences of the target audiences, therefore being more acceptable and, in the process, validating certain social and cultural hierarchies. This production work is often mediated rather than direct; other actors affecting the process will include the client(s), the PR team, designers, journalists, publishers, events managers, celebrities and opinion leaders and so on. Of these, the client is probably the most influential because PRP work will be largely dictated by their personal ambitions, organizational objectives and cultures (Curtin and Gaither, 2005: 100).
- *Representation:* PRPs represent the meaning of products and ideas by using a wide range of communications strategies and tactics ranging from preparing press releases and media kits for journalists, writing and publishing brochures, developing and maintaining websites, commissioning short films and videos, organizing seminars and events and lobbying and advocacy work. As in advertising, images and words are used together to communicate a particular message, although the written and spoken word (in the form of press releases, interviews, corporate documents and web-based communication) is usually the primary form of persuasion.
- *Consumption:* PRPs shape consumption by connecting new products and/or experiences to historically meaningful events or ideas for their audience. They

articulate meaning in relation to cultural and social norms that circulate among the audiences at particular times. Production and consumption do not exist in binary opposition to one another, but exist as part of a chain of intermediation, since consumers of PR messages are themselves also producers of meaning as they engage in making sense of the messages they receive, and PRPs use feedback from audiences to enable producers to shape their products, services and communication activity more appropriately (Curtin and Gaither, 2005: 101).

- *Regulation* addresses the limitations on PRPs and their field of practice (i.e. organizational limitations, budgetary constraints, technological infrastructure, institutionalized educational systems, regulatory bodies and other legal controls or cultural norms and expectations). The moment of regulation can be both constraining and facilitating. For example, new technology is able to empower PRPs working for activist groups by allowing them a more easily accessible means of having a voice in relevant debates. It also offers PRPs a means of communication that bypasses traditional media gatekeepers (Curtin and Gaither, 2005). PRPs, in turn, also play a regulatory role in shaping attitudes, behaviours and policies both formally through public affairs and political lobbying as well as informally through corporate culture and identity programmes (L'Etang, 2007).

- *Identity* refers to the meanings given to a particular object or group through the processes of production and consumption and is inherently subjective (Curtin and Gaither, 2005: 101). PRPs are implicated in this moment in three main ways: 1) the production of organizational/brand identity; 2) the construction of consumer identity achieved through the consumption of symbolically meaningful goods, services and ideas; 3) the construction of audience identities through segmentation and targeting practices. In addition, as cultural intermediaries, PRPs link identities (based on understanding of consumer lifestyles) with products (via market research knowledge) in order to produce goods and experiences for consumption.

Each 'moment' of the circuit of culture is connected with the others through a series of articulations, generating a complex web of what Edwards and Hodges (2011: 4), drawing on Dewey and Bentley (1991 [1949]), term 'transactions', through which meaning emerges. For these authors, PRPs' work becomes a 'locus of transactions' that produce emergent social and cultural meanings. These transactions are defined as engagements between individual actors (PRPs, clients, sponsors, audience members) and/or generalized others (PR consultancies, client organizations, employers, activist groups, government bodies, professional bodies or the professional field itself). In the act of engaging with these individuals and groups, PRPs not only act as cultural intermediaries in terms of their work at the different moments of the circuit of culture, but also are themselves transformed in the process. The meanings they create and disseminate in their engagements with others are part of their own lives as much as others'. PRPs, too, may adopt particular products, services or behaviours in line with the meanings associated with them.

Alternatively, they may alter their own practice on the basis of reactions to their work. In this way, integrating the concept of transactions into the understanding of the circuit of culture reinforces the interdependence of the moments and highlights meaning as continuously produced by PRPs within the interactions inherent to these relationships.

Making sense of these complex patterns and relationships requires in-depth study of PRP culture – their values, attitudes and behaviours, their perceptions of effective practice, their stories, experiences and visions for the future, and their perceptions of their relation to other fields (Hodges, 2006, 2012). Caroline Hodges defined PRP culture as a 'lifeworld': 'the way public relations people live, create and relate to the world of public relations work' (2006: 85). Given the degree of cultural relativism built into the circuit of culture, and the inherently subjective nature of lifeworlds, the need for an understanding of situation ethics as part of PRPs' cultural intermediary work follows (Curtin and Gaither, 2005: 104). PRPs are required to make choices about what form practice should take in a particular context (Burkitt, 2002). In her ethnographic work in Mexico City, for example, Hodges (2011: 37–38) found that PRPs' occupational ethos was one of human-scale, democratic communication and trust. The key word here, however, is 'ethos'. As several of the practitioners emphasized, it was sometimes difficult to uphold one's ethics in a country that had suffered so many brisk political and social changes and it often called for improvisation (Hodges, 2011). As this example illustrates, PRPs as cultural intermediaries may aspire to a world in which PR works for the good of society, yet the context in which they work may dictate otherwise.

Furthermore, despite the drive to be regarded as a legitimate and 'honest' profession, public relations remains an occupation that is regulated by the needs of its clients, with objectives and principles that are determined by, rather than independent of, organizations (Edwards, 2012). Here, knowledge capital – defined as formal professional education or informal education, skills and experience that are represented within the industry (Ihlen, 2009) – is also significant. Like other cultural intermediary occupations, a formal PR education is not required to work in the industry (Durrer and Miles, 2009) and so knowledge capital is a useful way to make sense of PRP expertise relevant to particular fields. In the charity sector, for example, an understanding of the social norms and regulations of the particular context, an ability to translate between the different approaches to living experienced by the 'clients' the charity serves, knowledge of how to gain media coverage, as well as how to lobby effectively would all be vital to PRPs' cultural intermediation – but are all ultimately determined by the client and industry context.

The moment of regulation in the circuit of culture also means that broader social hierarchies will frame, and are likely to be reflected in, PRPs' cultural intermediation. In the case of the UK, for example, PRPs are largely white and middle class, and the profession is heavily gendered, with men being over-represented at senior levels whilst women undertake the majority of the tactical roles (Bussey, 2011b; *PR Week*/PRCA, 2011). Exploratory research also suggests that the occupational body is privileged compared to the general population: PRPs' cultural capital (patterns of cultural taste, knowledge and activity as well as understandings of cultural and social norms) was consistent with that observed among more powerful social groups (Edwards, 2008, 2011; Durrer and Miles, 2009).

In summary, within the circuit of culture, PRP work is redefined as a cultural practice that is shaped by the context in which it is practised. This positions PRPs as cultural intermediaries whose 'promotion of particular products, ideas or lifestyles' contribute to deeper meanings, identity connections and understandings of any given experience via more personal and experiential approaches to communication (Negus, 2002; Durrer and Miles, 2009). Approaching PRPs in this way reveals a diverse range of intermediation, sometimes carried out by PR non-specialists (Edwards and Hodges, 2011), that needs to be understood in relation to its specific social, cultural, industrial and organizational context.

## ASSESSING IMPACT

As we saw above, the effects of PR are mediated rather than direct; that is, PRPs rely on the 'approval' of their clients and on the work of other cultural intermediaries such as journalists, publishers and designers to get their message across. However, a large body of critical scholars (Miller and Dinan, 2007; Moloney, 2006; Edwards, 2006; L'Etang and Piezcka, 2006; Weaver et al., 2006) concur that public relations involves the production of discourses that generate legitimacy for a particular point of view, sideling or negating alternative perspectives, and that PR therefore contributes to structural inequalities of power, prestige and profit in capitalist systems (Hesmondhalgh, 2002; Bourdieu, 2000: 57–58).

A PRP's role as a cultural intermediary is always bound up with self-interest for both their clients and for the profession itself. For example, in a study of the micro- and macro-level cultural intermediary role of a PR department within a UK rail transport provider, Edwards (2012) found that the PRPs were as much concerned with maintaining the symbolic value of the PR function within the organization, and therefore reinforcing its legitimacy, as they were with managing the reputation of the company amongst its various stakeholders. Their cultural intermediary practices, which focused on lifestylization and the quality of the consumer experience of rail travel rather than logistical aspects such as punctuality and efficiency of the trains, also had an impact on the industry in which the organization operated, challenging existing cultural and social norms about rail travel and validating neoliberal principles of consumerism and individual choice.

Whilst studies of the cultural effects of cultural intermediary occupations, like public relations, have traditionally regarded these industries as purely commercial, PR techniques *can* be used to assist a variety of actors in pursuing their interests. As Durrer and Miles (2009: 234) argue, the role of the cultural intermediary is not restricted to a shaper of taste and lifestyles but it can also extend to an arbiter of citizenship. A discussion about ways that public relations can contribute to the facilitation of social change has already begun (Hodges and McGrath, 2011; Dutta and Pal, 2011; Dutta, 2008; Molleda and Ferguson, 2004; Bardhan, 2003). For example, Caroline Hodges and Nilam McGrath (2011) set out to reconceptualize what public relations might be in a context where it forms part of a transformational process. These authors present their argument by way of a case study of a youth-led health communication project in a deprived community in the city of Iquitos, Peru. The purpose of this project was to inform and develop shared understandings of 'healthy community' and 'healthy living' and to encourage a change in policy and reallocation of resources. Using the information collected through participatory diagnostic workshops and meetings, 'popular communication' efforts (art, theatre, film-making, competitions, leaflets etc.) were developed by the young people as forms of communication and activism that were 'owned' by the community and shared with those responsible for making decisions about their welfare. PR professionals 'engage in relationships with media, community leaders, and other individuals on a daily basis' (Kent and Taylor, 2002: 30), yet this project was notable for the obvious absence of a formal public relations function. Instead, 'PR-type' tactics were carried out by project coordinators who, rather than operating as mediators to impart existing knowledge (common in western models of PR), engaged in a process of dialogue, reflection and mutual learning with the community. This case reinforces the transactional nature of PRP work and illustrates that there are multiple functions which PRPs can enact as cultural intermediaries beyond the creation of consumer lifestyles and disseminating information. These include advocacy, facilitating discussion and enabling processes of mutual learning. However, PRPs can only work in this way if political, economic, socio-cultural and legal structures allow.

PRPs, therefore, facilitate 'two conflicting trends' in PR (Ihlen, 2009: 71). As cultural intermediaries, they can work to provide already powerful institutions with opportunities to further consolidate their position of privilege within society whilst, on the other hand, they can support less powerful groups to challenge the status quo, promote participatory communication and lobby for policy changes (Bardhan and Weaver, 2011). If we return to the circuit of culture, the model recognizes that PRPs work across uneven playing fields, but those fields are not necessarily consistently tilted in favour of any one particular group. As Curtin and Gaither argue, '[t]he field shifts in any given articulation within the bounds supplied by the moments, meaning that the playing field is not always tilted in favour of economic power' (2007: 209).

# FUTURE DIRECTIONS

Research on PR should seek to engage with the practitioners themselves and to explore the relationships they have with their occupational activity, work environment and the profession, as well as the values and communication aims of the clients they represent. In closing, we suggest five directions for developing a more holistic understanding of PR and its practitioners as cultural intermediaries.

First, more insight is needed into public relations occupational cultures in different parts of the world. As researchers, there are certain questions we can ask which might help us to identify characteristics that are common, relevant and/ or particular to practitioner lifeworlds in varied social and cultural contexts (Hodges, 2006: 85): What sorts of people practise public relations? Do they have any common social and/or educational experiences? What meanings do public relations practitioners assign to what they do? How has the context(s) in which they work (cultural field, political field, organizational field, industry field) shaped these practitioners as agents and the occupational activities they carry out? How do practitioners subjectively and socially construct the meanings inherent in the practice they are involved in? What impact does the above have on the roles public relations practitioners play both inside and outside of work? How do the activities carried out by PR practitioners influence their role (actual and potential) as cultural intermediaries?

Second, scholars should explore the informal, untrained practice of public relations, paying particular attention to the growth in online opportunities (Edwards and Hodges, 2011; Demetrious, 2011). Much of the research, to date, has explored corporate practice operating within neo-liberal democracies when, as we have seen in this chapter, PR practices are applied in multiple contexts that are influenced by varied regulatory environments (Curtin and Gaither, 2005: 109).

Third, research should investigate how PR work negotiates complex intercultural transactions and crosses dominant and micro- or sub-cultures (i.e. organizational, national, ethnic, lifestyle etc.) (Edwards and Hodges, 2011; L'Etang et al., 2007; L'Etang, 2006). This would require emic research work that is more ethnographic in nature and acknowledges the integral relationship between both historical and future orientation (Hodges, 2012).

Fourth, there should be greater consideration of the moments of *production, representation, consumption, identity* and *regulation* in relation to a discourse analysis of PR and storytelling. Furthermore, a phenomenological perspective could be employed to explore the identities of PRPs in relation to the audiences they communicate with.

Fifth, wider application of the circuit of culture within the context of studies of diversity and power within the PR industry (Curtin and Gaither, 2007; L'Etang, 2009; Edwards, 2010) would be productive. As Curtin and Gaither argue, a growing body of literature has emerged which 'embodies the reconceptualization of publics [PR audiences] in terms congruent with the principles of the circuit and [this] represents perhaps the most prolific body of work within this paradigm to date' (2005: 109). Further work needs to be done which recognizes the 'multiplicity of identities and difference' that demands scholars theoretically address differences of race, class and gender simultaneously.

As we have seen, the circuit of culture offers a useful framework for analysis as it encourages researchers to combine theoretical ideas and epistemological perspectives and to consider varied contexts for exploration so as to investigate anything from 'everyday human agency and the making of cultural meanings' to 'social and organizational structures and economic relationships' (Negus, 1997: 69). These five starting points for research demonstrate the potential of the model as a means of envisaging research that can more fully inform our understanding of cultural intermediation through this important occupation.

# 9

# ARTS PROMOTION

## *VICTORIA DURRER AND DAVE O'BRIEN*

## RETHINKING CULTURAL INTERMEDIARIES, NEGOTIATING BOUNDARIES IN THE ARTS

Arts promotion, and in particular participation programmes in art galleries and museums, play a key role within arts institutions in attracting wider audiences. This chapter interprets the role of these individuals as cultural intermediaries. This interpretation is based on interviews held between 2006 and 2007 with 22 arts programmers in 10 different organizations in Liverpool which were, at the time, responsible for addressing targeted groups labelled 'socially excluded' under the direction of the New Labour Government's cultural policy in the UK. The view-points gathered from these interviews bring to light the significant role individuals within these posts may play as cultural intermediaries in building bridges into the arts for non-traditional audiences.

These individuals describe a desire to break down the barriers of the arts for individuals who may not typically attend. It is this desire and the processes by which they attempt to accomplish this task that has led us to re-examine the term 'cultural intermediaries'. This chapter uses the concept to both explain and challenge contemporary readings of the role of the art museum, gallery or centre and, in particular, speaks to the critique of arts policy as mere 'instrumentalism' (Belfiore and Bennett, 2008) or as a replication of Victorian social values (Bennett, 2000).

The chapter explains how these individuals' understanding of 'exclusion' as expressed within a cultural policy context translates to a deep understanding of a culture of elitism that has been longstanding within the field of the arts. It demonstrates that, by understanding such a barrier exists, these individuals may play unique roles as points of access for broader participation within, and thus greater promotion of, the arts. The form of arts promotion they advocate is one that is dependent upon a personalized approach that promotes dialogue, trust and relationship building. In taking this approach, we assert that they serve as cultural intermediaries who act as gatekeepers attracting non-traditional audiences into what many academics argue to be elite arts institutions. The focus here is on two aspects: how this approach is carried out by cultural intermediaries; and how these individuals are uniquely suited to carry out that role by their ability to traverse the arts' longstanding boundary of exclusion and inclusion. Tensions are seen to arise, however, and it is through these processes that the power of the arts world and its institutions (Newman and McLean, 2006) are both reaffirmed and challenged.

The data presented is drawn from the English context, where there has been substantial discourse and debate over the role of the arts, funding for the arts and the arts' relationship with various aspects of public policy (e.g. Gray, 2004; O'Brien, 2010). The debates in the UK, particularly with regard to the position of the arts in the economy and the associated discourses of creative industries (Miller, this volume), tie into global trends, particularly those with former colonial associations with the British model of policy making.

However, the English context, particularly the association of the arts with various forms of social policy, differed importantly from both Continental Europe and the US, primarily as a result of the specific relationship between the state and the arts in these three areas. Whilst it would be a vulgar distortion to speak of a single European 'model' for cultural policy, the role of arts organizations and their staff was associated with the ideas of 'art for art's sake' and the power of the traditionally conceived artistic director or curator (Luxford, 2010; Eikhof and Haunschild, 2007). Likewise the American experience, with its focus on philanthropic and civil society forms of artistic funding and organization, avoided the direct concerns with policy attachment and accusations of political control associated with arts policy in the UK at the time of this chapter's fieldwork (Mirza, 2006; Cowen, 2010).

The interview sample presented here was selected from both mainstream and traditional-style art galleries or museums in Liverpool with permanent collections as well as contemporary art centres and festivals (six types of organisation) that commission new artwork and are thus highly dependent on or subject to changes and trends in the international art market as well as from key, longer-established grassroots organizations (four) whose funding is less assured compared to the relative stability of the key cultural institutions in the city. Further, their aims tend to be based on, rather than responding to, ideas of social activism via the arts. Interviews carried out originally sought to investigate how individuals in roles of participation, education and outreach within these institutions felt they were addressing (or not) cultural policy aims for social inclusion.

# HISTORICIZING CULTURAL INTERMEDIARIES

In order to understand how we interpret the role of individuals in posts related to participation, education and outreach as cultural intermediaries, it is necessary to understand how art galleries, museums and centres have historically viewed public access to the arts. First, art galleries and centres have traditionally stood as elitist institutions. In their study of visitors to European museums during the early 1960s, Bourdieu and Darbel explained that art museums 'reinforce for some the feeling of belonging and for others the feeling of exclusion' (1991: 112). They argue that arts institutions are truly accessible only to those individuals who hold the appropriate cultural, social and economic capital and that those individuals who do not possess this capital feel that such institutions are 'not for the likes of us' (Bourdieu, 1990b: 56).

The very foundations of public institutions after the period of the French Revolution, and particularly those of the arts, have indeed been based on and organized by the wealth and knowledge of an elite whose private art and anthropological collections were obtained for the establishment of public museums (Macdonald, 1998) and stood as representations of national power and pride as well as political virtue (Graham et al., 2005). Those in power who possessed enough cultural capital and distinctive taste to truly appreciate art (Bourdieu and Darbel, 1991; Bourdieu, 1984) seemed to believe that art museums could express the goodness of a state or the civic-mindedness of its chief citizens who donated objects, art or even funds towards the construction of galleries (Moore, 2004). In turn, it was argued that through the consumption of the objects or the objectified ideals held within these institutions, the masses would benefit socially and morally (Arnold, 1993 [1867–69]; Cole, 1884).

Despite this belief system, which has rationalized the state funding of the arts, there exists a debate on how best to make art, once seen as privy only to the elite, more accessible to the public. Existing since the 19th century, the issue of accessing the arts has been linked to the notion that the arts are something of value to which everyone has a right (Kawashima, 2006). Yet, how exactly to promote the arts in such a way as to encourage atypical audiences to engage has been an ongoing debate (Durrer, 2008).

The evolution of art institutions in the UK since the 1970s has been motivated by a desire for widening participation, in both democratic as well as economic terms (McGuigan, 1996). In 1984, the Arts Council of Great Britain produced *The Glory of the Garden* policy document and funded new gallery education posts, aiming to further develop and promote the leisure services of the arts. Art galleries were reinvented as spaces for consumption. Visitor surveys were taken up; gallery cafés, blockbuster exhibitions and gift shops were introduced; major exhibitions were promoted (Kawashima, 1997); and technology was used to encourage more visitor interaction within galleries (Hannigan, 1998).

When New Labour charged state-funded organizations, such as art galleries, with the responsibility of combating social exclusion (DCMS, 1999, 2000), processes for promoting access for non-traditional audiences came under more scrutiny. Institutions and local authorities were encouraged to 'listen to and learn' from stakeholders and 'tailor' messages to specific audiences (DCMS, 2007). These approaches greatly affected the sector. Notwithstanding the election of a new Coalition government in the UK in 2010, the issue of access, which reflected New Labour's concern with social inclusion, has continued to be important in policy discourse. The Coalition, in keeping with broader Conservative policy, dropped references to social inclusion when they came to power, but the Arts Council England continued with one of its five core goals as 'Goal 2: More people experience and are inspired by the arts' (ACE, 2010: 12), within which 'more people are engaging in the arts in places where participation is currently low' (2010: 12), coupled with the aim of creating 'an increased likelihood of people's engagement in the arts, irrespective of their socio-economic or educational background' (2010: 30).

At the time of interview, 'social inclusion' was the preferred term for exploring issues of access and although the language of government has changed, the broader issues have remained. For example, whilst a range of New Labour's social and economic policies were to be socially inclusive, this presented problems regarding the capacity of arts institutions (which are by their very nature exclusive) to be inclusive to atypical audiences. As a result, the initial and thus implicit aim of arts institutions in delivering social inclusion became again associated with access (Kawashima, 2006). The role of cultural intermediaries in accomplishing this aim is understood here as crucial.

With this historical backdrop in mind, the following discussion proposes an examination of the activity of individuals within institutions traditionally associated with the high, or legitimate, culture which was the subject of much of the original Bourdeiusian investigations that gave rise to discussions of cultural intermediaries (Hesmondhalgh, 2002). The discussion of the role of staff within arts organizations shows their position not as mere translators of high culture for socially excluded parts of the masses, but rather as specific individuals who can traverse the worlds of state bureaucracy, the art world and the everyday lives of the individuals involved in the co-creation of their artistic programmes. Whilst the evidence shows the limits of this role, it moves beyond a narrow focus on class position and professional status to suggest the influence and potential of cultural intermediaries to challenge the structures of power within the contemporary art world, rather than acting as mere transmitters or translators engaged in the social reproduction of the existing powerful.

## MATERIAL PRACTICES

Through discussions around the interpretation of 'inclusion' within their practice, cultural intermediaries can be seen to have an 'empathy of exclusion' for non-traditional audiences. This empathy appears to allow a building of identity connection through a shared sense of exclusion, which in turn fosters relationship building. The nurturing of these relationships creates a bridge (Negus, 2002) between the elite field of the arts and the target audience.

# Building relationships

The empirical evidence used in this chapter demonstrates that relationship building is the key activity in which individuals in posts charged with outreach, education and participation engage in promoting the arts for new or atypical audiences. One senior staff member interviewed explained: 'In our case we use the education staff as the sort of storm troopers to bring those contacts about.' Relationship building is not a new promotion technique in the arts (Conway and Whitelock, 2005). Indeed, Boorsma (2006) argues in a discussion on arts marketing that art production and consumption are essentially communicative acts: artistic values emerging as a product of this interaction. As Boorsma suggests:

> The philosophical turn to the relational view of art implies that the art con-sumer has changed from a passive recipient into an active participant. Arts consumers provide a valuable contribution to the achievement of the artistic objectives. The audience takes part in the co-production of artistic value. (2006: 76)

With respect to the role of cultural intermediaries that we examine here, aspects of relationship building include: understanding barriers through dialogue and providing access; face-to-face meetings, either through outreach or at the gallery; establishing trust; and the nurturing of relationships. These approaches are taken based on these individuals' unique understanding of the lack of relationship atypical audiences feel they may have with the field of the arts. One administrator explains this situation:

> A lot of the time it's about people who have no understanding of contemporary art or, despite the fact that they might have come in touch with it, may not have been aware that they had and breaking down those boundaries. Making it feel like it's fun, it's, I don't know, it's safe, and approachable.

More specifically, when a group is identified as a non-traditional audience, cultural intermediaries explain that acknowledging and understanding perceived barriers to accessing cultural activity must first be achieved before a relationship can be pur-sued. One administrator explains:

> [First] I think maybe we look to see what those barriers might be and we ask people why they don't go to [art events] or what may make them feel uncom-fortable about it and try to change those things.

This process is about listening to and actively addressing the experience of exclusion those targeted audiences perceive. The value of dialogue and understanding is further explained:

> It's really important to talk to the people who are excluded [from the arts] and ask them why and to work with them to develop the tools to include them. It's also about sensitivity and thinking about what sort of thing might make people feel uncomfortable.

## Identity connections

Face-to-face meetings designed to promote personal relationships through trust are also key to breaking down barriers and promoting activities for galleries and art centres, implying a kind of identity connection via cultural intermediaries themselves. Trust is perceived to be incredibly important, and in being so, cultural intermediaries see their roles as quite personal ones: 'It's to be someone that people can go to if they have a problem.' One administrator explains: 'We do things like try to break down barriers between the community and artist by getting the community to meet with the artist.' Activities usually occur through two methods: they may involve a group working directly with an artist in the creation of something; or they may involve the group being in dialogue with one another regarding an extant work of art. Often the intention is to offer the freedom and flexibility to allow participants to shape the experiences that are being targeted at them: 'We always plan in such a flexible way. There's always the option for the participants to change things to make the project their's more.'

In an analysis of social inclusion work through sport, Crabbe (2007: 36) has argued that the individuals charged with delivering these activities for and with socially excluded groups are intermediaries who provide gateways between what are typically seen as 'alien and mutually intimidating worlds'. Similarly, as individuals who can empathize with the seeming irrelevance of the arts in the lives of some individuals, cultural intermediaries, who define exclusion in their practice as a lack of opportunity to take place in cultural activity, attempt to serve as go-betweens or interpreters for excluded individuals. This is accomplished through relationship building and, as Crabbe (2007) explains, working with such groups as well as identifying and targeting them constitutes an essential component of promotion.

The individual connections perceived to be made between the cultural intermediary and the excluded are critical. One cultural intermediary explained the results: 'So I think by meeting people running the project and seeing that we're just normal people as well, [they discover] stuff that they can get involved with.' Through establishing and making identity connections evident with non-traditional audiences, the cultural intermediary offers a means of co-producing artistic value (Boorsma, 2006), 'creating dialogue' and 'bringing people through the whole creative process'.

# Shared personal experiences

The position of a cultural intermediary is as someone who sits both within the arts but also understands the challenges in accessing that field. This understanding has come about for these individuals based on their desire to promote a more accessible and open field. Evidence gathered shows that this desire results from a personal feeling of exclusion within the arts. These feelings are manifest in personal histories of encountering the arts and in their current position in institutions as mediators for participating in the arts.

Initial discussions of social inclusion revealed how intermediaries saw their role as concerned with providing access to a broader range of audiences who may not be socially or economically excluded but who simply do not feel comfortable in an arts setting. For example, one administrator commented: '[The events] we provide are not seen as something [individuals] can readily approach or access.' Another stated that it is helping 'people [feel] comfortable coming to [the gallery] and accessing all areas of it and not feeling that because of anything about themselves that they can't.'

In fact, a number of individuals felt uncomfortable even using the term 'social inclusion' whilst recognizing the value of a highly personalized approach to such work, such as breaking down barriers and establishing contact and dialogue as a key means for providing access. These approaches combine professional perspectives on the meaning of inclusion with personal experiences of exclusion from and inclusion within the arts. As one senior staff member working in a grassroots organization put it: 'A great deal of what one does comes from one's own history.' He went on to illustrate how his personal history, his perspective on inclusion and the arts, is one of transition:

> I grew up in a family where it would have been unusual or unlikely for members of my family to visit a theatre or an art gallery or a concert hall so in a way [I] wanted to invent an arts centre where [my] own family would feel comfortable. And that immediately means that you are seeking to involve people who are outside the charmed circle of those people who are involved in the arts.

This individual's experience of barriers to inclusion have therefore informed his practice and his organization's understanding of the nature of the barriers that the arts can hold, or be perceived to hold, for people. His understanding is shared in the descriptions of many interviewees. One individual shared how her own experience with the arts as a college student has shaped her career choices as well as her interpretations of inclusion:

> I went to art college and studied art [to get] a fine art degree and failed it, which I find quite amusing. Part of the reason I failed is because I had this idea that art shouldn't be elitist and it should be something that everyone could do.

Her education and subsequent career in the arts provides her with the knowledge to work within the field, yet her explanation of why she may not have excelled in her fine art degree gives her the ability to identify with those who may not feel included within that field.

## The transformative power of the arts

The potential of a cultural intermediary to perpetuate established tastes, suggested by existing studies of cultural intermediaries (Bourdieu, 1984), is tested by a strongly held belief in the transformative role of the arts. This transformative role was a common theme within the interviews, particularly with those who work directly with non-traditional arts audiences. Cultural intermediaries described very personal stories of transformation based on gaining access to the arts. One individual explained:

> Arts changed my life. Going to the theatre made me realize there was something different out there, really, so the arts impeded [impacted] in my life and suddenly I started to invest in me through art, through going to the theatre, through reading, you know suddenly I became, I suppose, illuminated.

This sense of illumination was expressed by nearly all of the individuals who work directly with excluded audiences. One stated:

> There's something really lovely in work that just takes you away from life, and I always hope that my groups will begin to think of the gallery as somewhere they can come [to] just kind of escape from [what's going on in their lives] for a little while and that kind of potential of art to take you somewhere else and allow your imagination to roam is ... quality time that people don't often find in their own lives.

Because of their own feelings of transformation, cultural intermediaries are often sympathetic to the audiences (or non-audiences) to which Mason (2004) and Whitehead (2005) refer, who otherwise feel it is 'not for the likes of us' (Bourdieu, 1990b: 56). One administrator illustrates this point further:

> I don't think [the arts] is something that only certain people can do. I think it's broken down a lot but there's always been that separation of 'oh this is an artist and aren't they special?' I think that everybody has that in them. The difference is who chooses to do that but also who chooses to put that label on those things. I think because that [labelling has] happened it makes it really difficult then people that say, 'oh I don't understand that and I don't know anything about that,' and they look to other people to give them meanings or interpretations of work when actually everyone can go and do that themselves.

Cultural intermediaries appear to usurp traditional misconceptions of art, its institutions and its consumption. Whilst senior staff in the arts have critiqued the instrumentalism of recent cultural policy, the cultural intermediaries described here tend to stress notions that 'everyone is an artist' and 'everyone is creative'. Their articulated desire is to break down the barriers that oppose such notions. In this sense, their ambition is more fundamental than the organisations for which they work.

## ASSESSING IMPACT

The impact of these cultural intermediaries is located in their belief that they have the power and potential to challenge hierarchical structures within the arts. This power is enacted first through these individuals' own understanding of exclusion, many of whom acknowledge that they themselves feel or have felt excluded from the arts. As they feel they, themselves, are often negotiating their own positions within the arts (and even within their institutions), they are uniquely placed to acknowledge the barriers to accessing the arts that exist for many individuals, or non-traditional audiences. Steps involved in this approach include developing a dialogue with individuals and groups targeted as 'excluded' or 'non-traditional' through face-to-face meetings and discussions. This approach leads to a sense of identity connection and thus the building and then nurturing of relationships and trust. The potential impact of their efforts is a realization of the possibility for a more participatory and democratic approach within arts institutions. Cultural intermediaries can work with audiences to co-produce new understandings of value within the arts and thus challenge the field's longstanding power structures and ideology.

This work is not without its challenges, however, and there are tensions present in relation to understandings of value and quality, which cultural intermediaries themselves may be upholding. One explains:

> When I was in front of *Primavera* just a year ago I was standing in front of it thinking, 'you won't get a chance to see it, it will be so busy.' But the painting was empty and there were 40 people bending over [the museum label] and they want to know that [information], but they don't want to look at the paintings, which is a sad state of affairs.[1]

Even though this individual also described during interview his past experience of having to lead a 'secret life' appreciating the arts as a working-class child, his current position and appreciation of the canon perpetuates the accepted tastes of that field. This fact can be seen in the way he expresses 'sadness' at the inability of others in the gallery he visited to really 'look' at such a great masterpiece. The modest story told by this individual, the unease at finding a place across the frontiers of high culture, popular culture in relation to bourgeois, aristocratic and working-class identities, reflects the dynamic role of the intermediary within not only the art world, but also in English society itself (Friedman, 2012).

While cultural intermediaries are in unique positions to drive arts promotion, their very position to do so shows their mediatory position as privileged, thus reinforcing the arts as an elite arena. One cultural intermediary admitted the privileged position that exists in this role in 'bringing people into [the art] world', and another explained: 'You have that special background information [and] giving people that behind-the-scenes look at things is good.' Further, another individual illustrates the authoritative role cultural intermediaries have to judge the value of democracy over quality:

> We would never justify putting content out in to a public domain by the fact that it was the first [work] that that person had ever made. We would put it out into the public domain if it was good.

One administrator from a grassroots organization that coordinates participatory art projects, and the subsequent exhibition of work created, expressed a similar opinion: 'I think there can be a point where you go too far with democracy and you reduce the quality [of the artwork].'

While cultural intermediaries may be offering new audiences the freedom and flexibility to reach and value their own interpretations and even creation of art above or equal to professional artists, critics and historians, in doing so they risk simultaneously devaluing the institutions in which they, themselves, are situated. One administrator explains:

> If the money was cut, it would be very interesting to see what would take priority [the participation projects or exhibitions]. Where does the balance lie? Because without the high-quality contemporary arts experience provided by the gallery what are you getting?

These statements, with their associated recognition of both class position and mobility, are in keeping with recent work on the relationship between both trajectories of social mobility (Miles et al., 2011) and the relationship between taste, consumption and class position (Friedman, 2012). They also show the continued issue of the potential closure of the art world to those seen as outside a network of elites, including curators, dealers, art schools, government agencies and artists themselves (Griffiths et al., 2008), even when the intermediaries are constructing responses to this particular social fact.

It is the cultural intermediary who must negotiate the terms of inclusion, but who is also simultaneously limited in their ability to do so. This situation places them in a constant state of negotiation between: audience and institution; personal beliefs and structural beliefs; quality and democracy. One administrator explained the difficulty of this negotiation with regard to a participatory art project that was to go on display:

> People produce something and I feel that we come in and say this is how you
> have to show it off and I might be so concerned with how it's going to be seen
> and how it fits in with everything else that somehow it changes the whole
> meaning of the project and what they're doing.

The connections established with atypical audiences are affected by a context in
which the meaning attached to such production remains largely at the behest of the
host institution and the field of the arts. More explicitly, the cultural intermediary
is employed to maintain meanings within a predefined institutional arena. This
arena, and the cultural intermediary's own status or position within it, may allow
and/or constrict the potential impact of the relationship-building style approach to
arts promotion. One explained: 'Inclusion is also making sure that that does fit with
[our organization's] values and with our vision. So it's kind of finding the good balance but not going against anything we stand for.' This difficulty is especially evident
with respect to issues of the 'value' not only of artwork created by professional artists versus non-professional visitor but also the differing levels of value placed on the
two. One senior staff member who criticizes these notions explains: 'A lot of people
do not actually want to see [art] democratized. They do not want to see what they
would regard as the great unwashed turning up in large numbers.'

Nevertheless, this facilitation and manoeuvring is only possible with the presence
of a cultural intermediary, a gatekeeper that assists in negotiating and mediating that
difference. The empathy that cultural intermediaries hold for atypical audiences
allows them to identify with the targeted audience and take steps to building a
relationship and sense of trust with those individuals in ways that may challenge
perceptions of the arts as elite. This role is not necessarily one of manipulation. In
fact, these cultural intermediaries emphasize choice and opportunity with regard to
activities geared towards promoting access and participation. Another administrator
explains that arts promotion

> should be about giving people opportunities and making them feel comfortable
> about them, but not forcing people to do them or thinking that they have to
> do them because some people might be quite happy in their lives having never
> been to the [gallery].

The realization that the arts and perhaps visiting a gallery may not be an activity
desirable to all may appear problematic. In fact, the degree of choice available to
potential audiences, particularly when those under discussion are understood as
atypical art audiences, further highlights that these kinds of cultural intermediaries
are themselves best placed to promote activities for and to excluded individuals.
They are interpreters, as one administrator explained: 'Being able to speak the language of the different people involved [both within the arts and within socially
excluded groups], I think is a major role. I think it is kind of interpretation in a way.'
Indeed, as Powell and Gilbert (2007) suggest, relationships can provide a foundation

for genuine change. However, participation in the arts can never be entirely free from the type of constraints placed on participants by the need for knowledge and understanding of the rules and practices of the art world. One senior staff member illustrates the difficulty:

> The arts should be inclusive. Um, but I think there's a sort of black and white position, isn't there. It's either elitist or it's populist and actually it can be popular, but not by dumbing down. That's what I think a good arts centre or art venue should do is not compromise the work, but to find the ways through interpretation, through participation that you make it accessible. And the thing is you don't always get that right, but that's, you know, why shouldn't people from any background you know have access to the best quality ideas, even if they're difficult and awkward and problematic? You know, why make it so easy that actually you bleach out the problematic of the work? There's always art that's going to be awkward and ambiguous and the meaning isn't as obvious.

Connecting those excluded from the arts to 'awkward' and 'ambiguous' meanings inherent in some art works, then, becomes a difficult terrain to negotiate. The way in which cultural intermediaries, as empathetic members of the art world, carry out their roles as promoters of those works and of that elite world offers something of a bridge between traditional understandings of social stratification in relation to the arts and the culture of the arts.

# FUTURE DIRECTIONS

This chapter has presented the negotiated status of the cultural intermediary, between art world and non-traditional audience, between access and aesthetic excellence and between the needs of the participant and those of the organization. By acknowledging intermediaries' positions within elite arts institutions, the chapter moves beyond a viewpoint that often limits the discussion of the cultural intermediaries' role to one that reproduces power structures alone. Instead, by considering the personal viewpoints and the social interaction these individuals describe as occurring daily within their positions, we have begun to unpick the potential of these individuals to transform the elite practices of the art world whilst drawing on its resources.

The chapter suggests that the role of the intermediaries discussed today are close to the initial, pre-Bourdieusian, definition of the cultural intermediary as a translator, moving between communities and between worlds. The potential significance cultural intermediaries have in strengthening the bonds between public and institution is grounded in their role as translators between non-traditional audience and art world. This understanding of cultural intermediaries, as ambassadors between worlds, is especially important as they offer a chance to represent the value and worth of the art world to the public. The importance of this role is set against the retreat of the state as a direct funder of cultural institutions and programmes across Europe. In this context it is especially pressing for cultural organizations to make their case to the public, as competition for funds inevitably disenfranchises those institutions unable to convince the public and funders of their worth. For example, funding cuts to UK museums, such as Sheffield's museum service, means the role of cultural intermediaries as brokers between the public (as audience or not) and institutions will be especially important. Cultural intermediaries, as this chapter has shown, can make the case for the importance of cultural institutions in ways that connect to non-traditional audiences whilst representing the ideas, needs and experiences of those audiences back to the wider art world.

The chapter's use of the term 'cultural intermediary as translator' suggests that there is still a need for clarification of the meaning of the term 'cultural intermediary'. This provides the first possible area for further research, whereby clarification will respond to Hesmondhalgh's (2002) critique of the term. This line of inquiry could be further developed by a second strand of research, exploring comparative work with the other intermediaries described in this book and with other members of the art world, such as more senior curatorial staff. This chapter's discussion of relationship building offers a starting point for the third area of future research, whereby there is a pressing need to document the *practices* of cultural intermediaries and the way the material reality of intermediation may challenge elite power structures within the art world. Fourth, work engaging the audiences to understand the impacts and effects of intermediation will be an essential part of any future discussion of cultural intermediaries in the art world. Fifth, in the context of the redrawing of the state as a result of the ongoing global financial crisis, research on the type of cultural intermediaries represented here must explore the opportunities and threats created as state funding is reduced or superseded by philanthropy and a demand for more commercial revenue. It is our estimate that the inclusive practice of the cultural intermediary will be, at best, transformed or significantly reduced in the current climate, or worse be rendered peripheral as institutions struggle to survive (Lynch, 2011).

# NOTE

1    The speaker is referring to *Primavera*, also known as *Allegory of Spring*, by Sandro Botticelli. The work was viewed by the speaker at the Uffizi Gallery in Florence, Italy, as part of that gallery's permanent collection.

# 10
# FASHION

*LISE SKOV*

This chapter takes issue with Bourdieu's notion that cultural intermediaries always have a pedagogical agenda. Through an examination of the fashion clothing industry – one of the most market-driven among the creative cultural industries – an alternative understanding will be outlined of cultural intermediaries as detached observers of consumer markets, taking care not to impose their own values on their interpretations. From a macro perspective the difference may seem negligble: cultural intermediaries invariably process market information through mental grids, and facilitate a lash-up of supply and demand that is in no way automatic or natural. But in many cases, such an 'activist' analysis does not correspond to cultural intermediaries' own perception of their professional skills, and the commercial risk associated with 'misreading' the market. Thus this new departure matters for anyone who wishes to zoom in on the micro level of cultural intermediaries' experience and knowledge. It is equally important for those who wish to understand how power works in cultural industries or, for example, in the light of the growing concern with sustainability, how they can change.

Historian Regina Lee Blaszczyk coined the term 'fashion intermediaries' in her study of American consumer industries from the 1860s until the 1930s as a challenge to the notion that Fordism has been the main driver of business development (2000). In contrast to the Fordist principles of standardization, rationalization and economies of scale, consumer industries such as glassware, porcelain, jewellery, clothing and furniture continued to rely on small batch production and product variety. Blaszczyk shows how their dynamism was dependent on producers' skills in interpreting changing consumer tastes and communicating new lines to the market. According to her definition, fashion intermediaries are 'astute consumer liaisons whose jobs entailed studying markets, evaluating tastes and making product recommendations' (2000: 12). Obviously, this is not a formal job description, but an interpretation of a mediating function, which – to echo sociologist Harvey Molotch's informal definition of design (2003: 12) – makes otherwise loose elements lash up in order to produce something new.

Blaszczyk uses the term 'fashion' in the broadest sense, associated with all kinds of novelties and consumer trends. Indeed, many of the marketing initiatives she ascribes to fashion intermediaries (e.g. publicized product launches, elaborate displays in department stores and illustrated booklets) have been adopted and developed by hi-tech industries today as the principle of what ethnologist Orvar Löfgren has termed the 'catwalk economy' (2005). The present chapter, however, takes a narrower approach to fashion with a product-specific focus on clothing. The fashion clothing industry makes a good case study of cultural intermediaries because, on the one hand, it has been a leader in inventing marketing devices related to branding, events and continuous launching of new collections (for discussions of branding and clothing retail, see chapters by Moor and Pettinger elsewhere in this volume); on the other hand, it is a highly globalized industry with a web of intermediaries connecting the trendiest places in cosmopolitan style centres to newly industrialized backwaters in India and China. In Blaszczyk's case studies, fashion intermediaries are primarily men – owner-managers or marketing men – catering primarily to women consumers in the typical gendered organization that characterized early American consumer industries. In the more recent examples discussed in this chapter, cultural intermediaries are mostly women from Europe and Asia, working in the fashion clothing industry making clothes for middle-to-low-end retailers such as chain stores and supermarkets, whose consumers include men, women and children.

Given her empirical focus and the context of American business history, it is hardly surprising that Blaszczyk does not reference Pierre Bourdieu's discussion of cultural intermediaries and its consequent application in (mostly British) sociology and cultural studies. However, her book addresses many of the same issues, and in one area I believe that the American notion of fashion intermediaries can add a nuance to the European debate. Blaszczyk's notion of fashion as a unified approach to product development and marketing is based on a criticism of the tendency in design history to focus on aesthetic and social visions. In fact, her term 'fashion intermediaries' is intended to drive home their subordinate position: they are *not* 'taste makers' or educators. This marks a departure from a Bourdieu-influenced assumption that cultural intermediaries are always engaged in the pedagogical work of shaping consumer tastes (Smith Maguire and Matthews, 2010: 407–408). The difference is, perhaps, unsurprising, for as cultural sociologists Lamont and Thevenot point out, market-based criteria of evaluation are more often used in the US than in Europe, particularly France, where they tend to be secondary to moral arguments (2000: 14). But it is important to understand that when Blaszczyk says that fashion intermediaries are 'giving people what they want', she does not assume a laissez-faire approach. On the contrary, she shows that fashion intermediaries perform a complex task, requiring both sophisticated knowledge and personal authority within business networks, of anticipating changes in consumer tastes and coordinating diverse production and marketing processes. In short, it is a difficult job to make supply and demand lash up.[1]

# HISTORICIZING CULTURAL INTERMEDIARIES

The history of the clothing industry since the first decades of the 20th century can be conceived as an expansion of mediation processes, and by implication – as sociologist Keith Negus has critically argued (2002) – a growing distance between production and consumption both in social and geographical space. It is remarkable that technological development has played a negligible role in the development of clothing manufacturing. Economists Ben Fine and Ellen Leopold (1993) point out that the individually operated sewing machine has never been replaced by assembly line robots because of the difficulty of handling fabric, so that seamstresses' work time must still be factored into the price of every single garment sold. The critical dependence of labour accounts for the clothing manufacturing industry's historical tendency to cluster in low-wage regions, where it has taken advantage of immigrant or rural labour and, since the 1960s through outsourcing, global inequality (Green, 1997; Dicken, 2007). At the same time, because of the industry's sensitivity to wage pressure, it turned to intermediaries early on to ensure its profitability and growth by exploiting the characteristic of the labour-intensive manufacturing process – its flexibility. Innovation in the fashion industry has thus happened primarily in terms of mediation and (in contrast to manufacturing machinery) developments in communication technology.

In this historical development it is possible to identify a distinctive pattern in which male *business* intermediaries, who expand trade networks, are followed by female *fashion* intermediaries, responsible for product development and marketing within existing business structures. Leopold identifies the starting point in the New York City clothing industry. At the end of the 19th century, the jobber had organized newly arrived immigrant labour for contract work, but by the 1920s, this middleman role had been transformed into a much more powerful position: 'The jobber, freed from the technical and labour problems arising in the factory, was able to concentrate his attention on styles and sales' (Leopold, 1993: 107–108; cf. Fine and Leopold, 1993: 107). Sociologist Gilles Lipovetsky defines a second moment in the US and Europe in the 1950s, when department stores and large clothing manufacturers began employing fashion advisors to create seasonal displays, coordinate buying, and design garments for in-house production (1994: 90). They tended to be women of style, combining artistic education with business acumen.

The shifting gender relations, exemplified by these two moments, are typical, although highly variable according to sector and country. In general, there are more women in the fashion clothing business than it would seem from media readings, since fashion magazines tend to focus on designers with 'name' brands, and the trade press deal with company owners and managers. For example, men continued to dominate the world of Paris *haute couture*, while women took key positions in industry, retail and media. By the 1960s, several women designers who had worked for the leading department stores, such as Dominique Pecler and Li Edelkoort, set up independent *bureaux de style* offering trend information and design services to customers from consumer industries and service and hospitality sectors. Even today, when new business initiatives have moved online, the global leaders in fashion forecasting are women (Giertz-Mårtenson, 2010). In this respect, it is correct to link the emergence of cultural intermediaries in fashion to corporate growth, although it might be a stretch to call them corporate professionals, as cultural studies scholar Hesmondhalgh suggests (2006b: 219), since they tend to be contracted on a freelance basis.

The expansion of the education sector in the 1960s brought fashion design into formal education in many countries, although courses varied from vocational training with close industry ties to an art school curriculum which endorsed creative autonomy. While the UK integrated an academic approach to arts education early on, other countries in Europe, notably Italy and France, have continued to stress apprenticeship and craftsmanship. By contrast, the US has combined industry orientation with an independent academic focus, originating in domestic science. South Korea has also been one of the leaders in academization of design education to the extent that fashion design teachers are required to have an international PhD as a matter of routine. Since the 1990s, leading manufacturing countries, such as China and India, have also made considerable investments in fashion design education (McRobbie, 1998; Skov and Melchior, 2010).

The last point drives home the fact that today clothing manufacturing is concentrated in a few regions, particularly in Asia (Dicken, 2007). The geographical patterns of globalization have been shifting and complex, starting with the US import of garments made in East Asia in the 1950s and 1960s. The long-distance trade with East Asia has also been complemented by regional sourcing, connecting the US market to suppliers in Mexico and Central America, and Central and Northern European markets to suppliers in South and East Europe, Turkey and North Africa. Since the 1990s European and North American clothing companies have cultivated longer-term relationships with their suppliers who in turn deliver a bundle of financial and design services with the manufactured goods. As a result, financial risk and the management and technical issues related to manufacturing were pushed upstream in the value chain. This leaves brand owners in Europe and North America – to echo Leopold's (1993) description of how a similar logic was played out in an earlier period – free to concentrate on branding, collection development, promotional events and sales.

The precondition for these extensions of clothing manufacturing networks has been a massive knowledge transfer, which can be conceptualized with sociologists Callon, Méadel and Rabeharisoa as a process of qualification (2002). Although, as mentioned above, fashion intermediaries do not to see themselves as educators of the public, they have no qualms about teaching their suppliers upstream in the value chain regarding market requirements. The following example from my own research comes from an interview with a Danish fashion designer recounting her first trip to China soon after she had graduated in the mid-1990s. She accompanied her employer, a trader who, although he had been travelling to and from East Asia since the 1970s, had never employed a designer before her. In her first assignment in a factory in Southern China, she had to initiate the production of a line of underwear, destined for supermarkets and other low-end retailers in Europe:

> Almost immediately I had a clash with the Chinese factory's in-house designer over what shape the panties should be. He wanted them flat, but I insisted they should curve at the back. As I explained to him, Chinese women may have flat behinds, but European girls are round. He thought I was crazy – until next time I went out there when his attitude had changed completely. The factory had managed to get a very large order of panties from a Belgian customer because of the good fit. As a result, I was treated like a heroine.

Making the cheaper underwear sold in supermarkets just as comfortable as that sold in higher-priced lingerie shops was a means in order to reach the commercial goal of boosting sales, commonly shared by the European buyer and the Chinese supplier. Obviously, the relationship between the female European designer and male Chinese in-house designer is circumscribed by cultural and organizational power relations. She wins out the first time round because she represents the customer and, according to the role-playing of the service economy, is therefore right. But as sociologist Howard Becker has pointed out, this acknowledgement often comes with an undercurrent of resentment on the part of the supplier whose knowledge and preferences are degraded (1951). The second time round, her superiority is acknowledged without reserve because the factory had experienced that her designs gave it another entry to European markets. As knowledge transfer, the encounter was highly subjective and informal. In fact, it is striking that the clothing industry treats knowledge of body shapes and comfort in such a non-codified way, although they must be assumed to be central to consumer satisfaction (Borregaard, 2010).

What the European designer taught her Chinese colleague was pragmatic in the sense that he needed to be familiar with European body shapes only in so far as his company had European customers. Although this is a far cry from the idea of Europe spreading enlightenment and civilization, the discourse of 'Asia learning from the West' invariably carries a neo-colonial resonance. The superior position is held by countries with the consumer markets and cultural intermediaries who are able to profitably interpret these markets. Suppliers can only get access through submission to these cultural intermediaries and by emulating their knowledge. Paradoxically, it is exactly by accepting that they need to 'learn from the West' that suppliers can gain a degree of autonomy from specific customers, and independently offer styles that can attract other buyers. In my research on Hong Kong and

China, I found that the position as a 'global student' has a powerful imaginary hold in a supplier region (Skov, 2002). It endorses a knowledge asymmetry between buyers and suppliers at the same time as it enforces the notion of a collaborative partnership.

This example modifies the argument by Callon et al. that there is 'symmetry and similitude of behaviours of different economic agents engaged in qualification' (2002: 204). Symmetry only emerges out of an asymmetrical knowledge distribution in which cultural intermediaries *learn* from observing consumers and *teach* suppliers about market requirements. In this way new tiers of global suppliers have been brought into the shared understanding, which has enabled them to upgrade from producing to buyers' specifications to taking a more independent role as business partners. Their acceptance of this knowledge asymmetry is the precondition for their participation in 'the distributed apparatus of qualification' (Callon et al., 2002: 206).

## MATERIAL PRACTICES

In recent decades, skills of interpreting consumer markets has become relatively more important for fashion designers than their traditional expertise in hand drawing, drapery and tailoring. As a consequence of the changes in the organization of the globalized industry, fashion designers tend to work as a member of a product development team, which has enforced the need to standardize visual and technical communication through moodboards, computer drawings and spreadsheets. There has also been a huge increase in the number of annual collections from four in the 1980s to sixteen or more in the 2010s, resulting in shorter product development processes and more annual deadlines. In the 1980s a head designer of a national-level premium brand had some creative autonomy to put her personal fingerprints on the designs, whereas today's fast fashion brands require a more anonymous output.

As a starting point for the analysis of fashion designers' understanding of consumer behaviour, here is another example from my research on Danish fashion designers. An informant, who graduated in the late 1980s, described her first job as freelance designer for a casual menswear brand:

> Did we learn a lot! Our problem – and it's one faced by all fresh graduates – is that we believed we should go out and change the world. So we thought our first job for this company should be to change its style, which we felt was embarrassing and ugly. We knew nothing about things like target groups, even though the owner spent hours and hours talking to us about how the company owed its success to its understanding of its target group. Not that he managed to persuade us that he was right or anything like that. We were convinced that he could sell twice as much if he allowed us to design something cooler. Luckily,

though, he was prepared to spend a lot of time with us, and as a result, we learned in the end how to make use of our education and knowledge to appeal to his targeted customers. And that can be cool, too.

In industry-oriented design schools, marketing is included in the core first-year syllabus, but in artistic schools, like the one this designer attended, students typically graduate with only a vague notion of how markets work. They may only have learned to make clothes for themselves, and they may have developed a heightened sensitivity to their personal taste, so it requires a big mental shift to begin to use their skills in an instrumental way to evaluate market trends. In the informant's story that is the difference between designing 'cool clothes', which she did as a student, and her subsequent discovery that the work of the cultural intermediary 'can be cool, too', because it allows her to use her educated attention (Ingold, 2000) to tune in to different target groups and trends in the commercial market. This shift in focus from product to process is not a reluctant submission to market forces, although initially the designers were resistant, but a passage to a more sophisticated understanding of the role of the designer in the industry. In this perspective, demand is not an economic mechanism, but something cultural intermediaries need to engage with actively. They perceive it as a communication channel which, if they can get it right, connects them with potential customers.

The kind of informal education described here is similar to that analysed by sociologist Joanne Entwistle in the encounter between a small-scale name designer and a fashion-forward department store buyer (2006: 711; 2009). The exchange takes place in a more exclusive market segment and with a different contractual relationship between designer and market expert, but the direction of instruction from consumer market upstream in the value chain is identical. The same goes for the content. Entwistle describes how the department store buyer tells the designer to avoid too many sleeveless tops and make sure to include more wearable garments in her collection. If we were to map the range of tricks of the trade that are passed on in such informal settings they would include tips about good fit (as in the example discussed in the previous section), styles that are flattering to many body types (including those that deviate from the tall and youthful bodies of fashion models) and styles that are comfortable to wear.

These criteria can be summarized in the term 'saleability'. Of course, sales volumes that are considered successful vary from a small design-driven label to garments sold in supermarkets, and since clothing markets are highly segmented, criteria for commercial success is by no means trivial. As in other creative occupations, fashion designers acknowledge dual criteria for their work – creativity and saleability – but the two have different status. Most would agree that creativity can only be evaluated qualitatively, typically by experts, and possibly only on the basis of some insight in the design process. By contrast, sales are a matter of hit or miss. This gives us a hint as to why fashion intermediaries claim that their relation to consumers is based on neutral observation, rather than conscious intervention. They view the consumer market as a kind of testing ground for their work, but the test results are crudely binary.

Given the importance of sales, it would be a simplification to describe design as a trajectory 'from idea to product'. In the fashion clothing business, the creative process does not start inside someone's head, but with analysis of past sales and market trends. Although the term 'inspiration' is sometimes used to designate the initial phase, it is a highly routinized kind compared to the notion of inspiration in religion or romantic art, associated with an 'outpouring of a higher principle' and an 'inexpressible and ethereal state' (Boltanski and Thévenot, 2006: 159). In fact, the word is often used to characterize a derivative design method in which specific images and garments are used as direct templates for new products, but in a way that avoids copyright infringement. 'We do not copy the famous brands, we use them for inspiration' is a typical statement, which has significant legal implications. Another term commonly used for the production phase before a company has developed its own prototypes is 'research'. This term is appropriate in designating a systematic and objective study of the environment through immersion, but compared to academic research it is a more intuitive and eclectic process, and its outcome is not a better understanding, but a product prototype.

The research phase typically includes a trip to biannual fabric fairs, in particular Premier Vision[2] in Paris, and shopping for 'inspiration samples' in first- and second-tier fashion cities. These trips have an almost ritual meaning, as they symbolically mark a fresh start for a new season. For many young designers in Europe and Asia they are also considered major benefits, as visual gratification of trade exhibitions blend with vicarious shopping in fashionable shops and evening visits to the trendiest bars and restaurants, all facilitated by a company credit card. But even though spending limits can be generous (as they tended to be during the economic boom in the first years of the 21st century), time pressure rarely allows for serendipity. Typically such journeys are strictly planned with the assistance of trend consultants. In this respect, inspiration trips do not transport intermediaries into a world of spontaneity and transformation, but instead connect them with circumscribed information circuits. In reaction to this discovery, one young Danish designer commented bitterly:

> Didn't you ever wonder why one season you suddenly see neon yellow everywhere? You think it's amazing that they all had the same idea at the same time. But once you have been to Premier Vision and seen the exhibitions by the trend bureaux – 'if you want rivets go to booth 38 and 24' – then you know that designers have all the trends served up for them. And they buy trend books that cost thousands of euros.

## ASSESSING IMPACT

In her study of the fashion forecasting industry, ethnologist and fashion intermediary Ingrid Giertz-Mårtenson (2010) asked informants how they assessed their work to have influenced the clothing industry and consumer markets. Their answers show the extent to which fashion intermediaries perceive themselves as detached observers of consumer markets. They stressed that they cannot 'invent' new trends, and that they operate in a highly competitive market where a few mistakes can cost them their reputation. Giertz-Mårtensen for her part speculates that perhaps the trend bureaux can push individual trends to reach the market at an earlier stage than they otherwise would. In a similar vein, we might hypothesize that the current trend for sustainable fashion is partially supported by cultural intermediaries' concern with the negative environmental and social impact of the global garment business.

But an assessment of the impact of cultural intermediaries in fashion should not be limited to individual trends. It is ironic that even though fashion intermediaries can be said to be in the business of novelty, their practical theory of change is based on intuitive leaps rather than on action and causation in any sociological sense. They subscribe to a zeitgeist theory which goes something like this – change happens everywhere all the time. Fashion intermediaries can observe these changes in a neutral and objective manner in order to turn them into commercial products. They are not aiming to persuade their customers of any ideals or promote particular values; they are simply trying to lash up production with consumer demand. But while such an understanding of themselves as detached observers is a necessary component in the work of fashion intermediaries, it does not preclude that they have had an impact on business and society.

To see that we need to look to the long-term impact they have had in interspersing commerce into social life. Blaszczyk's study from the period before 1930 noted how fashion intermediaries had an impact by turning shopping into entertainment through events and exhibitions and by promoting gift-giving, in particular in connection with weddings. Events continue to be important for fashion intermediaries. In fact, the number of 'fashion weeks' worldwide has grown exponentially in the last decades as the catwalk show has proven to be well suited to presenting clothing collections to buyers and specialized media and at the same time promoting regional development, city branding and tourism.

When we look at the impact cultural intermediaries have had in the middle-to-low end of the fashion clothing business – the industry segment primarily discussed in this chapter – events are secondary to the overall commercialization of everyday life, particularly in relation to personal appearance, comfort and the body. Shopping has been promoted as a kind of self-care, in which practical and emotional concerns are enmeshed with spending. It would surely be an exaggeration to credit fashion intermediaries for having invented the novelty-seeking consumer, but they certainly offer a material and commercial direction for the search for novelty. One element is the continuous arrival of new stock in retail outlets; another is the specialization of individual garments. A senior designer in a Danish lingerie company described it like this:

> When I build a collection I think of a woman's life in twenty-four hours. She gets up in the morning, and perhaps she starts the day with a bit of fitness. So

she needs a sports bra. Then she goes to work in something classical, business wear with a feminine twist. In the afternoon she changes to something more casual to meet with her girlfriends. Then perhaps she is going out for dinner, and she needs something more romantic or sexy. Women have so many moods! I am not saying that I change my clothes four or five times a day, but I have two teenage daughters, and they certainly like to try on clothes! That's what keeps the wheels of the fashion business rolling – that we dress to express the different moods we have.

The overall long-term impact cultural intermediaries have had on the fashion clothing business thus lies in the boosting of sales volumes. In comparison to the middle of the 20th century, new clothes are cheap and easy to acquire, and as they tend to be conceived as a disposable, rather than a durable, consumer good, they are used less before they are discarded (Fine and Leopold, 1993; Klepp, 2001; Shove, 2004). As a result, textile waste has grown to the point that each person in Northern Europe is responsible for about 13 kilos of textile waste each year; the corresponding figure for the US is double that amount. It is in the structural formation of a 'fashion system' with near-continuous product launches and novelty offers, rather than in any pedagogical agenda or conscious intention of educating consumers, that the impact of cultural intermediaries on fashion can be found.

It is therefore possible to sum up their effect on the global economy in the following way. In so far as the current global financial crisis is caused by over-consumption in the west and under-consumption in China (Blackburn, 2011), then it is the web of mediators that connects the European or North American shopaholic, steeped in credit card debts, with the Chinese factory girl, whose low wage bars her from aspiring to a comparable consumer lifestyle even though she has contributed to her country's surplus. In this respect, cultural intermediaries can be said to have facilitated both the spending binge in the first part of the 2000s, and its recent collapse in a personal, corporate and national debt crisis. While financialization has created an economy given over to extreme fluctuations, economist Christian Marazzi (2011) points out that overcoming the crisis through re-establishing a more balanced relationship between real and financial capital will be extremely difficult, because it will depend on new rules to govern markets, new mobilizations about public welfare and new types of jobs. Added to the challenge is the need to invent new kinds of products and services that take account of high levels of material welfare today and have the potential to reverse global trade flows and minimize negative environmental impact. To meet such challenges we probably also need fashion intermediaries to lash up disparate elements in creative ways in order to produce something new. Cultural studies scholar Elizabeth Wilson made a similar point:

Capitalism maims, kills, appropriates, lays waste. It also creates great wealth and beauty, together with a yearning for lives and opportunities that remain just beyond our reach. It manufactures dreams as well as things, and fashion is as much a part of the dream world of capitalism as of its economy. We therefore both love and hate fashion, just as we love and hate capitalism itself. (Wilson, 1985: 14–15)

# FUTURE DIRECTIONS

This chapter has focused on the role of cultural intermediaries in facilitating product development, marketing and extending global production networks at the expense of examining their role in elevating the prestige and autonomy of a given cultural field. In fact these two roles overlap in the figure of the fashion designer, even though they rarely converge completely. The emerging field of fashion studies has tended to privilege 'creators' (as the French term would have it) or 'name designers' (whose personal names double as brand names) over those fashion intermediaries who, although they may earn a reputation in business circles, are essentially anonymous brokers in industry networks. With that in mind, we can identify several research questions that require further exploration.

First, cultural studies scholar Angela McRobbie (1998) has criticized the conservative celebration of the romantic artist that she has found in British design schools, as the emerging field seeks to model itself on high-cultural art forms. A first point of departure for further research is the question of how cultural intermediaries work to turn fashion into a field of creative autonomy, not only by acting as designer-artists, but also as critics, curators and policy makers. How does such a focus on fashion as a creative industry relate to the focus in this chapter on the clothes that people buy and wear?

Second, what is the relation between fashion intermediaries and local cultures? In recent decades there has been a growing cultural pluralism and polycentricity of fashion. In non-western countries this is often associated with an engagement with cultural and aesthetic traditions, while Europeans have only recently begun to cross the symbolic boundary between folk (or national) culture and fashion, even in the most deconstructionist way (Lindevang, 2012; Skov, 2011). This line of inquiry opens up for both local case studies and for critical reflections on how culture is commercialized.

Third, this chapter has shown that fashion intermediaries perceive demand less as an economic mechanism than a kind of communication channel. What would we learn if we bracketed the formalism of market concepts, and instead studied them in terms of experiences and skills? That could lead to a kind of ethnomethodology of economic life.

A fourth direction for future research follows the notions of Blaszczyk (2000), Lipovetsky (1994) and Löfgren (2005) of how fashion systems of continuous product development and novelty launches have been adopted and developed in other consumer and experience industries. This inquiry may go beyond the field of commerce altogether into fields such as such as education, management and health care, or examine Lipovetsky's argument that the changeability of fashion is constitutive for modern democracies.

Fifth, if fashion intermediaries produce value from observing consumer markets and anticipating changes, what other jobs can be said to work in a similar way? Sociologists Karin Knorr-Cetina and Alex Preda have made a similar argument in relation to traders in financial markets (2001). It would be interesting to do comparative case studies of fashion intermediaries, financial traders, futurologists, journalists and others, just as it would be important to develop sound theoretical conceptions of value creation through observation.

## NOTES

1   The empirical examples in this chapter are taken from my recent study of Danish fashion designers' careers, based on 45 life-story interviews (conducted 2009–2011) and my PhD 'Stories of world fashion and the Hong Kong fashion world', Hong Kong University, 2000.

2   Premier Vision is the world's leading international fabric fair, held twice a year in Paris and visited by European, Asian and North American clothing brands and manufacturers. As an institutionalized meeting place in the earliest phase of product development, it is also an important event for trend forecasting (Skov, 2006).

# 11
# POPULAR MUSIC

## CHARLES FAIRCHILD

I recently came across a story that suggests how tricky it can be to gauge the impact of the cultural intermediaries in the popular music industry. According to a well-documented story in *LA Weekly*, a key figure in the spread of West Coast hip hop was David Faustino, perhaps better known as Bud Bundy from the American television show *Married … with Children*. The alliance between a teenage actor on a poorly regarded show from the late 1980s on what was, at that time, a marginal American television network and 'an absolute who's-who of West Coast hip hop' (Westhoff, 2011: 17) seems unlikely. Yet Faustino and his partners appear to have had a significant impact in widening the reach of a form of hip hop which was to assert itself in no uncertain terms in succeeding years. Stories like this are common, but can be unreliable. They are often produced by the intermediaries themselves, or in this case a compliant chronicler. The work of these collaborating intermediaries is often shaped by demands more immediate than the reliable reporting of social history, in this case the righting of one intermediary's listing career trajectory. Examples such as this show how difficult it can be to research cultural intermediaries in the popular music industry. It can often mean dealing with an almost unmanageably broad range of sources, many of which are ephemeral and potentially untrustworthy.

While there are a large number of academic disciplines in which writing about cultural intermediaries in popular music is an acceptable pursuit, writing about these intermediaries more generally is spread across a multitude of non-academic forums that dwarfs the collected academic output. Sources include newspapers, magazines, trade publications, blogs, websites and the musician and music industry biography genre which might range anywhere from picture books for adolescents to door-stop-sized biographies and topical narrative non-fiction for adults about artists, bands, tours, industry executives, managers, producers, specific albums or recordings sessions, particular eras, well-known scandals, and a good deal more. The abundance of documentaries about the inner workings of the music industry only adds to the wealth of sources (Amoaku, 2005; Kirk, 2004; Moorman, 2003; Pray, 1996; Rushkoff, 2001; Timoner, 2004). This complex range of sources often makes it tough to figure out who the consequential intermediaries are, what practices might be more important than others, how these people and their work might relate to the historical contexts in which they act, and finally, what impact they might have.

However, things get a bit more clear when one looks less at specific professions and more broadly at the common goals, these intermediaries have pursued, the practices they have used to reach these goals, and the contexts in which they have acted. This chapter is intended both as a broad overview and a mild provocation. First, I want to suggest that the presence, importance and impact of cultural intermediaries in the music industry is, more often than not, drastically underestimated. The scope of their work is underestimated primarily in terms of its influence in shaping the broad forms of meaning that music takes, often implicitly and explicitly, regarding it as only a mildly consequential arena of social discourse. Second, one of the main reasons their work is underestimated is that the tremendous bulk of information and evidence available, such as those in the non-academic sources noted above, is too often ignored. Third, I want to propose that one of the main areas in which the work of these intermediaries is most underestimated is their cumulative influence on the content, character and mechanics of popular music itself. The one area of work that must become increasingly consequential for the work of cultural intermediaries to be assessed more realistically is that which traces the links between the material practices of cultural intermediaries in the music industry with actual musical content.

## THE FOCUS AND RANGE OF WORK IN THE FIELD

While it is reasonable to define a good deal of what cultural intermediaries in the popular music industry do as 'taste brokering' through a sometimes ill-defined balance of professional and personal judgment, it is clear that something much deeper is going on here. The goal of cultural intermediaries is the production of musical subjects (Born, 2005; DeNora, 2000; Hennion, 2003). They produce musical subjects by using a continually evolving range of tools for assessing and understanding what particular forms of music might 'afford' consumers. That is, music acts as a kind of socially organizing medium that helps people structure, share and make sense of their social experiences. Work that studies music as such focuses on music's potential to be used by subjects in this way (Born, 2005: 14; DeNora, 2000: 46–47). The music industry's cultural intermediaries exploit music's 'affordances' as thoroughly as possible by trying to create as many social, cultural and economic relationships with as many consumers as possible for as long as these relationships can be maintained. The exploitation of these relationships takes many forms, from the immediately obvious, such as marketing campaigns and product placement in films or television shows, to the less obvious, such as the contractually enforceable exclusionary relationships between record labels and retailers or broadcasters that ensure the required measure of market visibility is efficiently manufactured. Their work is a direct, strategic response to the substantial unpredictability of consumerism.

Importantly, the goal of cultural intermediaries in the music industry is not the production of a generic musical subject, but a paradoxical and contradictory musical subject that is both compliant and active, predictable and generative. This subject is an awkward necessity because consumerism depends on the widespread and continuous excitation of expressions of agency by consumers, but the consequences of this incitement to action are inherently unpredictable. The management of the inherent risk and uncertainty of consumerist public culture can only be accomplished if the complex of human agency whipped up into engagement and attention is successfully exploited. As such, cultural intermediaries in the popular music industry are employed to continually resolve the many paradoxes and contradictions thrown at them by the task of producing these contradictory kinds of musical subjects.

The range of academic work that explores the pursuit and construction of these musical subjects is broad and complex. I will not claim to provide a complete and all-embracing survey of academic work on the subject because many of the works cited here do not explicitly or directly analyse or theorize the work practices and impact of cultural intermediaries in the popular music industry. Despite this, the works surveyed here provide important and valuable work on such intermediaries, but sometimes in the service of another goal. Most academic works which examine cultural intermediaries, either directly or indirectly, focus on several key areas such as:

- policy and politics (Anderson, 2006; Bishop, 2005; Burkart and McCourt, 2006; DiCola and Thomson, 2002; McLeod, 2005; Tschmuck, 2009; Warfield, 2009; Williamson and Cloonan, 2007)
- the presentation of popular music in film, on television and on radio (Donnelly, 2005; Fairchild 2008, 2012; Hendy, 2000; Killmeier, 2001; Mol and Wjinberg, 2007; Smith, 1998; Vancour, 2009)
- the inner workings of record labels and their relationships with closely-related intermediaries (Dannen, 1991; Kloosterman and Quispel, 1990; McCourt and Rothenbuler, 1997; Negus, 1993; Segrave, 1994)
- music journalism (Brennan, 2008; Jones, 2002a; Kramer, 2002; Powers, 2010)
- the inner workings of specific music scenes and the categorization or codification of genres (Filene, 2000; Fonarow, 2005; Hamilton, 2008; Haynes, 2005; Pecknold, 2007; Thornton, 1996)
- the workings and effects of different branding, retail and sales techniques and environments from different historical periods (Gay, 1999; Meier, 2011; Miller, 1994; Suisman, 2009; Thompson, 1995)
- broad theoretical, analytical and historical overviews that incorporate some or all of the above areas (Garofalo, 1999; Kenney, 1999; Sanjek, 1996; Wikström, 2009).

By far the most populated area has been the history and theorizing of sound recording technology throughout the 20th century, with work focused on the role of the producer as intermediary (Hennion, 1989; Moorefield, 2005; Thebérge, 2004) and many others on contemporary transformations (Ayers, 2006; Bayley, 2010; Burkart and McCourt, 2006; Chanan, 1995; Coleman, 2005; Furgason, 2008; Gillespie, 2007; Haring, 2000; Jones, 2002b; Katz, 2004; Leyshon et al., 2005; Mann, 2000; McCourt and Burkart, 2003; Morton, 2006; O'Hara and Brown, 2006; Preston and Rogers, 2011).

Beyond these relatively well-established areas of research there are many research articles that provide thorough analyses of particular organizations or institutions (Bakker, 2006; Lanza, 1994; Mabry, 1990), individual intermediaries (Doane, 2009; Howe, 2003; Stratton, 2010) and what we might call marginal or unofficial mediators (Cooper and Harrison, 2001; Marshall, 2003; Serazio, 2008; Shiga, 2007). As noted, many of these works are only tangentially concerned with analysing or theorizing the work of cultural intermediaries in the popular music industry. Despite this, they still provide a wealth of information on the work of such intermediaries. Therefore, if we want to make use of this broad range of work in pursuing a better understanding of popular music intermediaries, we need to understand a few things.

First, one of the main consequences of the relationships between the music industry and consumers created through the work of cultural intermediaries is the production of a constant, socially determined variability in the perceived meaning and value of music. By this I mean, if we can accept that the context of any piece of music exerts some significant force on its meaning, then the meaning of music is at least in part determined by the ways in which it moves through the world. Given that the meaning of music plays a big part in determining its economic value, then the control over the channels through which these acts of musical communication and connection move is crucial to establishing its perceived value more broadly.

Second, we have to understand how intermediaries work to shape the context in which their relationships with audiences play out. While many models of analysis and critique seem to imagine a mostly ad hoc, chaotic context in which cultural producers endlessly chase some notional, elusive consumerist zeitgeist, a more substantial claim is that they act to construct and participate in what Bourdieu called 'habitus'. Habitus are 'systems of durable and transposable dispositions' developed throughout one's life which produce perceptions, practices and habits that 'generate and organize practices and representations that can be objectively adapted to their outcomes without presupposing a conscious aiming at ends' (Bourdieu, 1990b: 53; see also Bourdieu, 1984). Habitus is a 'practical sense that inclines agents to act and react in specific situations in a manner that is not always calculated and that is not simply a question of obedience to rules' (Johnson, quoted in Bourdieu, 1993: 5).

Third, when we understand the dynamic and contradictory nature of the form of musical subject noted above, and the contexts in which they are produced, then we can understand how habitus shapes the ways in which intermediaries construct musical subjects through the exercise of their necessarily mercenary intentions.

These intentions shape how intermediaries work to craft specific kinds of durable relationships with as many of these subjects as possible for as long as possible by inciting and rewarding particular kinds of subjective experience. This can help us understand something of the place of music in the relationships these intermediaries facilitate. The main questions we can ask then are: what might music afford a perceiver in particular contexts, and how is that affordance exploited? Answering these questions can help us understand the specific material practices in which intermediaries engage to reach their goals, and the contexts in which these practices are set.

# HISTORICIZING CULTURAL INTERMEDIARIES

There have been four major interrelated changes over the course of the 20th century that have to be taken into account to understand how the work of cultural intermediaries in the music industry has evolved since the late 19th century: globalization, technological change, a public culture increasingly crowded with competing and complementary communications, and the rise to dominance of the corporation. The first change is that the specific forms of economic globalization most people live under today have become a force that has altered the face of the planet. Globalization has meant that the market for all manner of goods and services has grown substantially, and in some periods exponentially, over the course of the last century. This process has been uneven, risky and tremendously challenging, but it has also provided extraordinary opportunities. However, 'globalization' should not be understood as a generic category merely denoting exponentially increased opportunities for interconnection across expanded distances. What has been widely termed 'neo-liberal' economic globalization has been effected through a fairly rigid adherence to so-called 'free market' principles. These principles include deregulation of markets and the reduction of the role of public institutions in commercial markets, especially the media market. The main goal of deregulating the media was to resolve perceived contradictions in the media marketplace between the public and private sectors by altering the role of the state from an adversarial role to that of market facilitator. Deregulation was intended to allow the unfettered use of both public and private resources by largely unregulated private corporations which have displaced the role of the public sector and now define the terms on which the pubic interest is served. These ideals were codified through multilateral and bilateral trade agreements as well as institutions such as the World Trade Organization and its many binding treaties, conventions and tribunal decisions (Iosifidis, 2011; McChesney and Schiller, 2003). The immediately relevant consequences for the music industry have been the consolidation and vertical integration of the entertainment and broadcasting industries. This has resulted in the dramatically increased interconnection of global cultural production which has made managing the experience of consumption not only much more specific and exacting, but also possible on a scale once unimaginable.

As the music industry became embedded in the larger structures of the entertainment industry, the context in which music producers and intermediaries worked became markedly different in a short period of time. The technocratic and bureaucratic processes of the neo-liberal form of globalization have run in close relation with a century of significant change in the technology used to produce, distribute and experience music. Also, the proliferation of multiple forms of technology for consuming music in a wide variety of forms and contexts has created an experiential terrain so crowded with so many competing demands for audience attention, that some of the most basic assumptions about what the entertainment industry is supposed to do and how it are supposed to do it have been starkly challenged. The much-discussed shift from a 'making economy' to an 'attention' or 'experience' economy has forced producers to work ever more laboriously to capture consumer attention.

Underlying all of these changes is perhaps the most pervasive and influential change of all: the transformation of the corporation from the late 19th to the early 21st century. At the turn of the 20th century the corporation was an important but still somewhat marginal form of industrial and bureaucratic organization. By the turn of the 21st century the corporation was established as the dominant form of economic and social power the world over. The institutionalization of popular music within corporations over the course of the last century has led to new divisions and models of labour within the music industry. It is these new models of labour that have shaped the material practices of cultural intermediaries in the popular music industry. Thus it is important to understand how these occupations and the tasks which define them have changed over time and have evolved to match market conditions.

## MATERIAL PRACTICES

The four broad historical changes noted here have definitively shaped the material practices of cultural intermediaries as well as some of the presuppositions that inform such practices. The key tasks of contemporary cultural intermediaries in the popular music industry grow from these historical dynamics of change and, in generic terms at least, can appear to be reasonably straightforward. They include finding music to bring to market; making sure that music is in some way acceptable to facilitate the construction and exploitation of that market; making sure that music can be heard in the right places at the right times and can move through the right channels in the right ways; making sure consumers recognize 'their' music when they hear it; and making sure the right people get paid in the right way to ensure that this process is sustainable and increasingly profitable (Ahlkvist and Faulkner, 2002; Forde, 2001; Fox, 2005; Hill, 2006; Zwaan and Bogt, 2009). The occupations through which these tasks get done are numerous, they are historically specific and they evolve as the music industry itself evolves. They include:

- independent entrepreneurs such as venue operators, promoters and impresarios, and those who manage the processes through which music can be contracted from professionals in a controlled environment (Elliott, 2005; Inglis, 2003)
- record producers and related liaisons moving between the label and the musicians to manage the actual sound of the product (Cunningham, 1996; Zak, 2010)
- 'the suits' or A&R people, copyright administrators, lawyers, political operatives and trade organizations like the IFPI or the RIAA who manage the global policy infrastructure to the advantage of their employers (Harker, 1997; Negus, 1999)
- a vast range of those who work to present music to the public in the most advantageous circumstances, including marketers and branding specialists, media buyers, retail buyers, music supervisors, radio broadcasters and 'street teams' (Carah, 2010; Fairchild, 2008; Klein, 2009)
- those who write about music who have varied relationships to the music industry, including critics, bloggers and social media draftees who undertake to push 'their' music to anyone within their online orbit.

While the literature cited above can provide an overview of these tasks, it is helpful to have a better understanding of one illustrative phenomenon to get a better view of specific connections between the practices of intermediaries and the music we experience. Music-based reality television is a pleasingly blatant example. Programmes such as *Idol* or *X Factor* are based on a paradox so obvious that it's surprising it is not commented on more often. Audiences are asked to accept the contestants 'as they are' and the contestants are constantly being counselled to 'just be themselves', yet the credibility and success of the whole enterprise depends entirely on the ability of the programme to transform 'ordinary people' into pop stars even as those producing this transformation must constantly try to understate, if not erase, the evidence of their own strategies and designs. As I have noted elsewhere, *Idol*'s producers in particular worked 'to naturalize the success of their "Idols" by asserting the unassailable credibility of their innate talent to render transparent the mechanisms used to construct the meaning and value of that talent' (Fairchild, 2008: 104). As a result, the successful contestants' job was to fit themselves into a pre-existing mould by establishing and confirming public expectations of what it already means to be a pop star.

The means by which the example I studied – *Australian Idol* – accomplished this feat were numerous. For example, as the contest wore on, contestants were increasingly surrounded by an educational infrastructure that included vocal coaches, choreographers, a movement coach, a music director, wardrobe staff and a so-called 'style team'. This virtual pop star academy was a frequent subject of behind-the-scenes aspects of the programme. In performance, the contestants also became increasingly surrounded by ever more elaborate staging designs and light shows as well as backing bands that routinely morphed from a solo piano or standard rock quartet to a full orchestra. Even something as obvious as the editing and camera work functioned as a defining experiential element of the programme, as these were central to establishing and maintaining the all-important '*Idol* journey' narrative.

Importantly, these extensive intermediations were the entire point of the enterprise. They directly produced that which we are meant to consume: a spectacle at the centre of which was music, but a spectacle that was in no way limited to music. The singular 'idol' the contest so assiduously sought was not merely a musician or a singer, but the result of a complex series of intermediations worked on an 'ordinary person' to construct and manage our perceptions, not only of the eventual 'idol' but of the process that produced them.

Despite the extraordinary changes the music industry has faced over the last 15 years, that industry's central tasks have not changed much, if at all. The music industry must still find music to bring to market, frame that music as both legitimate and acceptable and, most importantly, ensure appropriate distribution through channels that are secure and predictable. *Idol* managed all of these with remarkable skill and did so in a manner that was almost defiant of the challenges that new modes of distribution outside of the music industry's traditional supply chains presented, seeing off once-paralysing fears of 'disintermediation' with enormous sums of tacky acumen (Fairchild, 2008: 66).

## ASSESSING IMPACT

When considered simply as the isolated or idiosyncratic endeavours of a few people, the impact of cultural intermediaries in the popular music industry is easy to underestimate. However, when the work of intermediaries is considered in the broad context of a century of economic expansion, unprecedented forms of global interconnection, significant technological change and the pervasive influence of a consumerist culture that defines so much of our experience of the world, then the impact of these intermediaries becomes more recognizable. The work of cultural intermediaries consists of the very forms of labour that have effected the continuous expansion of markets and market assumptions all over the world. These intermediaries craft the laws, set the terms of trade, turn the evocative phrases, edit the imagery and prepare the terrain of consumption as part of a much larger, pervasive culture of promotion and market expansion that has shown no sign of exhausting itself. Their work has led to the ubiquitous use of music in films, television shows, advertising and a huge range of digital forms, all of which seem to morph and change their status and form constantly and unpredictably. Not surprisingly, this has also necessitated more careful and robust management of the global legal and political infrastructure of the music industry to effect ever tighter control over the channels and conduits of content and commerce. Despite this, the roles all types of intermediaries play in the rapidly changing worlds of managing music have received only tangential attention from most popular music scholarship, resulting in a serious misunderstanding and underestimation of their impact and importance. As the story of Bud Bundy, hip hop impresario suggests, the work of cultural intermediaries in the popular music industry often leads us into surprising and unexplored territory.

# FUTURE DIRECTIONS

There are several areas for future research that might address this problem. First, the field requires a far more robust use and development of what is sometimes referred to as 'post-Bourdieusian' theory in the study of art worlds in general and the study of musical intermediaries in particular (Born, 2010, 2005; Negus, 2002; Prior, 2011). Specifically, the field would benefit from much greater focus and depth, especially in the development of approaches drawn from the tradition of research dedicated to the sociology and anthropology of art. This work could profitably centre on what Prior calls an engagement with 'the specificities of musical objects' and 'the complex ways the social and the aesthetic are embedded in and activate one another' (2011: 122). Second, subjecting the proliferating collection of contemporary 'new media' neologisms to some rigorous attention would be very much welcome. Terms such as 'attention economy', 'experience economy', 'infotainment', 'democratainment', 'produser' or 'edutainment' are often bandied about with little justification or empirical specification. Given the rapidly expanding study of the use of music in a variety of digital cultures, work that explores how intermediaries use these ideas and similar forms of received wisdom in their work would be a major advance. Third, one very obvious area of work is the place of music in social media and cloud computing. While this area has been explored, surprisingly few works examine the new occupations, types of work and forms of social and economic interconnection these two arenas of cultural production and consumption might produce. No doubt these are being produced as I write. Fourth, one area that has been marginalized to the point of disinterest is the study of anti-corporate, grassroots cultural intermediation. While studies of informal, 'non-professional' or 'amateur' intermediaries have been noted here, these studies rarely go beyond chronicles of those who simply are trying to break into the mainstream using whatever tools might be available. If we want to thoroughly understand the work of mainstream intermediation, we must also understand the work of those who have no interest in joining the parade of corporate convention.

# 12

# LIFESTYLE MEDIA

## TANIA LEWIS

## FROM CELEBRITY CHEFS TO MAKEOVER GURUS – LIFESTYLE MEDIA AND EXPERTISE IN LATE MODERNITY

In 1997 a young Jamie Oliver, who was working at the time as a sous chef at London's River Café, featured in a documentary about the café. Despite being a complete unknown at the time, Oliver's combination of chutzpah, enthusiasm for cooking and sheer personality saw him land a television series that same year with the BBC. *The Naked Chef* was the series in question and Oliver has since gone on to international superstardom[1] not just as a food personality and television chef, but also, thanks to various food 'campaigns', as a lifestyle activist of sorts. For instance, he has set up a charity called the Jamie Oliver Food Foundation 'whose mission is to empower, educate and engage as many people as possible to love and enjoy good food' (www.jamieoliver.com/foundation/). At the same time Oliver is now a thoroughly branded celebrity expert, with multiple television series and books to his name and a range of branded products and services.

Oliver's often controversial career and his branded identity as an international celebrity chef and food guru provide a particularly apposite place to start thinking about cultural intermediaries and lifestyle media. Rather than discussing the lifestyle media industry in general, the focus of this chapter will be on the central role played by popular media-based experts or lifestyle experts today, and throughout this chapter I will repeatedly return to Oliver as a touchstone for understanding the complex socio-cultural role of the lifestyle media industry in late modern consumer culture. This brings me to questions of definition. In thinking about popular figures like Oliver as cultural intermediaries, my focus here is not so much on framing lifestyle media strictly within a cultural economy model in which particular occupational groups are seen as mediating between commercial interests, markets and the social and cultural realm. This essay is not an in-depth analysis, for example, of the professional world of chefs – though celebrity chefs *are* particularly interesting cultural figures today, to the extent that they have come to exemplify and embody a variety of contemporary shifts and tensions around work and leisure; branded, performative modes of selfhood; gendered regimes and hierarchies of cooking; questions of ethics and consumption; and cosmopolitan forms of culinary taste and cultural capital. Nor does this chapter focus on the producers of cooking shows or lifestyle programmes more broadly, as a major occupational group within the industry, though these figures are clearly also pivotal intermediaries in terms of shaping trends and content of lifestyle media, and I will briefly discuss some emergent research on these figures in my conclusion. Instead, my primary interest is in understanding the public or social status and function of figures like Oliver in a contemporary context in which, as Graeme Turner argues, the entertainment media have become key players in 'the construction of cultural identity' (2009: 3). More specifically in relation to lifestyle media, my concern lies with the socio-cultural role played by the swathe of 'ordinary experts' who now populate lifestyle media, a diverse cultural field which includes television chefs as well as a range of other lifestyle experts or advisors, from 'super-nannies' and fitness gurus to etiquette coaches and design mavens.

# FROM MANNERS TO MAKEOVERS: HISTORICIZING CULTURAL INTERMEDIARIES

Before I go on to discuss the practices and impact of these contemporary life experts, I want to contextualize the emergence of these figures. Much of the critical literature on lifestyle experts has tended to situate them in contemporary rather than historical terms, linking their emergence specifically to developments occurring over the past couple of decades. Here I want to briefly summarize that literature before mapping a longer historical narrative. While, as I discuss below, Bell and Hollows (2005) are among the few theorists who have sought to historicize the notion of lifestyle, they also acknowledge the distinct context that marks the contemporary turn to lifestyle (and to popular expertise), arguing that this turn reflects the growing dominance of a reflexive and de-traditionalized notion of selfhood. Individualized and consumer-oriented, this 'DIY' self is a site of endless choice, self-shaping and self-improvement while also being tasked with having to navigate a culture of risk and uncertainty. It is within this context that the recent proliferation of popular experts 'can be seen in terms of their role as an antidote to a growing sense of risk and doubt and as a source of new codes for living' (Lewis, 2008a).

Others have credited recent shifts in the social and economic role of gender in shaping the rise of lifestyle culture. Brunsdon, for example, argues that the surge of lifestyle and makeover television programming in the UK from the 1990s onwards represents a 'feminization of prime-time terrestrial television' (2003: 9), which she links, in part, to the rise in women in the workplace. Another key way in which the recent rise of popular lifestyle advisors has been understood is as in class terms. While the everyman persona of 'ordinary' expert figures such as Jamie Oliver can be read as signalling a refusal of social hierarchies and a democratization of taste, as numerous scholars point out, class and social distinction are nevertheless pervasive and in many ways constitutive features of contemporary lifestyle television and its brand of popular expertise (Lewis, 2008a; Palmer, 2004, 2008; Powell and Prasad, 2010; Skeggs, 2009). The rise and role of these tastemakers and shapers has also been centrally linked to a post-Fordist economic turn with lifestyle experts functioning as crucial guides and intermediaries in an increasingly aestheticized consumer market (Philips, 2005; Powell and Prasad, 2010; Redden, 2008).

While the critical literature on contemporary lifestyle experts links the rise of these figures to a complex conjuncture of contemporary social, cultural and economic factors, many of these accounts make the assumption that this phenomenon is peculiar to the mid- to late 20th century onwards, ignoring 'the longer historical reach' of present lifestyle concerns (Bell and Hollows, 2006: 3). In their edited collection *Historicizing Lifestyles* (2006), Bell and Hollows challenge this position, arguing for instance that Norbert Elias's sweeping work on taste and civility from the Middle Ages onwards might offer one historical context for understanding the contemporary lifestyle moment. Likewise, they suggest that Michel Foucault's mapping of the history of self-care, which in turn looks as far back as the Classical era, might also suggest an alternative genealogy for locating the emergence of a late-modern lifestyle ethic (Bell and Hollows, 2006: 13). In contrast, in my book *Smart Living* (2008) I locate the rise of contemporary lifestyle expertise within the broader context of Anglo-American modernity, tying the emergence of popular expertise to the rise of an urbanized industrial capitalism, associated developments in the media and marketing industries, and shifts within domestic familial relations (Lewis, 2008a). Expanding upon this line of argument, in this section I want to briefly review some of the main historical research on popular forms of ordinary and domestic expertise, from the 19th century to the present day, as a way of contextualizing and locating contemporary lifestyle media and popular advice.

Arguably the first modern precursors to contemporary lifestyle advice before television were the etiquette manuals of the Victorian era. The dramatic social upheavals that accompanied the industrial revolution in 19th-century Britain and America saw the emergence of a plethora of taste, etiquette and domestic advice manuals, with one of the most famous and lasting examples being Isabella Beeton's *Book of Household Management*, which sold 60,000 copies in its first year of publication in the UK (Langland, 1995: 32). The broader context for the rise of popular advice manuals was the emergence of a large aspiring bourgeoisie who sought to emulate the taste and manners of the aristocracy (1995: 25). Growing economic wealth in the late 18th century saw a relative democratization of consumption, with increasing class mobility making the role of consumption practices as a marker of taste and status even more pivotal (Bell and Hollows, 2006: 7). As Langland argues, as definitions of status became increasingly tied to the intangible symbolic realm of taste and manners, women (as bearers of good taste and morality) sought guidance in the 'detailed decorums' provided in the pages of etiquette manuals (1995: 26).

If manners defined the 19th century, the early 20th century saw a growing focus within popular advice culture on the modern woman and on rationalizing the role of women and the space of the home. The status of women in the modern home was marked by a sense of ambiguity as industrialism had freed them from 'the endless round of household productive labour' while at same time stripping them of the skills that had underpinned their productive role in the agrarian home (Ehrenreich and English, 2005: 17). This period saw the emergence of domestic science advisors, or 'domiologists', who attempted to marry a feminine focus on aesthetics and care of the self and family with the increasingly rationalized systems and technologies of modernity, tensions that were negotiated via the emergence of the housewife as the new feminine ideal (Leavitt, 2002: 54).

While early forms of domestic advice largely targeted women, the social upheaval of the 19th century also saw the rise of popular forms of instruction aimed at men at a time of instability around male codes of behaviour (Mechling, 2003: 13). Late-Victorian advice manuals emphasized the need for men to develop 'self-control and self-discipline of the body', traits seen as essential to being a morally upright and economically productive citizen (2003: 13). In the early decades of the 20th century, another pre-eminent site where popular advisors targeted male readers was through home improvement and domestic hobbies, offering the modern male a way to negotiate the feminized space of the home as well as the alienations of industrial labour. Through handicraft activities, such as fashioning small decorative objects for the home, a kind of 'domestic masculinity' emerged centred on pre-industrial manual skills (Gelber, 1999: 204), resulting in a craft movement that can be seen as a precursor to the DIY culture that later emerged in the US and elsewhere.

Moving forward to the 1950s, this is the period most often associated with the rise of a more recognizably lifestyle-oriented media, epitomized by the shift from plain-faced 'service magazines' to glossy lifestyle magazines whose advertorials encouraged readers to shift away from a culture of mending and 'making do' to a focus on buying new commodities (White, 1970: 123). The now familiar context for the huge growth of lifestyle and consumer advice media was a post-war economic and consumption boom that was accompanied by a massive growth in the advertising industry and a rapid expansion of a lifestyle-oriented middle class open to experimentation and new life choices. While women's magazines in the 1950s often continued to emphasize family-based female roles and values, magazines aimed at young working women, such as *Nova*, launched in 1965, began to tap into new social movements such as feminism, attempting to link feminine consumption to the new forms of agency associated with the progressive politics of the times. By the 1960s and early 1970s, marketers and advertisers were increasingly focused on the rise of the 'singles lifestyle', with magazines such as the hugely popular US publication *Cosmopolitan* introducing its female readers to the joys of instant gratification and spending for fun rather than for the home and family (Ehrenreich and English, 2005: 317). Consumer advice at the time thus began to broaden out from a focus on the household to targeting women as individual consumers of lifestyle-related goods and services.

The post-war period also saw an expansion – and a crucial shift in the mode of address – of consumer advice aimed at men, marked by a growing focus on the stylized male self. Men's magazines played a central role in addressing, advising and shaping the identity of the emergent male consumer, representing an important site for the development of a masculine culture of popular expertise organized around lifestyle consumption, discourses of individualization, and the 'stylization' of everyday life. The 1950s, for instance, saw the emergence of a growing advice literature expressing dissatisfaction with men's traditional 'breadwinner' role, with magazines such as *Playboy* and *Esquire* encouraging men to pursue 'self-fulfilment through leisure activities and consumption' (Gelber, 1999: 14). As Arvidsson argues, over this period, lifestyle magazines such as '*Playboy*, *Cosmopolitan* and *Ebony* became virtual instruction manuals for living', catering 'to an experimenting, interactive attitude' (2006: 28–29). Likewise Sam Binkley's extensive research and writing on alternative 1970s magazines, such as the *Whole Earth Catalog* produced by bohemian entrepreneurs based in the San Francisco Bay Area, demonstrates the depth and diversity of the models of selfhood and lifestyle offered to certain middle-class consumers at the time (Binkley, 2003, 2007).

As I discuss in detail in *Smart Living*, the 1980s and 1990s – the era of sophisticated lifestyle publications such as *The Face* – saw a further set of complex developments within advice culture in relation to design, aesthetics, commercial culture and new models of masculinity. A crucial development at this time, for instance, was the articulation of the visual and symbolic language of women's advice culture with a (masculine and elite) postmodern design aesthetic and with the increasingly sophisticated iconography of advertising (Mort, 1996). Men's lifestyle magazines, from *Arena* to *Loaded*, heralded the rise of new forms of consumer masculinity from the style-oriented male yuppie of the 1980s to the New Lad of the 1990s (Gill, 2003; Mort, 1996; Stevenson et al., 2003). While the New Lad was in part a reaction against the perceived bourgeois aestheticism and effeminacy of the images of masculinity found in the pages of *The Face* and *Arena*, this aggressive mode of 'new' masculinity also represented an attempt at negotiating a place for a more 'ordinary' male audience within an increasingly lifestyle-oriented consumer culture – a strategy that partly explains some of the cross-class popularity of Jamie Oliver in his more 'laddish' *Naked Chef* days. Through promoting male-friendly forms of lifestyle-based consumption, men's lifestyle advice magazines can be seen as playing a significant role (along with other factors such as the rise of the self-help movement and the men's movement) in the subsequent 'malestreaming' of domestic and personal advice that was to become increasingly evident within other lifestyle media contexts such as primetime television and broadsheet newspapers from the 1990s onwards.

# MATERIAL PRACTICES AND TECHNOLOGIES OF EXPERTISE: FROM CELEBRITY TO BRANDING

Having traced a modern genealogy for today's lifestyle experts, I want to turn now to the kinds of techniques and technologies used and dispositions expressed and embodied by contemporary lifestyle advisors, focusing in particular on the role of celebrity and branding and using Jamie Oliver again as my key example. As I've noted, a central and highly visible component of contemporary lifestyle advice culture is the figure of the celebrity expert, epitomized by individuals such as Martha Stewart, Nigella Lawson and Oliver. Experts on television play an important cultural-pedagogical role for late-modern audiences, but one that is far removed from the didacticism of earlier forms of 'how to' advice media. Celebrity lifestyle experts are exemplary here: their function is clearly not simply informational or mediatory; rather, they work to embody and enact particular models of 'consumer-citizenship' through their own much-publicized domestic and personal lifestyles, which are played out across their various personae as experts, celebrities and 'private' selves. As Smith Maguire notes in her study of personal trainers as cultural intermediaries, part of their legitimacy and efficacy stems from their use of 'their personal lives, bodies and tastes as crucial occupational resources' (2008b: 219).

Jamie Oliver is a model example of this kind of lived, embodied register of expertise. From his early days on *The Naked Chef* (1998), where we saw Jamie cook for friends in his funky London bachelor pad, to *Jamie's Kitchen* (2002) in which tensions arose between Oliver and his wife Jools over his far-from-family-friendly work schedule, to more recent television offerings such as *Jamie at Home* (2007) featuring an older, plumper Oliver presenting home-style recipes and picking ingredients from his own vegetable garden, his celebrity persona and expert role have from the outset of his career been intimately bound to his own personal life and lifestyle. Jamie's performative persona as a culinary everyman and media personality is also integral to his popularity and status. His much maligned mockney accent and frequent use of colloquialisms give him an aura of ordinariness that help him to negotiate his celebrity status and the often far from ordinary cuisine and culinary values he attempts to promote to a broad audience. As Hollows (2003) points out in her analysis of *The Naked Chef*, despite his extensive training and culinary credentials as an expert in Italian cuisine, Oliver works hard on the show to distance himself from the figure of the connoisseur, denying the 'poshness' of the food he cooks by self-consciously presenting his cooking as ordinary, as something anyone can do if they set their mind to it. Likewise, Oliver's particular mode of soft masculinity, at once playful and laddish but also domesticated and family-oriented, enables him to negotiate and re-badge ostensibly feminine skills and knowledge around healthy food, provisioning, cooking and entertaining as broader life skills, appealing to both male and female viewers.

Oliver's effectiveness as a cultural intermediary then stems in part from his ability to offer up his own lifestyle and embodied identity as a kind of extension of, and aspirational model for, the everyday lives of viewers. As neighbourly figures of trust, stability and familiarity, celebrity experts like Oliver can also be seen as idealized consumer-citizens or as what McCracken terms 'super consumers': that is, as both one of us, but also as 'exemplary figures because they are seen to have created the clear, coherent, and powerful selves that everyone seeks' (2005: 112). Within contemporary consumer culture, celebrity experts such as Oliver model idealized forms of lifestyle and consumption not only through the endorsement of certain kinds of goods and services, via perceived brand synergies between 'personalities' and products (i.e. Oliver and his 11-year association with the Sainsbury's supermarket chain), but increasingly through self-branding (Lewis, 2008a). Both Jamie Oliver and Nigella Lawson, for instance, have sought to extend their credibility as food gurus into the commercial realm through not only endorsing other companies' products but also producing their own products and in turn branding their own lifestyles. Like Nigella Lawson's kitchenware range (which comes complete with intimate personal quotes from Nigella about why each item is integral to her lifestyle), Oliver has also produced branded 'signature' product lines, his *Jme* cooking utensils and home wares. The Oliver empire has also extended to a home-selling consultancy business called *Jamie at Home* that employs ordinary women to act as party hosts, selling *Jme* products, at the same time as which, according to the promotion website, 'Jamie will pop in via DVD to demonstrate a gorgeous seasonal recipe to you and your friends' (www.jamieoliver.com/jamieathome/).

## ASSESSING IMPACT: ETHICAL EXPERTISE AND LIFESTYLE POLITICS

A host of programs and technologies have come to inculcate and sustain the ethic that individuals are free to the extent that they choose a life of responsible selfhood, and have promoted the dreams of self-fulfillment through the crafting of a life-style. (Rose, 1996: 168)

While figures like Jamie Oliver and Nigella Lawson can be read primarily in economic terms as performing, promoting and normalizing consumption-based lifestyles via various material and embodied practices, as I suggest in *Smart Living* these popular figures of 'ordinary expertise' play an influential role in shaping norms around social and cultural identity and citizenship more broadly (Lewis, 2008a). While on softer lifestyle television shows such as *Jamie at Home* the home is often positioned as a site of refuge from the pressures of late modernity, the flipside of this is the increasing surveillance and regulation of the identities, household practices and lifestyles of ordinary people apparent in fly-on-the-wall shows such as *Honey, We're Killing the Kids*,

*Life Laundry, What Not to Wear* and a host of other 'reality' lifestyle makeover formats. Drawing on Foucault's writings on governmentality, media studies scholars Palmer and Ouellette and Hay argue that, with the rise of neoliberalism, cultural technologies such as television have become important spaces for shaping people as citizens and governing their conduct (Ouellette and Hay, 2008; Palmer, 2003). For these scholars, reality and lifestyle television today addresses viewers (through psychologized models of self-help and self-actualization) as entrepreneurs of the self, capable of taking responsibility for and shaping their own destinies.

Thus, on lifestyle makeover shows such *The Biggest Loser*, a format that has proven highly popular around the world in a range of television markets, rather than portraying obesity as a product of western lifestyles or as a public health issue, the fat bodies paraded on the show are represented as markers of the failings of specific individuals. The experts on this show, the fitness instructors Bob and Jillian in the earliest incarnations of the US format, are integral to positioning the show's participants within a framework that is both about a liberated enterprising mode of selfhood and also about being a 'good' healthy citizen. Blending discourses of self-actualization and health and fitness, the lifestyle expertise provided by figures like Bob and Jillian emphasizes freedom and personal fulfilment through the regulation of the self. In the transition to a post-traditional lifestyle culture where consumer choice is king, lifestyle experts like Bob and Jillian step in to guide us towards the 'right' choices. Selfhood in the contemporary neoliberal moment is therefore an ongoing project that is at once voluntarist and at the same time profoundly embedded in a set of social and ethical duties and responsibilities.

As I have argued elsewhere, the contemporary 'ethical turn' has seen a particular emphasis on 'choosing' to live responsibly. This development, while linked to the rise of neoliberalism, also dovetails with the broader mainstreaming of ethical consumption and with the rise of a 'lifestyle politics' in which ethical and political concerns have entered into every aspect of people's daily lives, from people's eating and exercise habits to whether or not they buy ethical or fairtrade goods (Lewis 2008b, 2012; Lewis and Potter, 2011). It is in this context that figures like Jamie Oliver have come into their own, not just as lifestyle advisors but also as activists and agitators of a kind within a late-modern lifestyle culture in which consumption, branding, celebrity, politics and ethics have come together in often paradoxical combinations. While a number of celebrity chefs such as the UK's Hugh Fearnley-Whittingstall and Australia's Stephanie Alexander have also become involved in consciousness-raising efforts around food education, animal welfare and sustainability, Oliver's celebrity is increasingly as much linked to his campaigning on food issues and his involvement in broader social concerns as it is to his culinary skills. One of the first celebrity chefs to exploit the emotional power of the pop doc/reality format in foregrounding social issues, *Jamie's Kitchen* (2002) saw Oliver attempting to train a group of 15 disadvantaged youth to work in his new restaurant. In the face of growing un- and under-employment in capitalist economies, his various initiatives have received widespread acclaim and support.

Oliver's subsequent forays into promoting healthy eating, locally sourced and unprocessed food, and animal welfare have been rather more controversial. In *Jamie's School Dinners* (2005), Oliver, shocked by the poor diets of working-class children, put the spotlight on the deficiencies of the British school dinner system, which provides food to state-run schools. While much of the focus of the show, and Oliver's subsequent US series *Jamie Oliver's Food Revolution* (2010), is on educating school dinner 'ladies' and families on healthy eating (which invariably involves lessons in taste and aesthetics), Oliver does pay some attention to structural and political issues in relation to, for instance, government funding for school dinners, sustainable food sourcing, and the negative effects of globalized agri-business. A central theme on *Jamie's School Dinners*, for instance, is Oliver's often-caustic critique of commercial food culture. He is regularly shown rallying against the influence of fast and pre-prepared food on children – Jamie's *bête noire*, the 'turkey twizzler', comes in for a particular amount of flack and was subsequently withdrawn from UK supermarkets – while lamenting the lack of raw foods in the diets of the kids he meets. This is spelled out in a particularly effective scene with a group of children in which Jamie shows that, while they all recognize the logos of fast food outlets such as McDonald's, they have a much harder time naming the various commonplace vegetables he has brought into their classroom.

Oliver's role as what Hollows and Jones have nicely termed a 'moral entrepreneur' points to some of the paradoxes of a late-modern lifestyle culture that on the one hand encourages the hyper-consumption of branded images and products, while on the other hand promoting an ethic of consumer care, restraint and responsibility in the face of a growing awareness of the risks and limits of an unfettered consumer capitalism (Hollows and Jones, 2010). Figures like Oliver clearly are central cultural intermediaries today for a burgeoning lifestyle media industry, but what they increasingly seem to offer are not just guides for living and consuming in an uncertain world but also, to a certain extent, provocations to think differently about how to live. For instance, Oliver and Fearnley-Whittingstall's often controversial efforts to raise awareness about the conditions in which chickens are kept in the UK have been linked to a significant growth in the numbers of free-range products available in British supermarkets as well as decreased consumer demand for factory-based products (Hickman, 2008). Aside from selling ethical messages purely to individual consumers, Oliver and Fearnley-Whittingstall's campaigns (including the television special *Jamie's Fowl Dinners* (2008), where Oliver replicated the way male chicks are killed in carbon monoxide chambers for a visibly shocked 'live' audience) arguably have contributed to raising broader cultural and political awareness and 'responsibilizing' not just consumers but also producers, supermarkets and government. In the case of *Jamie's School Dinners*, for instance, following the success of the show, the British Government pledged to increase spending on school dinners with the then Prime Minister Tony Blair acknowledging that this was a result of Oliver's campaign (Oliver was subsequently named 'Most Inspiring Political Figure of 2005' in the Channel 4 Political Awards in 2006).

In understanding lifestyle experts as cultural intermediaries today, clearly the role and impact of figures like Oliver has to be understood in a cultural and political landscape in which a range of popular figures including celebrities have come to have considerable cultural authority within the contemporary media sphere and in which traditional forms of authority, whether of politicians, experts or intellectuals, have become increasingly linked to personalities and lifestyles through processes of celebritization. Lifestyle experts continue to act as mediators of manners, morals and markets and shapers of taste, as they have through much of modernity. However, as I have argued, their role as highly visible life guides and model consumer-citizens has taken on particular significance today in the context of a privatized, lifestyle- and consumer-driven political culture in which the entertainment media and processes of governance have become increasingly intertwined.

# FUTURE LIFESTYLES: RESEARCH DIRECTIONS

By way of conclusion I want to provide a brief summary of new and emergent scholarship on lifestyle media and popular expertise and suggested directions for future research. As I have outlined, there has been a considerable amount of scholarship investigating the contemporary and the historical role of lifestyle experts and lifestyle media in shaping social and cultural mores. One relatively new research domain, which I have briefly discussed here, is the role of popular food personalities such as Jamie Oliver and Hugh Fearnley-Whittingstall in emphasizing the ethical and political dimensions of consumption (Bell and Hollows, 2011; Hollows and Jones, 2010; Lewis, 2008a). Another related area, which remains critically under-examined, is the role of lifestyle media and its gurus in promoting green forms of lifestyle and consumption through unlikely television formats such as eco-makeover shows (Bonner, 2011; Lewis, 2008b, 2012; Thomas, 2008). More work is needed on the growing role and limitations and potentials of lifestyle media in mediating and promoting green, ethical and even anti-consumerist discourses and practices.

Finally, the globalization of lifestyle media and the role played by national and cultural differences in relation to lifestyle and consumption is another under-researched area. The focus in this chapter has been solely on lifestyle media in an Anglo-American context. However, the lifestyle media industry has become increasingly global. From Shanghai to Mumbai, glossy magazines and newspaper supplements promoting lifestyle-based consumption have a huge and growing readership, while lifestyle shows and reality makeover programming can be found on primetime schedules around the world – from the Indian version of *MasterChef* to Panama's local adaptation of *Extreme Makeover* (*Cambio Radical*). The global spread of these media forms raises the question of how and what kinds of lifestyle culture and consumption are promoted in these different cultural settings. While the global currency of lifestyle media has been interpreted by some scholars as a sign of the growing prevalence of individualized, consumer-oriented models of selfhood around the world (Bignell, 2005; Miller, 2007), there has been relatively little in-depth research in the field to date to support such arguments (Chua, 2000; Kraidy and Sender, 2011; Lewis et al., 2012; Xu, 2007).

A team of colleagues and myself are currently conducting the first comparative study of lifestyle television in Asia, which is also, as far as we know, one of the first such large-scale comparative studies in the world. Funded by the Australian Research Council, this project seeks to examine the various modes of lifestyle and selfhood promoted on lifestyle television across Asia by analysing a wide range of television shows and conducting interviews with television producers and audiences in China, India, Taiwan and Singapore. While the study critically examines both the role of television producers and lifestyle experts as 'cultural intermediaries', it also seeks to contextualize, denaturalize and/or provincialize such western frameworks in the context of a range of differentiated Asian modernities. In India, for instance, religious gurus, yoga teachers and Bollywood celebrities all lay claim to forms of popular cultural authority, variously framed through a performative mix of 'lifestyle' and self-improvement discourse and customary practices. On Taiwanese variety television, life advice experts likewise promote consumerist individualism while being addressed as 'class head' and 'teacher', suggesting the ongoing cultural potency in Taiwan of an ideology of hierarchical collectivism (Lewis et al., 2012). Such divergent cultural forms and understandings of everyday life advice and expertise complicate assumptions that a particular model of cosmopolitan middle-classness or neoliberal selfhood has become globally hegemonic, thus speaking back to conventional Euro-American assumptions about and models of consumer-citizenship and lifestyle under conditions of late capitalism. One of the central lessons of our comparative research then has been the need to pay close attention to the way in which media and cultural trends are articulated to specific historical, social, cultural and economic contexts, a situated and conjunctural approach I have sought to foreground here in this discussion of Anglo-American late-modern expertise.

## ACKNOWLEDGEMENTS

The author would like to thank Fran Martin for her critical feedback on this chapter and Wokar Rigumi for her diligent research assistance.

## NOTE

1  An Australian media and marketing website, for instance, recently referred to the 'Jamania' caused by Oliver's arrival on the set of *MasterChef Australia* where a couple of contestants reportedly collapsed onto the floor in excitement at meeting the 'cockney cook' (see http://mumbrella.com.au/jamania-77624, accessed 2 January 2014).

# 13

# JOURNALISM

## *JULIAN MATTHEWS*

The reader of *Distinction* (Bourdieu, 1984: 325) will recognise that the journalist –
or the 'journalist-writer, writer-journalist' more specifically – appears among other
occupations as a new cultural intermediary, conceived there as the critic who presides
over not-yet-legitimate cultural forms. Journalism scholars have been slow to follow this particular steer or Bourdieu's writings more generally (Benson and Neveu,
2004), despite embracing for the most part a sociological foundation for the analysis
of journalism (Gitlin, 1995). In contrast to the general reluctance by journalism scholars to adopt Bourdieu's ideas of the intermediary, this chapter considers journalism
as a cultural intermediary occupation with reference to recent developments in this
literature (see Smith Maguire and Matthews, 2010) and uses this lens to explore the
history, material practices and impacts of journalism in the UK.

Approaches used to study journalism up to this point have shaped our understanding of the knowledge and practices of these cultural workers. Often this
writing introduces the term 'journalism' to refer to the singular prestige form of
'news journalism' or simply theorizes journalist practice without reference to the
plurality of the occupation and the variety of its activities and forms. A view of
the journalist actor is further impaired when commentaries position them as the
subject of influence rather than the object of analysis. What journalists produce is
assumed to be the outcome of a mix of organizational, political, economic and
cultural influences on journalism production. It follows that most hold a less than
positive attitude toward journalists' agency. Accounts describe the potential of
these cultural workers with jaded reservation, and this view has become further
darkened within recent writing on the 'imminent crisis' that faces journalism from
changing markets, production dynamics and the challenge from the Internet
(Fenton, 2010).

In response, this chapter suggests that the lens of the cultural intermediary corrects
certain flaws and omissions in the study of the forms and practices of journalism.

This perspective emphasizes journalists' actions as an appropriate empirical entrance point for study. Literally, this opens the production environment to allow us to scrutinize journalists' performance in moments where knowledge conjoins with practice, and to acknowledge the diverse range of their devices and dispositions (du Gay, 2004). Accepting that ideas (dispositions) and writing tools (devices) vary according to the journalism specialism moves forward our understanding of journalist practice and the differentiated nature of journalism in the modern media ecology. In short, this perspective offers a common language with which to discuss the varied work of journalism, including the journalists' work situation, material practices and professional knowledge.

The cultural intermediary approach offers a new vantage point from which to view journalists' work situation. Journalists exist within structures that stretch beyond their organizational milieu, and as kindred to other intermediaries perform work as part of a chain of actors. This characteristic of their working environment is partially captured in studies that take seriously the non-journalist actor or news source as important and present in 'a tug of war' (Gans, 1980) or 'negotiation' over meaning (Ericson et al., 1991) with the journalist. All the same, the acknowledgments or likeminded insights from studies of news sources (Schlesinger and Tumber, 1994) or theories of elite influence on journalism (e.g. Hall et al., 1978; Entman, 2004) do not produce detailed analyses of the journalist actor working in connection with other actors. Viewing journalists as intermediaries then allows us to assess their overall contribution to the process of constructing meanings. Of particular interest is to view their relationship with others as negotiating a framing of reality that is finalized in journalism production, which brings us to consider their material practices.

In addition to the particulars of the journalists' location, this approach recognizes the material practices significant to the journalists' work and their outcomes, or what Smith Maguire and Matthews (2012: 5) summarize as the intermediary's accomplished framing work. Studies of journalism also view the practice of framing (Reese et al., 2001) as pertinent to the journalist, who negotiates and legitimates the use of frames in the general process of their work of mediation (Silverstone, 1999). Even so, the productive connection with the intermediary literature ends there, as journalism studies examine – more specifically, deduce – journalists' framing almost entirely from the analysis of news content while annexing interest in the practice of framing within theorizing of journalism production (e.g. Fenton et al., 1998; Kitzinger, 2000). Seeing the journalist as an intermediary, we can explore their framing practice and reveal how such activities will vary according to the conditions and networks in which they work (Smith Maguire and Matthews, 2012). This requires that journalists' activities be seen as the object of analysis rather than the subject of external influences.

Using this approach to study journalists' framing practices then positions the journalist to the centre of the production process. It focuses on the dispositions and devices that journalists use to accomplish framing and recognizes in the process the agency of the journalist actor in this context that appears as misplaced in journalism studies that attribute analytical priority to static bureaucratic structures and routines in journalism production (for a review see Cottle, 2007). The notion of disposition works in this context to highlight the wider professional knowledge(s) underpinning their practice, including the variety of knowledge associated with (i) different forms of journalism and (ii) individual journalists as human actors (Ettema et al., 1987). Turning attention to practices, the approach recognizes diversity in the writing devices employed by journalists who work with different dispositions. The device, translated crudely as writing techniques, characterizes the textual delivery of a variety of journalistic outputs, including for news journalism its popular and serious journalistic forms (Dahlgren and Sparks, 1992; Langer, 1998). In sum, the journalist as cultural intermediary is good for the study of journalists and demands that we adopt a widened historical view of the formation of this occupation.

## HISTORICIZING JOURNALIST INTERMEDIARIES

An expanded view of the history of this occupation provides insights into the origins of its now codified and routinized devices and dispositions. Of course, a history of journalism is really a comment on the development of the journalistic field (Bourdieu, 1998). Journalistic fields do not develop in uniform ways; as Hallin and Mancini (2010) explain in the case of Europe, these are based on national spaces, and vary considerably according to the circumstances of the journalistic market, the journalistic profession and those connections between journalistic forms and the State and political parties. It would be true to say to some extent that journalism takes 'on the form and coloration of the social and political structures in which it operates' (Siebert et al., 1956:1). Assisting then in our understanding of how western journalistic fields emerged from the 19th century onward is the co-incidental growth of the mass production of journalism and of democratic ideas, and the resulting liberal democratic reformers' campaigns for press freedom (Keane, 1991). Similarly important are later developments of the growth in variety of journalistic forms, objective reporting and the wider legitimization of journalism as a profession, to which we will now turn.

At what stage the occupation of journalism actually forms is a moot point – is it when individuals are paid to write, or much later during greater standardization and recognition of this type of employment? Putting this particular conundrum to one side allows us to observe those formidable developments that shape how journalists think about what they do. The rise of objective newspaper reporting is one such moment found in this history that Allan (2004) attributes to significant economic, political and technological factors operating at the time. In the 19th century, for example, the existing character of the press was undergoing transformation from the recent introduction of mass production optimized by new printing techniques, growing audiences and increased revenue from advertisers. Forms of journalistic writing developed as part of this context in ways devised to appeal directly to the public's newfound and growing 'demand for facts' (Allan, 2004: 15). The organized training of journalists followed. Based around news values and common forms of news writing, a standardizing of journalist practices materialized in conjunction with news agencies' information sharing that was facilitated first by the development of the telegraph. Later, processes of professionalization played a role in the development of the occupation. Both the newly formed National Association of Journalism (1884) and later-developed National Union of Journalism (1907) in the UK championed the use of standardized reporting practices in their claims for the professional status of journalism (Hoyer and Lauk, 2003). Further, the use of professional values was to accelerate after the First World War, with impartial reporting (a distinguishing of fact from value) joining other practices of objectivity to create journalism formed in the 'public interest' – as was recognized keenly in early broadcasting news (Scannell and Cardiff, 1991). These professional values continue to underpin claims to expertise made by journalists, despite journalists' access to professional knowledge and autonomy being shaped by their place in the occupational hierarchy of the media organization (Ursell, 2004).

The rise of different journalistic forms offers another insight into how the occupation has developed. Growing newspaper audiences and advertising revenues in the 19th century laid the foundations for the structured hierarchy of different popular and serious journalistic forms that exist today. Within broadcasting, journalism founded in public service and commercial outlets grew in opposition to each other through the 20th century. Collectively, these journalistic forms share evolutions in style and substance over time (Barnhurst and Nerone, 2001) which include general developments that differentiate between journalistic forms and others that erode distinctions between them. The wider 'popularization of journalistic idioms and modes of address' expressed in what Eide and Knight (1999: 525) entitle 'service journalism' is a pertinent reminder of the latter process. This popularization – identified with the uptake of 'content, format and accent' (1999: 525) common to tabloid journalism – has further spread to news forms as part of an ongoing change in style that began after the Second World War.

Notwithstanding the importance of processes of the personalization or tabloidization of journalistic forms for shaping journalists practices, the occupation of journalism has been further formed according to the growth in media outlets. Opportunities to write on the problems of everyday life have emerged from the rise in newspaper supplements and magazines over time. In charting this increase, Puddefoot (1970) describes how enhanced printing techniques and an increase in consumers laid the foundations for 'women's coverage' in Sunday supplements of the UK quality newspapers of the 1960s and a raft of magazines. A staple ingredient of this new content was 'advice and exchange of views on emotional, social and family matters' (1970: 79), a feature of journalists' work that has steadily grown in presence in publications. Currently, the media ecology is peppered with journalists who dispense advice and shape tastes on cultural matters in their role of self-portrayed 'expert' (Lewis, 2008a; McKay, 2008). The opportunities from which these journalists benefit continue to widen on account of publishers' views of their audiences that Conboy summarizes as 'consumers and as lucid participants in the selection and maintenance of specifically gendered lifestyles' (2004: 145).

A diversifying of journalistic forms has accompanied the growth in media outlets. The rise in magazine publishing, for instance, has produced new forms of writing that are delivered with a variety of conventions. Journalistic writing on film and music, as one example, uses distinct modes of address and styles of commentary including the form of the review and the interview (Laing, 2006). Styles of food journalism have followed a similar upward trajectory, emerging from the women's page in newspapers to something 'that occupies an unrivalled centrality to our lives' (Bell and Valentine, 1997: 3). Jones and Taylor (2013) outline how the ever-increasing opportunities for the food journalist emerge from the growth in trade publications, magazines directed to food consumers and newspaper-based articles. Such writing, they explain, follows the marked forms of the cookery column, the restaurant review and the feature article about food. A similar analysis of publications for other specialist journalisms including sports, automotive, fashion, travel and wine journalism to name a few (see Turner and Orange, 2012) uncovers opportunities for journalists to pen work in differentiated styles and formats. In sum, journalists' dispositions and devices emerge from historical shifts that include the rise of forms and ideas of journalism. Now it is time to examine how knowledge and practice fuses in the making – or more specifically, framing – of journalism.

## MATERIAL PRACTICES

In accomplishing their work, journalists must decide on the material to write about and how it will be presented. Although these decisions characterize journalists' daily activities, the responsibility to take them is not given to all journalists. Production activities differ between organizational employees, freelancers and others situated higher within the structure of the media organization. In the case of freelance journalists, it is their position as an outlier that excludes them from a publication's policy-making decisions and those general in-house processes of organizational work common to it, for which responsibility rests with various editors and copywriters. This distance to the story-producing machinery of the publishing organization explains the form and intensity of their connection with a community of other writers and sources (Forde, 2003). Acting as substitutes for community interaction with institutional workers, these connections facilitate an audience for freelance journalists' writing and one that provides a flow of specialist knowledge on which to write. Close relations with institutional actors upstream in particular remain integral to the practice of journalism. Nevertheless, the work of freelance and regularly employed news journalists is separate to this. Mindful of the boundaries defined by those professional values central to their particular disposition, news journalists self-enforce a distinction between the sources of their information and their writing community. Let us now look closer at the processes of selection and presentation.

Framing begins in an interaction to select material. In their position as the receivers of information from sources, journalists are required to engage in a 'struggle over meaning' (Wolfsfeld, 1997) and over what can be said. Connections with 'appropriate sources' and the journalists' knowledge and reputation shape the quality of resources that the journalist will acquire in the course of their work. Whether the framing changes beyond the original negotiation with the information source and how it does so depends on a journalist's autonomy to make decisions different from those of their commissioning institution. The relative freedom to shape commissioned work is available to those recognized as specialists in a field, for instance, in contrast to contemporaries who work on non-commissioned ideas or articles and are subject to review by in-house actors. Others embedded in media organizational life experience similar forms of autonomy to select material free from the editorial gaze. Also seen as specialist journalists (Tunstall, 1972; Mellor, 2008), such as war and foreign correspondents, these journalists benefit from an organizationally sanctioned freedom to determine the direction of their work within accepted boundaries. Still, maintaining a focus on journalists' autonomy overlooks the dispositions that they share, negotiate and implement on a daily basis.

Accomplished framing work relies on applying a shared professional disposition. Although working dispositions vary, they take their steer from the values of a corresponding media organization and details of the journalistic form under production. These dispositions operate in production to provide guidance on what is appropriate for a publication and its audience, and for us their presence in journalists' activities challenges views of production knowledge as abstracted and encoded within organizational processes and structures such as the news routine (Rock, 1983). Journalists share collective understandings of the journalistic form for which they write, and use them in dialogue with other journalists. Daily, they will visualize and retell features of their writing in their interactions over the 'ideal' article, review or news agenda and as part of their evaluations of other journalists' writing. A shared conception of the news consumer and their preferred informational likes and dislikes underscores these wider ideas and, in turn, assists in the everyday practice of journalism.

My ethnographic research into journalists working on a BBC children's television news programme helps to show how disposition operates in media production (Matthews, 2010). These journalists were observed throughout the news day, and were found to use their shared disposition in the practices of their work, including moments that demand production knowledge be introduced and reaffirmed with others. Two selected moments in the production cycle of the programme, which I call 'production rituals', demonstrate how this is achieved: (i) the selection of prospective news stories and (ii) the reviewing of the previous day's news programme. When at these times journalists discuss the appropriateness of a news story, they demonstrate their knowledge of the preferred characteristics and inscribed imagined audience of their journalistic form (programme). In dialogue with others, they revisit the ideas that underpin their decision making and thus participate in rich and detailed exchanges over news selection that leave explanations based on static and generalized 'news values' looking simplistic. Additionally, witnessing these actions helps to understand how journalists' dispositions change over time. The conclusion reached at the end of these newsroom dialogues is often one to reaffirm the importance and application of their disposition. However, on occasion moments in these processes allow for a challenge to existing ideas that underscore journalists' practices and thus, when successful and agreed upon, these interactions allow for an incremental change in the content or delivery of their journalistic form.

Practices of presentation finalize the framing process. Significant to this closing stage of production are dialogues between journalists and editors over the preferred presentation style. These exchanges are based on those corrections to writing generated as part of a 'blue pencilling' process which many, following Breed (1955), view negatively as the locus of organizational control over journalists. A focus on power and control alone at these moments restricts our understanding of the negotiation over what is produced. Therefore, it is more profitable to view these dialogues as moments in which aspects of the disposition are shared and reviewed. To construct a review article, for example, journalists will follow agreed considerations of its form and accept editorial advice on how its presentation can be fine-tuned. Their shared knowledge of the preferred journalistic form is integral to producing these and other formats as examples reveal. For instance, the significance of the review article for the journalist and their publication's identity in context of their community of critics, followers and audience demands the journalist and editor craft the review's written judgements to follow the preferred 'highly individualized and self-conscious style' (Wyatt and Badger, 1990: 338). The interview is another significant format finessed in discussions between those editors and journalists working for fashion, music and film publications. Attention here is directed to producing writing that dwells on the 'personality' rather than the idea of the 'artist' for those under the spotlight (1990: 338). A more general consideration for these discussions is how formats of writing must capture the correct mode of address for their audience.

All journalists personalize their writing for audiences, and practising tabloid journalists offer a good example of this. They phrase their writing to appeal to a segment of the consuming news audience imagined by them as the everyday person on the street (Conboy, 2002). Based on this view their working disposition contrasts sharply with those of quality newspaper journalists and informs practices to cover issues of the private sphere, reaffirm accepted values, include the voices of ordinary people, and pen news with a partisan and engaged style (Cottle, 1993). This was made clear when I examined the devices journalists used to develop a campaign on the 'UK asylum system crisis' (Matthews and Brown, 2012). Journalists framed these stories similar to other depoliticized tabloid content (Sparks, 1992) despite their political nature and used the same disposition and devices for the task. Retold over a period of a month's coverage, the asylum crisis (defined as an inability of government officials to deal with an unprece-dented rise in economic migrants) was personalized to the reader as a problem developing despite shared 'common-sense' solutions and one as affecting their rights as 'citizens' to welfare services. Journalists used humorous writing devices to pour scorn on the already defined 'incompetent' government officials inef-fectively handling those 'bogus and manipulating' asylum seekers. Additionally, and in accordance with their disposition, they introduced the 'ordinary' voices of the public into their writing in ways to reaffirm their framing of this issue. As this example shows, journalists' dispositions vary according to the characteristics of the product for which they write.

Further, it is the knowledge and credibility associated with journalists' reputations that underpin their ability to accomplish framing work. Network connections and published work in a specialist field reinforce the status of the journalist as 'established critic', whereas the news journalist gains affirmation through rehearsing values cen-tral to their journalistic form. These sets of professional knowledge shape the mate-rial that journalists produce. The value of impartiality – the effort to separate fact from opinion – for example cuts across and informs several forms of journalistic writing. Objectivity, on the other hand, is significant for the practice of news jour-nalism and is used, many suggest, as a strategic ritual to safeguard journalists against criticism (Tuchman, 1972). However, when objectivity is considered in context of a wider professional disposition and as negotiated rather than simply present and mediating, it produces a detailed picture of journalists' intermediary work. Here, we recognise that news journalists negotiate the connection the news story makes with wider, often contested, positions and identities that exist in society. My study with Simon Cottle that examined the production of UK news programmes introduces the role played by journalists' shared dispositions in selecting how to frame news stories (Matthews and Cottle, 2012). Journalists' selections over the period of the study, we demonstrate, affect the introduction and shaping of news story topics, their ordering of news voices and their representation of cultural identities.

Therefore, it is important to recognize that journalists negotiate with profes-sional values in the course of their framing work. Of the many journalists working in the journalistic field, those with greater autonomy to define their work – such as the specialist correspondent – feel the weight of these decisions most acutely. My recent research conducted with war correspondents, for example, introduces this process (Matthews and Fisher, forthcoming). This finds that in performing framing, journalists negotiate tensions between cumulative experiences of the con-flict situation and the professional values used to report them. It is the decisions they reach after this negotiation that shape their practice. The choice to report war in terms of its 'human cost' is an outcome from this process that not only guides their reporting but also helps to justify in their mind their continued presence in the conflict zone.

Seen more widely, war correspondents' application of the 'human cost of war' frame underscores an ongoing critique of the relevance of established professional values for their work, including their frustration with the hackneyed view of the correspondent who reports on conflict situations from a distant and emotionally disengaged position. Journalists' regular witnessing of killing on a mass scale informs their negotiation with professional values such as impartiality and their view of these as extremely difficult to deploy in conflict situations. What follows from this negotiation produces heightened emotional reaction in news presentation and, where possible, a steadied focus on the plights of victims in reports. Studying journalists' devices and dispositions uncovers then-pertinent negotiations between professional ideas and practices. These processes produce recognizable impacts also, which we will consider next.

# ASSESSING IMPACT

Discussions of journalism talk generally about its impact as part of the occupation's significance as a social and cultural force in society (McNair, 1999). These statements about the impact of journalism are relevant, of course, but the lens of the cultural intermediary allows us to think specifically about the nature of these impacts and their location in the chain of meaning production.

Journalists occupy a position upstream from which possible impacts take place. Without making explicit reference to the connections that bind journalists with actors upstream, Davis (2003) introduces how a relationship with elites is sustained by their privileged access to this sealed arena. When in situ, they engage with elites (politicians, institutions, non-government organizations as well as elite media) and facilitate interactions between them, the outcomes of which appear explicitly and implicitly in their writing that addresses contested ideas and meanings. Although we need to know more about journalists' actions, reactions to and participation within these ongoing dialogues with elite audiences, we can see how their efforts to reveal illegality and wrongdoing in a democratic sense can produce tangible impacts on policy and the political lives of elites (Thompson, 2000) as well as play a role in shaping the future course of societies.

It is equally important to examine how other relationships are configured in this chain of actors. Journalists working for non-news publications enter into different relationships with upstream actors, formed in part by their action to review cultural forms or consumer goods. Of significance to their dialogues with the PR/marketing delegates, for instance, is a negotiation with those frames designed specifically to assist in a product's or form's journey to and within the marketplace. In one sense, reviewing products or forms characterizes their place in relation to others available in the market. Some, of course, become rarefied in the process and positioned in the canon of legitimate forms or products in sharp contrast to others that do not. In another sense, this work participates in a wider dialogue with other writers. Reaffirmed within these exchanges are the structures and narratives that journalists use to mark the boundaries around the available meanings that can be associated with goods, ideas or services.

Additionally, impacts occur downstream from the journalist at moments when audiences engage with journalists' accomplished framing. It is too simplistic to use the traditional label of 'media effects' to understand these intersections. We should not see audiences as limited to using journalists' frames to understand and make choices about the world around them. Instead, these consumption moments involve a process of negotiation over meaning. Audience reception research, even when presenting its most simplistic permutation of this connection in the form of the marked subject positions audiences use to respond to frames (Morley, 1980), recognizes audience agency in this engagement with journalism. Audiences negotiate journalists' frames using their existing knowledge, including their media literacy and those characteristics that shape their perceptions of social reality, including ethnicity, class and gender. However, a step closer to the idea of a fixed impact is taken when we accept that audience engagement with framing is not unconstrained. A negotiation with frames will always be restricted by the material that journalists produce, and despite instances where frames are resisted or subject to contrary readings, these still convey 'facts' and in turn influence 'their [audiences'] ideas, assumptions and attitudes' (Eldridge et al., 1997: 160). Additionally, impacts take different forms than those assumed to set an agenda of issues or mark audiences' understanding of them. Journalists' framing fits into the routine pattern of everyday consumption (e.g. newspaper reading as an activity) and expresses the world in commonly accepted ways, which assist in reaffirming audiences' general 'ontological security' (Giddens, 1991). In other words, journalism makes and remakes the world to appear recognizable and largely predictable for its audience.


## NEW DIRECTIONS

Using the framework of the cultural intermediary brings a fresh perspective with which to understand journalists' activities. As suggested, this recognizes the devices and dispositions that characterize the process of producing journalism, and offers fertile ground on which to develop our understanding of this occupation. To promote this agenda the following discussion outlines a number of avenues for the further study of the journalist as intermediary.

To enhance the understanding of journalism as an intermediary occupation outlined above, future research would need first to audit the journalistic field to discover the variety of cultural intermediary work that is taking place, and establish as part of this overview the interconnections between various journalistic forms and the devices and dispositions that create them. Second, a more thorough account is required of different dispositions, including journalists' use of professional credibility in their work. This analysis would need to be mindful of journalists who develop credibility claims through their expertise in a field and those who use claims based on journalistic values. Journalists' engagement with professional values is a third important avenue for study. Of interest here is how journalists' personal habitus impacts on the application of professional values in their work and the cumulative influence these decisions have on journalists' understanding and use of values over time. Fourth, looking beyond the immediate context of these intermediaries' work, research needs to analyse the chains that various journalists inhabit, including the connections and negotiations that take place there with other journalists and sources of information. Indeed, this should take into account how these relationships differ according to the various types of journalism operating in both new and old media. Fifth, research should aim to develop international and historical comparisons between journalistic fields to expand our view of the occupation and of the practices of journalists operating in the same chain and across chains of meaning production.

# 14
# FITNESS

## JENNIFER SMITH MAGUIRE

Commercial fitness is a useful field through which to consider the work of cultural intermediaries. Taken most broadly, the work of cultural intermediaries involves the construction of legitimacy (Smith Maguire and Matthews, 2012). Such work is critical to all cultural fields: no matter how established a field's claims to social prestige (e.g. in the case of art or gastronomy), it will be characterized by struggles over positions of relative dominance (e.g. Ferguson, 1998), with new or not-yet-legitimate cultural forms (such as outsider art or nose-to-tail cooking) vying for ascendancy. The field of physical fitness is no different. The social esteem associated with purposive physical exercise is well established: individual fitness has long been linked to worthy goals through, for example, the Rational Recreation and Muscular Christianity movements of the 19th century and the emphasis on daily exercise in health promotion initiatives since the 1970s (Green, 1986; Smith Maguire, 2008a). At the same time, the particular objectives and practices associated with physical exercise continue to change over time, promoted and given credibility by a range of different experts and entrepreneurs.

The cultural field of commercial fitness is populated by a range of cultural intermediaries who, in addition to their role-specific activities, carry out the more general work of framing physical fitness as a socially valued pursuit, and the fit body as an esteemed form of capital. While the work of fitness magazine writers, health club representatives or the presenters of television exercise programmes might ably serve as examples of fitness cultural intermediaries, this chapter focuses on the occupation of personal training. Personal trainers are key frontline service workers in the commercial fitness industry. Paid to design and facilitate personal fitness programmes on a one-to-one basis, personal trainers perform the 'relational work' (Cochoy, 2003, in du Gay, 2004) between consumers and health clubs, exercise equipment retailers, fitness media and other exercise-related goods and services.

The chapter draws on previous research on personal training in the US (Smith Maguire, 2001, 2008a, 2008b). However, it is important to note that while commercial fitness and personal training are global in scope, they are not globally homogeneous (e.g. Ginsberg, 2000; Spielvogel, 2003). The particular, local characteristics of personal training – how the occupation is organized and to what degree it is professionalized; how it is experienced by practitioners and clients; how it relates to other health, fitness and exercise activities and experts – will be informed by its societal context, including the established leisure and physical culture traditions, and patterns in the demand for and provision of personal services. An American case study thus offers to highlight aspects of a phenomenon that may resonate with, but not directly translate to, other national contexts.

The chapter provides an overview of a number of problems that characterize personal training. These include the problem of health (e.g. the challenge of exercise in an increasingly sedentary world) and the problem of appearance (e.g. how to achieve a valued body shape and look), which set the historical context for personal training's contemporary expansion and professionalization. The chapter then considers the material practices of personal training, with particular attention to how the problem of credibility (e.g. strategies to lend legitimacy to personal trainers' claims to professional expertise) and the problem of selling (e.g. the tension between those claims to professionalism and the obligation to sell goods and services) give rise to particular embodied devices and dispositions. And finally, the chapter highlights how, in addressing the problem of motivation (e.g. how to effectively mobilize consumers to take up a fitness regime by serving as role models), personal trainers have the potential both to challenge dominant notions of 'fit' legitimacy, and to experience emotional burnout.

# HISTORICIZING FITNESS CULTURAL INTERMEDIARIES

In the early 1990s, personal trainers were heralded as a 'new breed' of expert in the field of fitness:

> Exercise enthusiasts are becoming more educated about fitness and health, more insistent on an exercise regimen that caters to their schedules, and more adventurous and versatile in the activities in which they participate. Emerging from the demands of these individuals is the need for fitness instructors conversant with a variety of sports and activities and willing to meet clients at the fitness center, in the home, or elsewhere to personally guide them through an exercise program designed specifically for them. This has generated a new fitness niche, and we are witness to a new breed of fitness instructor – the personal trainer. (Marks, 1991: xix, in Sudy, 1991)

Available in over 90 per cent of health clubs (their main employment setting), personal trainers have become a staple of the fitness industry. In the US in 2011, 231,500 people were working as fitness trainers and aerobics instructors, up from 189,220 in 2005. The number of clients is also growing: approximately 6.5 million in 2011, up from 4 million in 1999.[1]

A decade earlier, the popular press had reported on personal trainers, but within the narrow parameters of an elite service for celebrities, athletes or yuppies, and these fitness experts were sometimes celebrities in their own rights, with their own training studies, training manuals and exercise videos. In the late 1980s and early 1990s, competition increased within the commercial health club industry (fuelled in part by economic recession and the increasing popularity of at-home exercise equipment). Reflecting the consumer market's emphasis on frontline service workers as a means to add value and competitive advantage (e.g. Pine and Gilmore, 1998), the health club industry identified service as key to competing for consumers' disposable income and time, recruiting and retaining members, and generating revenue through the sale of ancillary services. These are some of the conditions for the expansion of the occupation. Once aimed at a niche of elite clients, personal training became a service aimed at a mass, middle-class market.

The 'new' personal trainers were often drawn from the health clubs' existing ranks of exercise and aerobics instructors, a group that had expanded over the 1970s with the popularity of 'aerobic dancing', and were already organized as a quasi-profession. The leading occupational organization for aerobics instructors, IDEA (the International Dance-Exercise Association) began in 1982 as part of the growth of aerobics instruction. Through its conventions and publications, IDEA involved itself in such topics as exercise science research, questions of professional ethics, liability insurance and marketing strategies. In 1985, IDEA created a separate organization, the IDEA Foundation, to oversee questions of professional training and certification. In 1990, the IDEA Foundation (later renamed the American Council on Exercise – ACE) began offering an exam specifically for personal trainers.[2] The ACE exam was accompanied in 1991 by the publication of ACE's *Personal Trainer Manual* (Sudy, 1991), the official companion text to the exam – the preface of which contained the above quotation. IDEA also began publishing a six-page monthly newsletter, *IDEA Personal Trainer* (*IPT*), in 1990; it became a 40-page full-colour magazine in 1994, and in 2004 was re-launched as *IDEA Fitness Journal*. By 2000, ACE had certified 44,000 personal trainers.[3]

Various devices (organizational entities, certifying examinations, training manuals, occupational statistics, professional codes of ethics) have played a part in the construction of personal training as a distinct occupation, and the legitimation of claims to professional status and expert authority. The relative success of these strategies, on the part of organizational groups and individual trainers, is far from assured (e.g. certification is not legally mandatory); however, their accumulated impact is to make relatively secure the idea of fitness instructors as a cadre of experts.

An account of the development of personal training extends beyond the aerobics instructors of the 1970s. Earlier examples of figures who traded on physical capital and persona to claim exercise expertise and promote fitness and physical culture include: Jack LaLanne, with his television show first airing in the 1950s; and Charles Atlas, with his bodybuilding manual that achieved such success in the 1940s; and Eugen Sandow and Bernarr Macfadden, with their physical culture magazines in the late-19th and early 20th centuries. Earlier still were 19th-century physical culture movements (such as Muscular Christianity, Rational Recreation and the Playground Movement) and physical education reformers such as Martina Bergman-Österberg in the UK and Dudley Allen Sargent in the US (Green, 1986; Riess, 1989), establishing durable links between exercise and self- and social-improvement. Recognizing these predecessors necessarily entails an appreciation of the historical and cultural context for today's personal trainers. While it is beyond the scope of the chapter to offer a detailed history of fitness culture, we can briefly take note of two dimensions of the longer-term roots of personal training, with regard to health and appearance.

On the one hand, the development of personal training has been contingent on exercise being regarded as a problem. Advances in domestic, medical and agricultural technologies have greatly reduced the manual labour of everyday life, the risk of death by communicable disease, and the likelihood of malnutrition. As a result, we now live long enough – and under conducive conditions – to develop chronic, degenerative diseases such as heart disease and cancer. These changing patterns of illness, in conjunction with the lack of passive cures (e.g. inoculations) for chronic diseases, and a government- and research-led emphasis on active measures of disease prevention, have led to the endorsement and promotion of 'healthy lifestyles' that include regular physical activity. Thus, whereas physical exertion was once a taken-for-granted part of daily life, it has become a problem of purposefully including exercise within daily routines: a problem with scientific legitimacy and political-economic urgency. The credibility of personal training as an occupation with claims to professional expertise has thus benefited from this general consensus that 'exercise is good' for both the individual and society.

On the other hand, like health, appearance has also become a particular type of problem over the modern period, with the sort of physique (e.g. toned, slim) that results from physical exercise being regarded as a marker of social status and mechanism for social mobility, especially for the middle class (Bourdieu, 1984). The development of the fitness field must be understood relative to the expansion, class position and dispositions of its consumers (especially the upper, professional/managerial strata of the service class) and its producers (the personal service occupations, such as personal trainers and aerobics instructors). By 1930, almost half of the US labour force worked in service occupations, with that proportion rising to over 60 per cent in 1970 and 75 per cent by 2000 (e.g. Lash and Urry, 1987; Godbout, 1993; Bureau of Labor Statistics, 2001). The shift from producing things to producing impressions and interactions has necessarily involved changes in the organization of labour and the definition of productive skills and capacities. An attractive, 'fit' physique takes on additional value in such a context, as a desired result (for clients) and as a symbol of credibility (for the personal trainer, whose physical shape literally embodies his or her expertise).

These two concerns with health promotion and appearance improvement have been mutually reinforcing stimuli: improving both one's health and one's appearance have become obligations for 'promotional' subjects (Wernick, 1991) who are 'incited to live as if making a project of themselves' (Rose, 1996: 157). While creating a demand for therapeutic experts such as personal trainers (and other lifestyle experts – see Lewis in this volume), these concerns have also shaped the material practices of personal training in specific ways. The problem of health has informed the definition and legitimation of personal trainers' claims to expertise; the problem of appearance has shaped their performance of that expertise.

# MATERIAL PRACTICES

What do personal trainers do? Typically a first meeting with a client will involve a 'fitness assessment' to outline an exercise programme based on such factors as the client's health concerns, lifestyle issues and personal goals. Following the assessment and programme design stage, a personal trainer will then 'coach' the client through a workout, correcting technique, adjusting equipment and providing guidance on the pace and progression of the workout. In subsequent sessions, the trainer will update and adjust the exercise programme to match the client's physical progress and to counter boredom. The particular practices and forms of knowledge associated with personal training are drawn from exercise physiology, kinesiology, anatomy and biomechanics, some or all of which normally form the abstract knowledge tested through certification.

However, equally significant practices and skills for personal trainers are those associated with frontline service work (Leidner, 1999). For example, as one personal trainer described his work to me:

> You become their coach. You are their teacher. You become their coach, their shrink, and their slave driver [laughs]. You have to stay on top of them. If they come in, and they're whining that they're tired and don't want to work out, you have to know how to cope with that. You're dealing with people's personalities. They come in, they've had a bad day, their boss yelled at them, and they don't want to work out. You have to know what to do to make sure they have a good workout. I'm their mentor. I'm Yoda! [laughs] I tell them, 'You want to be a Jedi? You have to listen to Yoda.'

Trainers provide motivation, talking to clients about fitness and non-fitness issues, and offering positive feedback and encouragement. Repeated sessions often give rise to a quasi-personal relationship in which fitness instruction blurs with gossip, cheerleading and coaching as the trainer continues to motivate the client to pursue their fitness goals. Devices such as sending clients birthday cards, providing wake-up calls and reminder messages, accompanying clients to try out new equipment, and emailing exercise tips to clients away on holiday or business trips are all service strategies for motivating and retaining clients, and distinguishing the trainer in a crowded marketplace.

Research on fitness instructors has largely focused on the lived experiences of the trainers, and the immediate trainer–client interaction (George, 2008; Greenleaf et al., 2006; Haravon Collins, 2002; Markula and Pringle, 2006; Smith Maguire, 2001). However, the material practices of personal training are not only those involved in the service encounter. The study of cultural intermediaries is increasingly interested in the role of non-human actors and devices in enabling and constraining the work of cultural intermediaries, and rendering it relatively durable (Latour, 1991). Thus, an appreciation of the material practices of personal trainers also requires attention to devices for regulating and reproducing an occupational identity, specifying and codifying forms of expertise, promoting and making visible a (quasi) professional status, and legitimating and circulating benchmarks, tools and protocols for practice (cf. Moor, 2012). These devices will include professional development conferences, training manuals, occupational journals and certification courses: field-specific texts (Ferguson, 1998) that standardize and disseminate the forms of expertise, conventional devices and endorsed dispositions that characterize the work, and thus specify the resources or forms of capital by which the field is stratified.

In the case of personal training, such field-specific texts include the aforementioned *IDEA Personal Trainer* (*IPT*). An analysis of *IPT* issues from 1990 to 2000 (Smith Maguire, 2008a, 2008b) highlighted four recurrent themes in defining the occupation: the technical skills and specialized knowledge required for designing exercise programmes; interpersonal skills needed to deliver the service and motivate clients; skills and capital needed to establish the credibility of the trainer and the occupation; and entrepreneurial skills required to sell the service. The remainder of this section examines the latter two themes, with regard to how personal trainers and *IPT* authors articulate the problems of credibility and of selling, and the devices and dispositions that arise as resolutions to these problems. (The problem of motivation will be returned to below, with regard to assessing the impact of personal trainers.)

## The problem of credibility

Personal trainers are involved in the framing of fitness products, services, ideas and behaviours as legitimate and worthy points of attachment for their clients. However, personal trainers cannot take for granted that they wield such authority. As a service occupation, they have (at best) a quasi-professional status; they lack the established legitimacy of health professionals associated with exercise, such as physiotherapists, and their social status may be outranked (outside of the health club, at least) by their professional/managerial clients (Hutson, 2012). Therefore performing professional authority is a major aspect of personal trainer work (George, 2008).

Certification is one method of addressing the problem of credibility. In the US, even though there is no standardized qualification requirement in order to work as a personal trainer, certification is the norm, promoted by both occupational organizations and health clubs, many of which make certification a condition of employment.[4] Certifications are a device for demonstrating quality and supporting claims to professional status; they also create a logic of career advancement and a justification for fee structures (cf. Lloyd, 1996). Nevertheless, like health clubs that have become indistinguishable on the basis of equipment, certified personal trainers are largely interchangeable in terms of their technical knowledge. As such, the institutional capital afforded by certifications is a necessary but not sufficient basis for establishing credibility.

As *IPT* articles and interviews with personal trainers make clear, expertise also rests, crucially, on embodied resources, including the body itself. As the following trainer explains, being credible entails both maintaining and displaying his physical capital:

> Exposure on the floor as an exercise trainer is one of the best ways to get a client without making a heavy sell. And when you work out here during your time off, people are looking at you, seeing what kind of body you have. People look really different out of uniform, and so if you're working out in a tank top, and you're really working and getting sweaty, people see that you have a good body.

In the same way, another personal trainer remarked upon the importance of her fit physique: 'You should look at a trainer and say, "That's the body I want."' A further trainer was equally explicit about the exchange value of his body: 'A lot of it is a form of self-advertising. If people look at you and say, "Oh, well, he can do this, he obviously knows what he's doing."' Therefore personal trainers are encouraged to objectify expertise – and cultural ideals that fit-is-good – in their own bodies.

This emphasis on physique is not unlike the role of clothing choices for sales assistants' displays of 'fashion competency' (Pettinger, 2004: 179; see also Pettinger, this volume). It highlights the precarious balance that personal trainers – and cultural intermediaries more generally – must strike between two dimensions of their authority, grouped loosely as 'professional' and 'personal'. To make credible their claims to expertise in matters of value and taste specific to their cultural field, personal trainers draw on both abstract devices such as 'professional' qualifications and standardized fitness assessment measurements, and 'personal' devices such as working on one's fit physique during time off. Indeed, personal trainers are exemplary cultural intermediaries: they become devices themselves, their biographies, attitudes and embodied capital serving as occupational resources and guarantors of credibility.

## The problem of selling

Personal trainers are shaped by their location within a commercial field – as opposed to, say, an educational, military or medical field. As a result, the work necessarily involves a promotional dimension: personal trainers must recruit and retain clients in order to make a living; the majority of personal trainers are employed by health clubs, which thus involves them in the frontline promotional service work of representing and promoting their employer (cf. Witz et al., 2003); and many trainers are also involved, formally and informally, in the promotion of the goods and services of the fitness industry more generally. However, this obligation to sell poses a problem for personal trainers, placing the service-oriented ethos of the professional in direct conflict with the economic rationality of the entrepreneur, who must exercise (some) self-interest when recruiting clients, setting fee rates, selling membership and training packages, and so forth.

This tension around the issue of selling is explicitly acknowledged by *IPT*:

The word 'sales' has a bad reputation in the fitness industry. However, selling personal training is something that many of you are doing daily without even knowing it! Most of you truly love your work. You represent a healthy lifestyle, a fit mind and body, and a positive self-image. Selling often becomes second nature when you present the concept of personal training to someone else. Your own personal commitment generates enthusiasm and sparks an interest.[5]

Or as a club manager noted in dealing with his trainers' discomfort with the idea of selling memberships and training packages: 'Many of them are uncomfortable when you first suggest it, because they have this image of selling as selling used cars. You have to explain to them that they're selling health and fitness. You're selling something you believe in.'

As suggested in both examples above, personal trainers are encouraged to adopt a vocational disposition (Weber, 1946a) – an idealized notion of living 'for' rather than 'off' fitness. Regarding one's work as a calling that relies on personal belief results in the blurring of professional and personal life, as this *IPT* article suggested:

You communicate your energy and intentions through your demeanor, through your honest enthusiasm for helping others improve their lifestyles and reach their fitness goals, and through the activities you pursue to develop yourself personally and professionally. When people meet you, they should feel your competence, enthusiasm and values.[6]

Indeed, this endorsed attitude is to be considered a device in its own right – an occupational 'formula' (Negus, 2002) for both selling services and performing professional credibility. Circulated by occupational texts, it is internalized by personal trainers, many of whom understand themselves as 'fitness people': 'It's how you look, it's enthusiasm, how aware you are, and what you know. That all comes across. It has a lot to do with your spirit' (female personal trainer).

The vocational disposition ideally resolves the problem of selling by appealing to a personal belief in and the moral ideology of fitness lifestyles as socially 'good'.

While such a disposition does not feature in the objective basis of wages or certification, a personal trainer's authority status and occupational success ultimately rest with his or her ability to convey a sense that their work is a sincere extension of their personal taste and lifestyle. In this way, personal trainers exemplify Bourdieu's suggestion that cultural intermediaries are ideal needs merchants 'who always sell themselves as models and as guarantors of the value of their products, and who sell so well because they believe in what they sell' (1984: 365).

## ASSESSING IMPACT

Two scales of impact merit highlighting here. The first and more diffuse has to do with the governmental role of personal trainers in mobilizing others (Miller and Rose, 1997) by creating durable attachments between consumer fears and desires, and the fitness field's dominant values and practices – so ably embodied by personal trainers themselves. The problem of mobilizing (or in the parlance of fitness, 'motivating') consumers is a key issue for personal trainers. Communication, performance and self-presentation skills, and the ability to exert interpersonal influence (cf. Goffman, 1959; Hochschild, 1983) are central to accomplishing this indirect management of others (Burchell, 1996).

As discussed above with regard to the problems of credibility and of selling, personal trainers rely on the relative congruence between their physiques and dominant bodily ideals, and on a disposition that regards work as an extension of personal belief. As this personal trainer noted, her motivational position as a role model also required her to look – and live – the part:

> If I let myself go, everybody thinks they can let themselves go. So, it's an image. It's an image because if I don't show them that I can do this, then what makes them think they can do it? I practice what I preach … well, most of the time. It's a lot easier talking about it than doing it! [*laughs*]

Typical of the governmental therapeutic expert who influences and exhorts rather than directly intervenes, personal trainers lead by example – here, in the case of having and working on a fit physique.

Personal trainers may be implicated in the reproduction of dominant ideas about what a fit body should look like and the ends to which it is directed. However, as governmental subjects entrusted with their own self-management, personal trainers may also potentially challenge and disrupt established notions of legitimacy. For example, personal trainers and other exercise instructors may enact their expertise and leverage their position as role models to challenge the dominant consumer body culture and promote a more empowered, mindful approach to the body that eschews idealized images and focuses on non-instrumental enjoyment (e.g. see Greenleaf et al., 2006; Haravon Collins, 2002; Markula and Pringle, 2006).

The second scale of impact that merits mention is the impact of the work on the cultural intermediary him/herself. There has been some consideration of this aspect of cultural intermediary work, such as the constraints of maintaining a seemingly obligatory personal lifestyle (McFall, 2004), the ongoing changes to a cultural intermediary's own sense of taste and aesthetic legitimacy (Entwistle, 2006), and the high turnover of lower-status work that demands personal investment but offers little security and satisfaction (Pettinger, this volume). Along these lines, consider that a personal trainer's physical and emotional investment in their work is both an occupational necessity and hazard. This is made clear in *IPT* articles such as this:

> How can you serve your clients if you are not mentally, emotionally and physically prepared? People in our industry give and give and give and then give some more. We have to be positive and upbeat at all times. At the end of the day, we can be exhausted.[7]

In much the same way, this personal trainer reflected on her obligation to be upbeat at all times:

> You are always on the go and you've got to be exciting, you're got to be energized and you've got to show people that they can do it and you have to be working with them and, oh, by the end of six hours, 'Hello! I can't do that anymore!' You have to be supersonic all the time.

Belief, affect and personal disposition may be resources to be used for occupational ends, but they are also exhaustible resources.

The risk of emotional exhaustion for personal trainers is mediated by the conditions of their employment: the problem of burnout is associated especially with the regulation and bureaucratization of emotional management (Hochschild, 1983). On a positive note, the flexibility of the trainer–client service interaction means that formulaic scripts are impossible for management to impose (except perhaps in the first 'fitness assessment' meeting). Formulae – if they are imposed – are reserved for the exercise programmes, and the service of motivation is largely left to the trainer's discretion. Thus, at least in terms of interpersonal interaction in the role of motivator, personal trainers' emotional labour is conducive to job autonomy and satisfaction (Smith Maguire, 2001).

Nevertheless, the degree of autonomy varies widely within the occupation. While self-employed trainers have relatively high levels of control over their work, most personal trainers are employees of health clubs and fitness facilities. In such cases, a trainer's autonomy is constrained by the need to comply with the employer's dress code, fee scale and demand for income generation. Especially in lower-status, sales-driven health clubs, trainers are paid less, and tend to have less intellectual capital (with fewer, if any, certifications beyond the club's own 'training' programme) and less control over client appointments; their pay may be almost entirely based on client fees, thus intensifying the promotional drive; they may have requisite quotas of sales per month to retain employment; and they may have quotas imposed on their free time, as some clubs require personal trainers to work out at the club for a certain number of hours per week, in addition to their client hours.

Personal trainers are also differentially constrained by the emphasis on a fit physique and lifestyle that is associated with the occupation. As this trainer remarked, reflecting on why she left personal training:

> I knew I was getting to the end of working only as a personal trainer when I was no longer willing to maintain my own looks in order to maintain my business. I still train a few clients, because I can draw on my experience, my education. I have a lot to offer. But most trainers have to rely on their body, their appearance, to get clients.

The obligation of taking up a particular lifestyle organized around the maintenance of a fit physique places constraints on personal trainers, limiting who is likely to be credible and for how long.

Yet, the endorsed vocational disposition and obligatory lifestyle may also work in tandem to afford personal trainers distinctive points of attachment to their work, thereby enhancing their capacity to be credible, sincere mediators. While a personal trainer may experience the occupational necessity of working out during non-paid hours as a negative encroachment of work into leisure time, they may also experience it as an advantage of their chosen occupation, and an opportunity to extract added value from their leisure pursuits.

# FUTURE DIRECTIONS

Several themes to be addressed through further research on personal trainers – and cultural intermediaries more generally – are suggested by the chapter. First, comparing cultural intermediaries within the same field: What are the differences and points of interaction between personal trainers who operate at different positions within the fitness field? How are personal trainers stratified by such factors as job autonomy and occupational security, and by their stocks of cultural capital (embodied, objectified, institutionalized)? Is there a continuity between personal trainers with the greatest capacity for shaping their own tastes into new fitness practices, and those who are delivering someone else's fitness programme to customers? Or is there a point of rupture between low-impact cultural intermediaries and (merely) frontline service workers?

Second, examining occupational dispositions and formulae: How is the vocational disposition internalized by personal trainers, and does it relate to habitus and dispositions that preceded the occupation? In what way does habitus inform the 'self-selection' of individuals for work that requires such a mentality? Personal trainers' subjective, consuming passions play a role in softening the edges of and delivering instrumental agendas (of commercial health clubs looking to make a profit; of governments looking to health promotion to reduce the costs of a sedentary population): how do they understand and articulate the place of economic rationalities in 'personal' interactions and 'caring' services?

Third, focusing on devices: what devices are developed and conventionalized by individual trainers, and by those involved in the meta-construction of the occupation, to define, objectify and defend forms of specialist expertise? Devices may assist cultural intermediaries, but they may also push them (Muniesa et al., 2007: 2). To what extent do endorsed, conventionalized devices (from the knowledge validated through qualifications, to the emphasis on physique as a display of competence) come to exert their own impacts, enabling and constraining particular consequences of personal training for practitioners and consumers? What devices are associated with relatively successful or durable challenges to dominant body ideals and the legitimation of more 'mindful' approaches to fitness (Markula and Pringle, 2006)? And linking this to the impact of work on cultural intermediaries themselves: What are the devices for coping with the problem of emotional burnout? Do such devices include relatively standardized career trajectories and exit points? How do the forms of capital prized for the role of personal trainer (such as physique, impression management skills, an upbeat persona) get translated into currency for other, subsequent positions within the fitness field or other cultural fields?

# NOTES

1   Industry statistics taken from the International Health Racquet and Sportsclub Association (www.ihrsa.org) and the Bureau of Labor Statistics (2001) (www.bls. gov).
2   In roughly the same time period there emerged the National Register of Personal Fitness Trainers in the UK (1992) and the Canadian Personal Trainer Network (1993).
3   Information on ACE certifications from *IPT* ('Evaluating personal trainer certifications' 2000: 20). According to an ACE 'certification specialist' (via an email exchange, February, 2002), ACE was certifying over 5,000 trainers a year in 2002.
4   For example, a 1997 IDEA survey suggested that 94 per cent of personal trainers had been certified (*IPT*, 1997, 8 (May): 25–40).
5   *IPT*, 1993, 4 (June): 1.
6   *IPT*, 1994, 5 (November/December): 33.
7   *IPT*, 2001, 12 (February): 35.

# 15
# CLOTHING

## LYNNE PETTINGER

Clothing, the 'quintessential global industry' (Larner and Molloy, 2009: 41), is an interesting case through which to consider the interconnections between activities that are readily understandable as cultural intermediary work and activities which might be more contentious to read in this way. Cultural intermediation occurs throughout the cycle of production and consumption. The clothing industry makes use of branding, marketing, advertising, of product and store design, of business management, forecasting and strategic planning. It also requires large numbers of workers to produce and sell products. In this chapter, I will sketch an outline of the clothing industry, looking at what the obvious 'cultural intermediary' occupations contribute. It may be presumed that the shop floor plays little part in mediation within the branded garment retail (BGR) industry (Aspers, 2010), given how much of store identity is set elsewhere. However, I will argue that retail sales assistants in clothing stores have a specific cultural intermediary role. I suggest that the bodies of shop workers are part of the symbolic mediations through which brand values are produced and reiterated, and that in providing customer service (and on occasion refusing to do so), sales workers contribute to the distinctions that characterize consumer culture.

The conceptual confusions over the term 'cultural intermediary' have been discussed elsewhere in the reader (see Smith Maguire, Nixon, McFall). This chapter adheres neither to the Bourdieusian account, with its very specific presumptions about class, nor its common adaptation (e.g. Nixon, 2003) as a way of understanding a particular set of 'creative' occupations whereby agentic workers intervene in markets to set symbolic meanings and create tastes. I prefer to consider the mediation that happens in markets as more diffuse, 'mutually constitutive relationship[s] between production, mediation and consumption' (Molloy and Larner, 2010: 374). Cultural intermediation is not confined to one occupation or space, but is extensive and diverse, so that 'the boundary between culture making, cultural mediation and cultural consumption is blurred' (2010: 362; see also Cronin, 2004b). This framing makes possible an understanding of the complex and ongoing qualification of value in markets as generated by a range of actors and devices, not solely by powerful, knowing agents at set moments in a circuit of culture. This means that sales workers can be understood as contributing to the production of value in competitive clothing markets.

Clothing retail is a buyer-driven industry in an unpredictable market, fragmented into stores targeting specific customer groups. Store identities, or brands, may overlap (most obviously, there are several stores targeting young, fashion-conscious women). 'Retailers carve out niches, which they essentially hold from year to year (or from season to season). This is to say that identities of branded garment retailers are formed in continuous processes' (Aspers, 2010: 36), intended to generate a coherent narrative of the firm. The BGRs discussed in this chapter are national, sometimes international, chains with standardized stores and products, marketing to an identified target market. They sell relatively affordable clothing, in standardized stores to a defined target group that are promoted in national advertising campaigns and drawing on global buying chains. The organizations have a complex structure, with departments for different intermediary occupations (2010: 15). Many are 'factoryless firms', subcontracting the production of branded goods, or acting as an organized buying group. Garment production, often carried out in Asia, is thus kept at a distance – although suppliers must respond rapidly to the demands of lean retailers (Abernathy et al., 2004). BGRs focus on honing the branded presentation, in a dynamic between product, store, advertising, marketing and branding, and the consumer.

# HISTORICAL PERSPECTIVES

## The clothing industry

Clothing retail changed with the development of a consumer culture. Department and multiple retailing were the significant innovations, both for how they influenced shopping practices by consumers and for how they influenced production. Department stores were the new and significant form of retailing in the late 19th century, and multiples in the early and mid-20th century, although any periodization should be taken lightly. Department stores and multiples had similar business methods, such as standardized work practices, central buying, and cash sales. Some had control over production (Shaw, 1992: 137). Their growth was contingent upon a growing consumer base with disposable income (and the desire to spend it, turning luxuries into necessities), on wider economic and political developments (from regulations on imports to changes to the organization of firms) and on technological developments in production and retailing. Technologies specific to clothing retail, including sewing machines and pattern-cutting aids, made clothing production faster and cheaper, and transferred it outside the home (often into small-scale factories in the 'garment districts' of western cities; much of this production, still small-scale factory work, had moved to Asia by the 1980s). Clothes came to be made to standardized sizes (and changes to the 'normal' measurements of men and women prompt periodic reassessment of this: Laitala et al., 2011).

Part of the developing consumer culture was generated through the activities of a range of cultural intermediary occupations, including advertisers and other 'puff merchants', scientific marketers and other consumer expertise. Department stores, named designers and fashion magazines made visible a fashion and consumer culture (Rappaport, 2000). The department store educated and seduced middle-class shoppers, particularly women, into a consumer culture where personal adornment was key.

Multiples stores such as Marks & Spencer and Burtons (in the UK, with equivalents elsewhere) were able to produce cheap-enough ready-made clothing to suit the pockets of more and more of the working classes, because of the economies of scale in production and retailing methods. Montague Burton, 'the tailor of taste', made suits for the ordinary working man (Mort, 1996: 134–143). Such an apparent 'democratization' of clothing retail reflects a particular mass market: branded products were mass produced and sold in branded stores. British stores adopted the American emphasis on interior design and exterior positioning, including branded delivery vans and functional signs in store (Winship, 2000), whilst making reference to national identity in their brand stories, as in the case of the old Marks & Spencer's own brand slogan 'St Michael's goods are British made'. Recovering from the impact of wartime rationing on clothing consumption, stores such as Burtons expanded in the 1950s and 1960s. New competitors emerged, often aiming to reach increasingly niche markets.

From the 1970s onwards, clothing production and retailing fragmented into smaller niche markets with specific brands. Fordist production methods, where clothing was produced well in advance of the time when customers might purchase it, was vulnerable to overproduction of unpopular items and underproduction of popular ones. Smaller production runs were possible in the 'post-Fordist' era, increasingly made by firms subcontracted by BGRs (Piore and Sabel, 1984). This made responding to consumer demands easier and contributed to the fragmentation of retailing: young women could shop somewhere quite different from their mothers. Post-Fordist consumerism and commercial leisure demanded more work from the sophisticated marketer, and different kinds of sales workers.

The contemporary high street or shopping mall is largely made up of BGRs targeted at specific markets, a small number of larger chains which blur the boundaries between chain and department store, selling several brands under one roof, and a small number of independent stores. Some of the former will be global firms, often those with a strong lifestyle brand (e.g. Gap) or an innovative mode of organizing production (e.g. the fastest of the 'fast fashion' stores, Zara). Others are national brands.

# Working in clothing retail

An historical perspective on the many forms of mediation relevant to this story about the emergence of a consumer culture and retail industry can be found in other chapters in the reader. Here, I consider sales workers specifically because of how their work has been positioned in relation to the changing context of consumerism. Early department stores found their new sales force somewhat problematic, requiring careful training into deference and service work. Whilst 'silent salesmen' (branded packaging and store display) replaced some of the workforce in multiples, contemporary sales workers remain objects of close concern and management by their employers. Sales workers' consumption behaviour was significant to their employment, showing how work is caught up in the development of consumer culture.

Workers in clothing retail were the object of commentary and concern in part because of their position at the forefront of a consumer culture. As modern retailing first took shape, commentary concerned pay and conditions (e.g. Bondfield, 1899), the moral standing of (women) workers constantly exposed to the seductions of consumerism, and the challenges to middle-class shoppers of extracting sufficient deference from those serving them (Rappaport, 2000). These concerns reflect the different class, gender, status and employment conditions of clothing retail workers when compared to other intermediary occupations. Some concerns related to how sales work could and should contribute to a consumer culture: How is deference ensured? How are the emerging consumer desires of working-class women to be managed? For workers, sales work was often seen as preferable to factory work and certainly to domestic service, and required some potential recruits to disguise the poverty of their origins: 'Dirt – the mark of poverty and domestic labour – was incompatible with the aura of ladylike respectability which a salesgirl in a large departmental store should exude. These gradations of status were quickly learned', writes Alexander of the working-class London women she interviewed (1994: 209).

The first department stores expected assistants to stand behind the till and wait for customers to come to them, displaying goods at the customer's request. From the 1920s, retailers came to focus more intensely on understanding and persuading consumers, instead of thinking of themselves as an agent for manufacturers. 'This new active type of selling demand salespeople who were more carefully selected and trained' (Porter Benson, 1992: 171), with skills in handling people. Despite the stress on selling skills, sales work had then (and still has) low social status, but in the micro conflicts between workers and customers, workers and management, a more complex story about the power of the sales worker emerges. The complex hierarchies and negotiations made between workers and consumers reveal ambiguities in the social position of the shop worker. Whilst customers and sales workers judged each other by their own class values, sales workers acquired power by policing merchandise and ignoring troubling customers, to the frustration of management (Porter Benson, 1992). Clothing sales workers operated at a troubling meeting point between work and consumption, raising anxieties around status and distinction. For the clothing sales worker to play a part in convincing customers that something is worth having, he, or mostly she, had to learn how to speak to middle-class consumers. With the increase in targeted branding to specific consumer groups, the sales worker came to provide a stronger form of mediation, by signalling something about the BGR where she worked. I now turn to the contemporary practices of clothing retail, and the nature of this signalling.

# MATERIAL PRACTICES

There are a range of material practices within BGRs which produce a branded selling environment. The design and production of clothing to sell, and the signs, fixtures and fittings, carrier bags and other features of store design demand work by cultural intermediaries to produce the retail environment as a space that offers desirable goods to customers. In this section I examine the material practices that go into producing this space. I discuss the contributions of designers, buyers, marketers and branders to this. I pay particular attention to sales workers, and suggest that they play an often unacknowledged role in mediating the selling space by enacting the brand of the retailer. I consider how sales workers' dispositions as consumers may contribute to their hiring, and to the kinds of work they do: their interactions with customers and the appearance of their bodies.

## The cultural intermediation of clothing retail

The clothes sold in BGRs, whether 'fast fashion' or comfortable casuals, are designed by a mediated process that involves translating between the BGR's identity, current and future fashion, and the customer. Designers plan for future seasons and production must be organized to get goods to market at the right time. BGR designers work in teams, so that the vision of one designer does not trump a collectively generated understanding of what suits 'our customer': 'BGR designers have only a limited aesthetic freedom; their designs must be in line with the aesthetic identity of the BGR's previous seasons, as well as with consumer trends' (Aspers, 2010: 99). Further, design is connected in complex ways to other parts of the brand production network: from the marketers who 'understand' the customer to those developing the 'brand message', BGR clothing design is rather different from understanding of 'creative' design work that entrants to the fashion industry hold (McRobbie, 1998).

The organization of production in a BGR affects what intermediary workers do. Whilst many BGRs manage and commission design and production of 'own label' goods, some use buyers to negotiate with suppliers according to their understandings of the customer and the direction of fashion (Entwistle, 2009). Buyers make calculations about what will work (2009: 94). Stores which specialize in producing cheap versions of catwalk trends do not have buyers, but may have trend spotters and designers whose work is to interpret and translate. Here a strong intermediation between understandings of the market and design work is needed in order to produce clothing at the right time, and in quantities and styles that will capture customers. Relationships with suppliers can vary depending on whether production is 'in-house' or subcontracted, and extensive negotiation takes place between fabric producers, designers and garment manufacturers and so on (Aspers, 2010: 102–117). In negotiations between buyers and designers, where the former stress the commercial and the latter the aesthetic, the essential ordering principle is 'a shared vision of who their customer is and what this customer likes/ dislikes' (Schulz, 2008: 395).

A range of cultural intermediation is brought to bear on clothing retail in addition to design and production. These may be considered the more 'standard' forms of mediation. Longstanding cultural intermediary occupations such as journalism, advertising, marketing and branding are relevant here, as well as new ones, including trend analysis, social media marketing, personal shopping, web design of online shopping portals and such like. The networks of interconnections between these activities, some within the BGR and some outside it, are complex and require extensive negotiation. For example, on an advertising campaign shoot, the representation of the brand is negotiated between photographer and models, ad agency and designer (Sommerlund, 2008).

BGR shops are created as particular selling spaces. Lighting, fixtures, mirrors, walls and other material dimensions of the space are debated and decided on as part of the brand identity. Even 'the musical-technical devices by which shoppers may be emotionally conscripted by the retail environment' (De Nora and Belcher, 2000: 82) are part of the brand aesthetics. As Böhme suggests, 'Giving commodities a staging value makes up an essential part of their production' (2003: 72).

In BGRs, brands are understood not only in their own terms, but also in relation to competitors (Aspers, 2010: 76) and the market: 'the constitution and construction of a commodity are the result of who sells it and wears it (which is related to their status) as well as its relations to other commodities as perceived by actors in the market' (2010: 51). I have discussed a range of activities that contribute to making consumption happen. The account presented so far in this section suggests that 'how' clothing is sold, not 'who' sells it, is what matters. In the next section, I will consider in more detail the question of how exchange happens, to explore the impact of 'who sells' on the identity of the BGR and on the consumer.

As stated in the introduction, conceptualizations of the cultural intermediary cannot easily be used to understand low-status, low-autonomy and low-paid sales workers. In part this is because the class position of the conventionally defined cultural intermediary is decidedly *not* that of the shop-floor workers. It is also because such workers may be presumed to have little say in how selling or taste-making happens. They enact brand strategies, but do not define them. Reframing sales workers' bodily presence on the shop floor as part of the array of mediating devices directed at selling the brand (Pettinger, 2008) achieves a different perspective. The material practices and dispositions of workers contribute to the symbol-making and cultural mediation that happens on the shop floor, where customers encounter goods. Sales workers in BGRs do three forms of labour that contribute to cultural mediation work: they manage and manipulate the selling environment; they provide 'customer service'; and they embody some features of the brand through their body labour.

## Mediating exchange

There is extensive academic understanding of retail sales work as a form of service work which, whilst providing clear insights into the emotional demands of the work and its low pay and poor conditions, tends to neglect its engagement with markets (e.g. Grugulis and Bozkurt, 2011). Understanding clothing retail work demands attention be paid to the location of this work within a specific market order, not least by recognizing that workers are also consumers. As Harvey says, subjectivities and consciousness are 'forged in the fiery crucible of the labor process, the passionate pursuit of values and competitive advantage in the labor market, and in the perpetual desires and glittery frustrations of commodity culture' (2000: 13); work and consumption do not exist in separate spheres, and their interconnections are translated by retail organizations into 'branded workers'.

Small actions – such as the ongoing tidying work that needs doing every time a customer replaces a rejected garment where it suits them rather than in its correct place – are materializations of an array of practices and devices through which BGRs try to facilitate shopping. From the laminated training sheet telling new workers on how to tidy a rail, to the sales worker who sighs when confronted with the undoing of her work, to the assistant manager to says 'Well, it only takes one customer to mess up a rail', to the choice of hanger and fitting, there is a lot of disguised work in making shopping happen. In laying out products in the stores, cleaning and tidying the fittings and rails, unpacking deliveries and putting up window displays, the store is actively made by sales workers into its branded form. This work is low-status and the most mundane part of retail work, requiring little initiative, only response to a design brief and a managerial directive. But it is central to the materialization of the brand. Such routine, invisible work is part of how consumption is made possible, and how selling spaces (and hence the commodities within them) become desirable.

## Customer service

Customer service is a way of intervening in symbol-making and mediates culture/economy. There is longstanding managerial interest in promoting a customer service ethos within BGRs (Sturdy, 1998), often as a part of brand differentiation. The sales worker may promote extra sales, find alternatives, recommend and advise. In cross-selling and advising, tastes are discussed and assessed. Standing at the fitting room entrance, counting garments in and out to guard against theft, the sales worker may flatter the customer, or help by finding another size. Not every customer demands or is offered such interaction, and the attempts may not result in sales, but such encounters are part of ordinary service provision in clothing retail and deserve recognition for their contribution to the broad promotion of consumption. Advertising campaigns will not count as successful if customers cannot find the jumpers they saw modelled.

Retail sales work has been conceptualized, like other kinds of service, as requiring emotional labour. Hochschild's original formulation of this captivating concept defined it as work 'to induce or suppress feeling in order to sustain the outward countenance that produces the proper state of mind in others' (2003: 7). When sales workers maintain deference, excitement and enthusiasm or manage frustration, irritation and competing demands, they do emotional labour that forms part of the affective production of the branded selling space. Workers are usually trained to meet branded customer service norms, for example greeting customers as they walk through the store (Williams and Connell, 2010). Interactions between the sales workers, who are the public face of the brand, and customers with specific demands, mark the moments where selling happens. Korczynski (2005) frames this as the 'enchantment' of customer service – and in doing so fails to recognize how enchantment is built through more extensive mediation work than customer service alone. The emotional labour done on the shop floor is part of a wider generation of affect as it makes the brand, and its products, seem desirable. The production of affect is a significant part of cultural intermediary work. Sales workers, in managing their own feelings and in generating feeling states in customers, are part of the affective landscape of the BGR. Appropriate emotional responses to products are needed to present their desirability. Responses to customers are supposed to be appropriate (although they are often not). Demonstrations of deference to wealthy customers, argues Hanser (2008), produce class distinction. At a high-end private department store in China, 'class entitlements were enacted – by the wealthy – and class recognition extracted – from working salesclerks' (2008: 119). Deference was refused to customers who seemed unlikely to buy. Those deemed rude, or wrong for the brand, can be slyly punished by sales workers (Johnson and Sandberg, 2008).

## The branded look

Sales workers can be seen as providing mediation between production and consumption through the look and sound of their own bodies: their aesthetic labour. In earlier work (e.g. Pettinger 2004), I compared BGRs and suggested that brands were signalled through the bodies of sales assistants, whether 'modelling' the store's products or wearing a uniform. This thesis can be presented in the language of actor network theory as part of the 'qualification' of the brand, whereby working bodies are market devices (Pettinger, 2008). Through being certain kinds of consumers, and through reflecting something of their employer's target market, sales workers produce consumption. Some stores recruit their customers from the shop floor (Williams and Connell, 2010), and there is even legal precedent for making workers conform to branded service image (Avery and Crain, 2007, cited in Williams and Connell, 2010: 351).

Consumer research shows that customers notice these branded performances and are influenced by 'the fit between the sales associate's appearance and the store image' (Kim et al., 2009: 412) and to differences between stores (Birtwistle et al., 1999). As Williams and Connell found, 'What distinguishes upscale retail jobs is the weight that managers in these stores place on hiring people with the "right look" – to the exclusion of almost all other qualifications (although workers' scheduling availability is a close second)' (2010: 353). Most research into the idea of the 'branded' sales assistant has looked at high-end branded stores: 'style' outlets. Here, the fashion orientation and stylish performances of workers are a form of technical expertise, relying on a worker who is comfortable with and understands fashion. Such ability to present one's body in a suitable way – to manage emotion and aesthetics in order that the affective attributes in the store be demonstrated – are critical ways in which sales workers mediate sales. It relies on the body itself taking suitable form: usually as young, slender and attractive. To some extent, the cultural value of young, attractive, fashionably dressed women and men outweigh assessments of the low-status and low-paid occupational characteristics. Workers become the upfront embodiment of the BGR's identity.

## Dispositions

The material practices of producing stores, providing service and performing the brand demand workers with an appropriate orientation to consumption. Specialist retailers have long known this, hence musical instrument shops are staffed by musicians (Sargent, 2009) and 'retro' shops by 'creative' vintage clothing aficionados (Crewe et al., 2003). In clothing retail, an orientation towards consumer culture is presumed, and proximity to objects of desire through work may change worker's own tastes, as for the 'lifestyle management consultants' studied by Sherman (2011). In many instances, there is an implicit or explicit 'matching' between workers and target customers, mediated by management. Retail workers want to work in some kinds of outlet, and not others, because of their self-identity as consumers (or desire to be consumers) of such products. Williams and Connell contend that

> workers consent despite the deplorable conditions because these stores resonate with their *consumer* interests, not with their interests *as workers*. The typical high-end retail employee represents what we call a hybrid 'worker-consumer' who identifies with and finds pleasure being associated with particular brands. But this consent is typically short-lived, as their dismal working conditions almost inevitably produce disillusionment and result in extremely high turnover. (2010: 351)

A willingness and ability to carry out the body labour needed to suit grooming standards, and hence an acceptance of (always gendered) ideas about appropriate image, is a necessary disposition and again reflects an orientation towards consumer culture: time must be spent applying make-up before work. Even in discount BGRs, where there may be insufficient staff to provide personalized service, consumer orientation is visible in sales workers' appearance, and in their clothes outside and inside work. Their working/consuming dispositions are formed in social groups that may include colleagues, as sales workers often socialize together and use friendship networks to get jobs.

A growing number of studies have framed such behaviour not as mediation but as co-production, drawing on autonomous Marxist theories, in particular their stress on 'immaterial labour' (Lazzarato, 1997). Land and Taylor (2010), for example, demonstrate how the workers in a company making and selling clothes for surfers have their leisure activities co-opted into the company's brand story. In this account, consumerist dispositions and actions form and produce part of the surplus value, separate (and prior to) the wage relationship. Workers are always working to produce value, whether paid or not. The thesis expressed in this chapter would seem to suit this reading: workers are employed because they are consumers. Yet retail work also provides a good illustration of the problems of conceptualizing value like this, given the complex networks through which value and meaning are generated. The gain of the immaterial labour perspective is the recognition that production co-opts such a swathe of workers' subjectivities, capacities and life worlds (e.g. see the special edition of *Ephemera*: Dowling et al., 2007). Setting aside disagreements over the correctness of immaterialist interpretations of Marx's labour theory of value (Sayers, 2007), it seems to me that the specifics of the case of clothing retail suggest a significant problem with theories of immateriality, and that is the loss of understanding of the specificities of what labour does to mediate consumption at different moments. The risk of immaterial labour is that differences of institutional location, labour process (including the kinds of affective labour demanded) and such like are lost.

# IMPACT

The complex mediation in clothing retail has three particular impacts. First, clothing retail makes up a significant proportion of global trade and national GDP, with a general flow from Asia to Europe and North America. In 2003, China contributed 23 per cent of clothing exports; the US took 30.2 per cent of imports, the EU 25.6 per cent (Dicken, 2007: 251). Export-oriented economies such as China and Malaysia rely on sustained globalized consumption of products to maintain their 'economic miracle' (as well as on the continued existence of a female workforce willing to do this low-paid work). Clothing production and retail is an excellent example of the globalized economy, and from anti-sweatshop campaigns to 'reduce, re-use and recycle' ones, it is one where arguments about the ethics of consumerism and of capitalism are played out (Littler, 2009). The various cultural intermediary activities considered here contribute to the excesses of consumer capitalism (the advertising that encourages us to buy, the accessories that someone has placed next to the queue for the tills). However, some cultural intermediary work, and even new intermediary occupations, may respond to anti-consumerism campaigns. Examples such as 'green' branding consultants and, companies that promote the use of fairtrade cotton, and such like, demonstrate the ongoing cultural intermediation within consumer capitalism to incorporate resistance and opposition, and provide a consumerist 'solution' to the ethics of buying cheaply made products in large amounts.

Second, the argument that sales workers contribute to the production of symbolic value in a cultural economy has implications for understanding work. Sales work tends to be considered low skilled, despite the centrality of the 'soft skills' of emotional and aesthetic labour. Nickson et al. found that 80 per cent of employers surveyed about recruitment said personality was either 'essential' or 'very important', and 68 per cent said having the 'right' appearance was either 'essential' or 'very important' (2012: 9), calling attention to the implications of this demand for soft skills that are not easily incorporated into education and training courses for access to work. If access to sales work relies on embodying consumer culture, then the unemployed will struggle. So too might those with 'unacceptable' body shapes or who are seen as too old. Such workers are excluded from this part of the labour market because they do not consume correctly.

Third, as online retailing grows, some cultural intermediary work has changed, and web designers should be added to the set of occupations that contribute to mediating taste and selling clothes. The development of sales assistant avatars and virtual fitting rooms replicate consumers' offline experiences, to some degree. Given presumptions apparent in the political sphere that real world retail in redeveloped urban spaces is the solution to joblessness and economic decline, it is to be hoped that the development of online retailing has some limits. Online retail demands that selling is organized differently: jobs in distribution centres and delivery services increase, and the traditional cultural intermediary occupations need to adapt to new technologies.

# FUTURE DIRECTIONS FOR RESEARCH

It is common (still) for researchers into retail to comment on the lack of critical academic research into the sector. In this final section, I make three suggestions for what direction this research might take, considering the importance of thinking about and theorizing work in the context of consumer capitalism.

First, there is a need for cultural sociology to pay more attention to low-status work, such as the sales work discussed here. This involves thinking about what kinds of mediation happen when goods are rendered saleable. Such a perspective would enhance the sociology of work's interest in the labour process, and would provide a more nuanced understanding of how culture is made, not merely by privileged taste-makers but through the rather mundane material work of the runners on the television show and the interns at the fashion house. This might involve a more extensive assessment of the idea that target customer markets reflected who is recruited to face customers, and an exploration of its limits. In the case of sales, exploring mass market products and ordinary consumption rather than exciting 'lifestyle' brands would be interesting. In the case of clothing, studies that contrast different BGRs would be useful, in particular, that explored the different workings of the international brands and those which are local. A study of the impact of a global brand newly entering a particular market on local understandings of sales and service would be fascinating.

Second, the implications of the kinds of technologies that are used in the production, distribution and consumption of clothing needs further elaboration. The devices that mediate markets act to constrain subjectivity in complex, if hidden ways. Fuller and Goffey (2012) point to the need to understand 'grey' media such as online forms and data mining techniques to develop recommendation systems and so on, to see how culture is made through software and digital artefacts. Such hidden mediators are significant.

Third, theoretical development is important. This may include assessing arguments about 'immaterial labour', exploring the usefulness of actor network theory, arguing against the Bourdieusian conceptualization of the cultural intermediary, and thinking more carefully about the materiality of consumption.

# 16

# BOOK RETAIL

## DAVID WRIGHT

## IDENTIFYING MEDIATION IN 'THE WORLD OF BOOKS'

Placing a book in the hands of a reader depends upon the fluid interaction between different types of worker doing different types of work. Production involves authors, agents, publishers, commissioning editors, copy-editors, proof-readers, production specialists, typesetters, designers and marketing professionals, paper manufacturers and printers. The supply of books to shops or libraries subsequently requires the interaction of logistics firms, wholesalers, haulage companies, postal workers, sales representatives and the use of computing technology and the associated support professionals of that field. Not all of these kinds of work would fall under Bourdieu's original definition of cultural intermediary, emphasizing as it does 'presentation and representation' in the processes of the supply of 'symbolic goods and services' (Bourdieu, 1984: 359). As Negus (2002) has pointed out, though, the term does not encapsulate important agents in the broader *field* of cultural production – such as accountants and financiers – whose work, whilst not symbolic in any obvious way is nevertheless crucial to the process of mediation. This notion of *field*[1] is also important to understanding the specific dynamics of the focus of this chapter: work in book *retail* – one field within this broader system of interlocking and overlapping fields concerned with book production and circulation.

Studies of different mediating roles in publishing (Coser et al., 1982), academic publishing (Thompson, 2005), literary prizes (English, 2005) and marketing (Squires, 2007) pay detailed attention to the distinctiveness of these sub-fields but also reveal that agents in these settings articulate their day-to-day work in terms which are similar to each other. These terms include a belief that their working roles require distinctive relationships with books, a belief in the place that books have (or don't have, or *should* have) in the broader culture of which they are a part, and the tensions between 'culture' and 'commerce' that continue to serve as the over-arching narrative for the cultural industries as a whole. All these claims about the 'world of books' recur within the retail book trade, and this chapter will touch on what is at stake in them in articulating the forms of mediation in this specific sub-field. The focus will be on the British bookshop and its workers, following research conducted in chain retailers at the turn of the 21st century (Wright, 2004, 2005a, 2005b) but, as the chapter will outline, given the changes that have occurred in the book retail industry in the last quarter of a century there are also new forms of mediation in book retail which challenge the forms established within the bookshop. These new forms of mediation will be outlined briefly with a view to considering future directions for research on cultural intermediaries in this field.

The place of books within a field of cultural products also reminds us that book retail is a sub-field of *retail* – and needs to be considered in relation to other similar looking forms of retail. For all that books are imagined as 'different', they are bought, sold and circulated through techniques which have similarities to other commodities. Nevertheless, although we may talk about the 'worlds' of fashion, home decoration, and home entertainment, the 'world of books' evokes a particular imaginary of the trade therein – and obscures our understanding of it as a workplace. Orwell's image of the bookshop as 'so easily pictured, if you don't work in one, as a kind of paradise where charming old gentlemen browse eternally among calf-bound folios' (1968: 242) persists in the contemporary industry. This image is fed off in the contemporary retail trade, even amongst those chain retailers who combine the construction of an amenable atmosphere for the disinterested browser with marketing techniques geared towards the rational bargain hunter. It is to the organizational development of this distinctive place of the bookshop that we now turn.

## HISTORICIZING CULTURAL INTERMEDIARIES IN THE RETAIL BOOK TRADE

An historical account of the emergence of the current division of labour within the book trade needs to recognize that the trade and circulation of books is bound up with grand narratives about the development of modernity, at least in the west. The invention of the print-capitalist supreme, Johan Gutenberg, is credited, in the cultural imagination of Western Europe, with catalysing the spread of Enlightenment notions of free speech, rationality and democracy. A discrete role of 'bookselling' as a separate part of the process to printing and publishing is part of this genealogy of the trade. In post-Gutenberg Europe 'the bookseller' was as likely to be writer, printer, publisher and distributor rolled into one (Mumby, 1910) – a vertically integrated business model *avante la lettre*. The separation of the roles – from writer, via literary agent, editor, publisher, printer, book retailer – came later and was only really cemented in the 20th century.

It is perhaps these historical traces, though, which allowed Thomas Joy, former head of the British Bookseller's Association, to claim that 'the selling of books ranks with the highest intellectual pursuits and good salesmanship entails much more in book-selling than in many other forms of retailing' (1974: 61). Despite the many changes experienced in the book industry in recent decades, and continuing changes which might be interpreted as rationalizing out this claim to distinctiveness, it remains a key part of occupational identities. Even if we are sceptical of Joy's self-aggrandizing tone, there is an identifiable role for bookshops and bookselling in the slightly more mundane creation of the contemporary field of retail. Although the trade has been consistently constructed, often from within, as gentlemanly, old-fashioned, inefficient and in need of modernizing, there is an argument that bookshops have been a social, cultural and technological cutting-edge. Bowlby (2000: 193) argues that the bookshop was an early model for the kinds of retail space that came to typify the contemporary high street – especially the 'self-service' of displayed goods to a sovereign consumer. The bookshop was the first to make use of shelving that was not confined behind a counter and that was designed for display and for browsing without the immediate assistance of a shopkeeper. More recently book retail, through the development and growth of Amazon.com, was at the forefront of the technological revolution of online retail.

Whilst the evidence of the book trade as a source of innovation is compelling, the more familiar narrative is one of perennial decline. That story would include reference to a romanticized past when there were specialist, 'independent' bookshops which were profitable, although their profitability was not an aim and was largely ensured by the price maintenance policies which 'protected' books from the market. In the light of the collapse of price maintenance, these shops were driven out by large chain retailers who were able to discount best-selling books and provide a wider range of titles through centralized methods of ordering and aggressively re-negotiating terms of trade with publishers. Even these 'real-world' retail channels are subsequently threatened by online retailers whose potential access to all books in print, combined with aggressive discounting of best-sellers, have beaten chains at their own game.

There are elements of truth in this story, but also elements of myth. Specialist bookshops were few and far between in the UK in the immediate post-war period – certainly beyond the South-East, Edinburgh and the major cities of the North and the Midlands. In this period books tended to be sold through newsagents and stationers – including the large chain stationer WH Smith, for many years the dominant firm in the UK book market with a strong presence at UK railway stations. Accompanying these outlets were the small, specialist, locally run 'independent' bookshops, department stores or large, well-established specialist shops such as Hatchards in London. The subsequent ascendancy of the chains in the latter part of the 20th century was helped by the end of the Net Book Agreement (NBA) in 1995, which allowed for competition on price in book retail and made it more liable to benefit from economies of scale and subsequently more attractive to investment capital. In the UK, the NBA had been established at the turn of the 19th century with the specific aim to insulate books from competition as a means of preserving profitability and thus preserving the trade. The Society of Authors proclaimed in 1897 that 'books cannot claim to be published until the booksellers are interested in them; and no bookseller will be interested in a book unless he gains a fair profit from selling it' (quoted in Joy, 1974: 24). Alongside this economic concern was a cultural one, connected to the notion of preserving the cultural contribution of literature through the operation of the judgment of the specialist bookseller, 'the well educated men and women who, with their staff are trying to serve the community well and make bookshops a centre of literary and artistic interest and enlightenment' (Joy, 1952: 95). Critics of price maintenance argued that it supported inefficient and poorly organized publishers and booksellers to the detriment of the consumer and, moreover, preserved literary taste, as expressed through the commercial circulation of available titles, as a product of cultural elites. This was ultimately detrimental to both the business and cultural aims of the trade if it meant that consumers were intimidated by entering specialist bookshops. Terry Maher, former head of the Dillons book-chain and a key challenger to the NBA in the UK, explained how, under the price maintenance system, 'bookshops had a narrow appeal. Most people never entered a bookshop in their lives. There was a feeling within the trade that people who buy books know what they want and know where to find what they want. And the rest didn't matter' (Maher, 1994: 54). The abolition of price maintenance is not unique to the UK, having been preceded by similar changes in the US (Miller, 2001), but it does mark out the UK retail book trade from similarly sized national economies within Europe, notably France and Germany where price maintenance on books remains an important element of national cultural policies informed by a continued desire to 'protect' books from the market and the belief that this serves a broader cultural purpose (Canoy et al., 2006).

The economies of scale evident in the contemporary trade might, for some commentators and some consumers, be *overly* rationalized in a manner which obscures the distinctiveness of the trade from other forms of retail. It might not be rationalized and efficient enough for some. Such is the discursive terrain upon which this particular field of cultural production is perpetually played out. The following sections will outline how these changes, and these discursive struggles, feed through to the front line of book retail.

# MATERIAL PRACTICES: FOR LOVE AND MONEY

The development of retail in the UK since the 1980s has been characterized by shifting expectations of workers. Rational, centralized and electronically managed systems of stock control and distribution systems have limited the possibility of worker engagement, whilst, somewhat paradoxically, retailers have at the same time attempted to *re-enchant* the process of shopping as a symbolically important leisure activity – a process which in part demands the appearance that workers are engaged, committed and passionate. The creation of a 'culture' within large retail organizations that integrates workers' aspirations with broader company goals is a central management aim, as both customers and workers are assumed to benefit from the sharing of their passions (see du Gay, 1996; Korczynski, 2002). For book retailers, this culture of commitment was not imposed through managerial technique – it existed already through the historical narrative of the symbolic importance of books. The patina of work with things which both management and workers view as 'important' allows chain retailers to construct bookshop work as a potentially attractive short-term career for young, educated people, albeit one in which wages are low. Figures from the Booksellers Association suggest that entry level pay for a bookshop worker in 2008 was from £12–14,000 per annum – in a year when the median annual salary was £25,000. One consequence of this is the creation of a different kind of emphasis in management cultures. Unlike other retail sectors, training in the book retail industry need not convince workers that their work is meaningful. Instead, it needs to convince them that they are not, in the words of one manager I spoke to, 'customers who take money occasionally'.

Given these tensions, the idea of the retail book trade as a long-term sustainable career, or as a kind of apprenticeship for a career in publishing, rather than as an example of the kind of flexible, short-term insecure jobs typical in the service sector, is less tenable in the contemporary trade. Bookshop work becomes a stop-gap for literary-minded workers, students or 'pin-money booksellers' – workers who are financially secure either through a partner's income or through a career elsewhere – who are sustained in the job by virtue of their existing levels of capital. This is a significant shift in book retail which for many years clung to a belief in its professional status, partly informed by the perceived requirement to *know* about the books being sold – a status augmented by the presence of an industry-recognized diploma in bookselling run by the Bookseller's Association. The bookshop workers in my study had a clear perception that their work was more complex than that undertaken in other retail, which was perceived as 'just standing behind a till all day'. Knowledge of such things as the terms and conditions of dealing with publishers and 'margins' between cost and retail price were cited, even at entry-level bookshop work, as important elements of the day-to-day operation of the role. Alongside these business-oriented forms of knowledge was the sense of trust which emerged from relationships with like-minded customers. This was not an expertise based solely on knowledge of product lines, but on an enthusiasm for books that they were able to exercise in the day-to-day performance of their roles. A *genuine* appreciation of books – as opposed to one that might be informed by the commercial imperatives of their employers – was considered crucial. As one worker, an English graduate with four-and-a-half years' experience of work in the town-centre branch of a chain retailer, described it: 'You can have all the blurbs you want but you can't beat actually speaking to someone who has read it. I don't think you can really fake it.'

The perceived role of bookshop worker expertise is compromised by the changing structures and practices of the retail trade. In her account of the historical development of the US book trade, Miller describes this shift in the context of broader social and economic processes. The practical organization of the bookshop, its stock, its use of space and how it views its customers are all informed by more general conceptions of the relationships between cultural producers and consumers. 'A prior assumption that booksellers should steer the public towards "quality" reading material', she suggests, 'has been eclipsed by a vision of the consumer as having the right to freely choose cultural goods without interference from cultural elites' (Miller, 2006: 56). Thus the bookshop is implicated in the shifting sands of cultural authority and the democratizing power of the market as reflection of popular taste. 'Guidance', should it come from the bookshop worker, is not from a position of authority or expertise. It should not be concerned with edifying or enriching the lives of readers but should direct the customer to find what it is they want – assuming that, as rational, autonomous consumers, they know what that is. This conceptual shift is accompanied and enabled by organizational and technological developments. The increased size and power of the chain-store retailer generates centralized forms of stock management and distribution, which reduces the level of local autonomy over stock decisions. This affects the range and variety of titles stocked, as large publishers are in a better position to negotiate rates of margin and discount at a national level. It also has effects on the character of bookshop work itself, as any claims to embodied expertise on the part of the worker are compromised by the fact that decisions about ordering and reordering stock are taken at a distant head office or automated through electronic point of sale systems (EPOS).

This removal of autonomy can be interpreted as a fundamental challenge to the distinctive atmosphere of the bookshop. Centralized, automated forms of stock management, alongside aggressive price promotion of best-selling titles, remove the expertise of the bookshop worker from the process of mediation. This dialectic between the salesperson as facilitator of sales or as barrier to the efficient, rational management of the sales encounter has been a feature of the retail space down the ages – as noted in Susan Porter Benson's (1998) history of the department store. In the context of book retail, though, it has a particular resonance in teasing out the rational, economic pressures which shape the trade and yet which are hidden – by both workers and employers within narratives of its 'difference'. These automated methods have consequences for how those involved in the work of mediation can feel about their work.

All these changes to the practices of the face-to-face sales assistant and to the technical and organizational forms of mediation that underpin the diverse forms of contemporary book retail reflect both changes to the internal organization of the book trade and broader cultural changes. Internally specific technologies, techniques and devices involved in the process of placing a book in the hands of a reader emphasize the rational and the efficient. Externally the challenge to the authority of cultural elites upon which the position of the bookshop worker was allowed to rest has been undermined by a consumer-oriented republic of taste in which informed customers know what they want and just need help to find it. If the romantic imaginary of bookshop work has been reduced to 'just' a process of passing a bar-coded product through a till scanner linked to a database, the other mediating roles in the broader field of retail also exhibit an intensifying tension between the poles of culture and commerce that shape the field of cultural production (Bourdieu, 1996) under these new organizational conditions. The final two sections of the chapter will explore the impact of these changes and suggest new directions for research into mediation in this field.

## ASSESSING IMPACT

There are two levels of impact to emphasize in this section. In building on the place of the retail worker within the established systems of a rationalized retail space I briefly consider the ways the presence of the bookshop worker transform the shop. First, though, I want to consider the role of the shop in the transformation of the field of books. Bookshops and bookshop workers may be the end of the chain linking author to reader but in recent years they have become a key, determining link in it. Book retail chains, in their online or offline variants, are able to dictate the terms of trade with publishers in a way unique in the history of the book trade. The effect of this is to shift the power dynamics in the field of book retail away from the publisher as arbiter of cultural value. Depending upon your position this can be either towards the customer in a democratic republic of tastes or towards the powerful retailer homogenizing tastes for more profitable 'middlebrow' books at the expense

**Table 1**    UK book retail market share by company 2007

| Company | Market share 2007 |
| --- | --- |
| Waterstones | 20% |
| WH Smith | 13% |
| Borders * | 8% |
| Other stores | 4% |
| Other specialists | 6% |
| Tesco | 5% |
| Other supermarkets | 5% |
| Amazon | 16% |
| Other internet | 5% |
| Book clubs/mail order | 10% |
| Others | 8% |

*Ceased trading in 2009.

*Source:* 'UK Book Sales – Retail 1999–2009', The Booksellers Association, http://www.booksellers.org.uk/industryreports (accessed 16th August, 2011)

of complex or difficult 'literature'. The discursive complexities of these positions are beyond the scope of this chapter, but it would be difficult for even the sternest critic to substantively claim that the re-shaping of the book industry in the last twenty years has not *increased* accessibility to books. The nature and make-up of this access is more debatable. We can chart the effects of some of these changes through the early 21st century with data on the shape and size of book retail in the UK. Tables 16.1 and 16.2 contain some industry derived data on the spread of retail book trade across its various sectors from 2007–2011.

In the UK in 2007, Waterstones represented the largest single firm. The experience of this firm has become emblematic of the transformation of the book retail land-scape in the UK – both through its size and through the range and variety of books its particular business model is able to offer customers. For most of its history, it oper-ated an expansive strategy, resulting in takeovers of a series of competitors of varying sizes (Dillons, Ottakar's, Books etc) which have left it as the single dominant special-ist UK chain. In 2009, as part of parent company HMV Group Plc, it operated through 314 branches with an online presence (Datamonitor, 2010). In 2011, in the wake of the financial difficulties of the economic downturn, HMV sold Waterstones to the investment fund A&NN, but it retains around 300 branches across the UK. This picture of a single or few dominant chains is echoed in the US (Barnes & Noble, Books-A-Million), in Canada (the Coles and Chapter brands both operate under the auspices of Indigo Books & Music) and in Australia (Dymocks, Collins).

In the most recent data, the rise of the chains appears to have plateaued. Whilst the UK market share of the chain retailer rose by 18 per cent between 2001 and 2005 – reaching a peak of 43 per cent in 2004 – it has been in decline since 2008 and, by 2011, was no longer the single largest sector of the UK retail market. This trend is evident in similar markets (see Turner-Riggs, 2007; PwC, 2011) where the consolidation and competition from online retailers has led to the closure of sig-nificant brands (e.g. Borders in the US, UK and Australia) and an incorporation of

**Table 2** Percentage of market share (value) by type of outlet

| Type of outlet | 2008 % | 2009 % | 2010 % | 2011 % | Change 2008–1 |
|---|---|---|---|---|---|
| Large Chains | 40 | 40 | 36 | 33 | −7 |
| Independents | 10 | 11 | 5 | 5 | −5 |
| Bargain Bookshops | 3 | 4 | 4 | 4 | +1 |
| Supermarkets | 10 | 10 | 10 | 9 | +1 |
| Other Shop | 9 | 7 | 8 | 8 | −1 |
| Direct Mail | 12 | 11 | 6 | 6 | −6 |
| Internet | 17 | 17 | 31 | 35 | +18 |

*Source:* 'UK Book Sales – Retail 2008–2011', The Booksellers Association, http://www.booksellers.org.uk/industryreports (accessed 28th August, 2012)

elements of online 'clicks and mortar' retail by the established chains. Angus & Robertson, the single largest Australian chain, for example, became an exclusively online retailer in 2011. In the UK, the relative decline of the chains, as Table 16.2 illustrates, is contrasted with the substantive rise of Internet retailing. This growth is also at the expense of the direct mail book club and the independent bookshop. It is accompanied by the steady presence of the supermarket, whose share of the market doubled from 2004 to 2009 and has remained constant at around 10 per cent since. The browser of 'calf-bound' folios, then, is only one customer of the retail book trade. The online bargain hunter and the supermarket impulse buyer might require different forms of mediation, even than those recently established by the chain bookshop.

As Miller's (2006) history of the US retail trade reveals, fears about the effects of scale on retail enterprises recur in the realm of cultural consumerism (or, more pejoratively, *mass consumption*). These fears include the threat posed by the ability of powerful retailers to force down margins on the most profitable books as well as on more immediately accessible works, and to squeeze the profitability of books which are difficult or radical. The effect of this, in retail as much as in publishing in general, is to make the trade in books subject to the whims of *economic* capital as expressed through the quest for profitable titles, as opposed to mindful of the values of *cultural* capital connected to the contribution of specific sorts of books to the broader culture. Size and power in the context of commercial organization might be associated with homogeneity. At the same time, more efficient means of distribution have produced, for all the powerful narrative of decline, a wider range of available literature either on the high street or at least a few clicks of the mouse away.

The place of bookshop workers in this reshaped trade is interesting to reflect on. As suggested in the previous section, the logic of rationalization is de-skilling, much as the logic of concentration is decreased variety. Both processes are occurring unevenly as the bookshop worker retains a key role in shaping the discursive space of the bookshop. This is recognized and exploited by firms, and welcomed by workers as evidence that they are not *just* doing retail work but also connected to the more established meanings of book retail as being partly about expert guidance. A visit to my local branch of Waterstones reveals, scattered through the shelving on four floors of prime city-centre real estate, a series of hand-written recommendations, labelled with the names of workers, pointing browsers towards the preferred titles of the shop staff ('books we love', 'books we wish we had written') away from the stacked tables of bestsellers or new releases. Browsing the website of the same retailer reveals that bookseller recommendations (complete with name and branch of individual booksellers) are a feature of this service interaction too. There are subtle negotiations at play in these forms of recommendation. For workers they allow a sense of creative involvement in narratives which distinguish book retail from other types of selling. They allow a performance of knowledge and expertise from workers who tend to be educated and articulate, as well as enthusiastic about specific products – the residue, perhaps, of the historical journey from bookselling as intellectual pursuit as constructed by Thomas Joy, to service provider for the rational, knowledgeable book consumer. For particular kinds of customers, seeking in the bookshop a refuge from consumer society even as they participate in it, the hand-written review evokes an 'authentic' form of interaction, not driven by marketing priority but by a heartfelt desire to share a treasure. For firms, the embodied expertise of the sales person is part of the process of production of meaning around the product, and by extension, producing meaning around the space of the shop.

That these attempts to shape the bookshop space as meaningful occur at this period in the history of book retail is interesting. Collins (2010) and Thompson (2010) outline the paradox between the increased range of books available in contemporary retail environments and the narrow focus of publishers on pushing fewer and fewer best-sellers. The appearance of variety and the aesthetic pleasures of rows of books shape the chain bookshop as a consumption 'experience' but are in contrast with the economic imperatives piling tables with celebrity biographies, television tie-ins or big name best-selling blockbuster authors. Similarly, the patina of intellectual work crystallized in the action of hand-held recommendation or, moreover, the decorative performance of the bookshop worker as an expert, works for firms, customers and workers as a means of distancing themselves from the rational consumerist model of books as *merely* commodities to be bought and sold like any other. Such phenomena point out the extent to which the field of book retail has transformed the broader field of book production.

## IF YOU LIKED THAT, YOU'LL LOVE THIS: FUTURE DIRECTIONS

The above discussion has outlined how transformations in the book industry, principally concerned with processes of rationalization, have played out in the shape of the book retail trade and in the possibility of retail work as a form of mediation in this field. The final section will sketch how these transformations might continue – and how book retail as a mediating process might need to be re-thought.

First, digital technologies are being incorporated into the practices of book retail as both an opportunity and a threat. The rise of the e-reader opens up new and profitable avenues for publishers and retailers, which are beginning, after an uncertain start, to make considerable contributions (Gabatt, 2011). Not untypically within the history of the book trade, such changes are met with anxiety and appeals to the 'authentic' nature of the smell and feel of the 'real' book – as object experience. The evidence of the music and home entertainment industry in recent years suggests that digital forms of distribution and circulation have the potential to remove human intermediaries from the supply chain almost entirely, allowing in its most extreme manifestation the possibility of authors meeting readers with only the mediation of a self-publishing platform such as that provided through Amazon's Kindle device or equivalent. Given the commercial tie-ups between e-reader manufacturers like Kobo or Kindle and bookshops like Indigo (in Canada) and Waterstones (in the UK), it would be interesting to see if the hope, expressed by Waterstones' CEO James Daunt, that such tie-ups will mean that the best e-readers 'will be married to the singular pleasures of browsing a curated bookshop' (Waterstones, 2012) is realised, drawing as it does on a romantic connection to the aesthetics of the physical object as part of a reading 'experience'.

One snag in the digital transformation of book retail is the physical difficulty of converting publisher's sizeable and until now profitable back catalogues. This has implications for the speed at which a range and variety of books that is equivalent to, for example, iTunes for popular music is made available for electronic books. How such a future and present-oriented catalogue might relate to the formation of notions of literary value and the literary 'canon' itself would be interesting to examine. The forms of digital distribution and circulation at play in the music industry – and already emerging through the Amazon model of online retail – points to the second broad area of development. The process of recommendation in cultural consumption is less dependent in the online environment on the established channels of expertise in the definition of 'value' in cultural life. The continuing diminution of the role of the expert bookseller in a republic of taste is evident in the automated forms of recommendation that lead readers, algorithmically, to books they might buy based on books they have bought – or more tellingly on books bought by other people with shared tastes. Such new technologies of recommendation (see Wright, 2012) effectively make the consumer his/her own intermediary.

These developments feed through into the idea of mediation-at-a-distance, achieved not through any face-to-face interaction between individuals but between the platforms of recommendation provided by television book clubs or the circuit of promotion provided by literary prizes (English, 2005; Squires, 2007) and their audiences. The success of initiatives such as Oprah Winfrey's book club in the US and Richard and Judy's book club in the UK have as good a claim as any 'new' technology initiative in driving sales in retail and shaping the reading habits of a broad spectrum of society. The influence of these kinds of initiative in shaping the priorities of publishers to 'readable' books that attract what English refers to as 'journalistic' capital within a competitive environment for media products might mean that skills of promotion, marketing and branding become even more central to the forms of mediation in the book industry. Jim Collins' (2010) recent account of the transformation of the US book industry reveals the explicit attempts of contemporary book publishers and retailers to market books alongside other forms of 'lifestyle' products. Books and reading are imagined as different from other sorts of 'things' but they are bought, sold and circulate through techniques which have similarities to other fields of consumerism. The continuing effect of this on how those involved in these processes articulate their work would also be interesting to monitor.

Alongside mediation-at-a-distance, though, is the final key point about the place of work. This chapter began with a reminder that there are forms of mediation which are outside the definition of cultural intermediary framed by Bourdieu around presentation of the symbolic. All of the processes of rationalization outlined above can also be interpreted as a shrinking of the circle of cultural mediation in the retail book trade; that is, fewer people with accredited forms of expertise are required to mediate given that the channels of circulation are less reliant on the 'friction' of intervention. However, the same digital technologies that enable efficient and responsive stock management in online retail, as Striphas points out, 'empower management to monitor worker productivity to an astonishing degree. Amazon's implementation of these everyday – often unnoticed – commodity codes has resulted in a workplace increasingly suspicious of and hostile to living labour' (2009: 106). Autobiographical accounts of work within Amazon during its mercurial rise (e.g. Marcus, 2004; Daisey, 2002) reveal a sharp division of labour between what we might identify as 'tiers' of intermediaries. James Marcus, a 'literary editor' in an organization which, like bookshops and book chains, recruited people for their 'passion' for books, reports an early task of 'reviewing' 17 volumes of Patrick O'Brien novels in an afternoon. He also points out the division of labour within this new part of the retail trade identifying, for example, the crew of book cover scanners who 'worked in semi-darkness like trolls in a fairytale. It was strictly manual labour of a dull, quasi-Dickensian sort' (Marcus, 2004: 30). Mike Daisey's time in customer services at the Internet giant included a similar mechanical task – a weekly shift in an ongoing project to disconnect links to Amazon.com from pornography websites. Further empirical examination of these new *hidden* forms of mediation, still essential to the production of the meaning of service interactions in the retail book trade, might shed important light on the possible meanings of work in this field of cultural production.

# NOTE

1   See Thompson (2010) for a fuller discussion of the place of 'field' in understanding the contemporary book industry.

# 17

# FOOD AND DRINK

*Richard E. Ocejo*

## CULTURAL INTERMEDIARIES IN THE FOOD AND DRINKS INDUSTRIES

In his classic work, *Distinction* (1984), in which he first proposes the concept of cultural intermediaries, Pierre Bourdieu considers attitudes towards food and drink as well as eating and drinking behaviors as insightful indicators of class standing. Members of the working class, for instance, whose behaviors often include functional meals and lower expenditures on food and drink, indicate a 'taste of necessity', while members of the upper class, who spend more on food and drink and discuss their own tastes and preferences through symbolic language, are more likely to demonstrate a 'taste of luxury'. Bourdieu identified that food and drink are important markers of lifestyle and of class position, with strong relationships with economic and social capital. Since his initial analysis scholars have examined the important role food consumption plays in shaping social status and self-identity (see Johnston and Baumann, 2007, 2010).

It is unlikely that Bourdieu had workers in the food and drinks industries in mind when he discussed the emerging group of cultural intermediaries within the 'new petite bourgeoisie'. The manufacture and service of food and drink represent established economic sectors (agriculture, hospitality, industry) with traditional occupations (farmer, server, distiller). Food and drink are not among the typical 'cultural industries', such as music (Negus, 1995) and advertising (Nixon, 2003) that have dominated the cultural economy literature on intermediary roles and occupations (du Gay and Pryke, 2002b).

But today in western culture we can identify three key transformations that have introduced cultural intermediaries and intermediary work to these industries: the decline of traditional food and drink cultures, such as French cuisine and European wine, as dominant culinary authorities in society (Kamp, 2006; Kuh, 2001; Levenstein, 1989) and the subsequent emergence of 'cultural omnivorousness' in food and drink, or the consumption of previously 'lowbrow' tastes by high-status groups (Peterson and Kern, 1996; Peterson, 1997, 2005); the rise of artisanality, authenticity, and 'localness' in terms of production and provenance as indicators of value and taste amid popular critiques against corporatized agribusiness and conglomerations with controlling interests in the industry, as well as moral, political, economic, and ethical concerns over environmental and health impacts (Heying, 2011; Pollan, 2007); and the shift in occupational practices, roles, and self-identities of workers in certain segments of these industries (Ocejo, 2010, 2012b).

With the loosening of formal cultural rules, a 'democratization' of consumption practices that has reconfigured the relationship between lifestyle and status, and a new-found attention to production processes and the origins of goods, the food and drink industries have developed numerous cultural intermediary roles and occupations to construct and add value to products and services, communicate symbolic meanings behind products and services to consumers, and shape consumer tastes and preferences.

This chapter focuses on the cultural intermediary occupations that have emerged in the food and drink industries. 'Food and drink', of course, are very broad categories that occupy multiple economic sectors (e.g. agriculture, manufacturing, trade, and service) and are represented by numerous industries (e.g. poultry, wheat, coffee, beer, wine, and fruit) and even smaller sub-industries (e.g. organic produce, natural wines, and gluten-free foods). Each industry encompasses a wide range of occupations, from farmers, immigrant laborers, and chefs to CEOs, accountants, and exporters. Each also has a range of positions that engage in cultural intermediation. Jennifer Smith Maguire (2010), for instance, identifies multiple occupations within the wine industry that engage in forms of promotion, including winemakers, publicists, retailers, distributors, and writers. There is also differentiation within industries in terms of the type of intermediary work that is conducted. As Heather Jamerson (2009) indicates, the intermediary work of winery hosts (i.e. the strategies they use to convey the value and knowledge of their brand's product to consumers) varies depending on where it is located within the wine industry's 'artistic classification system', or its universally recognized hierarchical system that is constructed by symbolic boundaries and rituals, norms, and sanctions (DiMaggio, 1987).

Based on existing literature as well as my own research on and knowledge of work within several of these fields, in this chapter I focus specifically on occupations within food and alcohol companies, workers who engage in the actual production of goods and occupy a dual role as producer and intermediary, and people who work in the service industry. The following discussion of forms of mediation within food and drink industries thus introduces a spectrum of cultural intermediary work from corporate environments to retail service that have developed in western societies (Negus, 2002).

# HISTORICIZING FOOD AND DRINK'S CULTURAL INTERMEDIARIES

Determining when cultural intermediary work became a part of the food and drink industries presents a challenge. In her research, Liz McFall (2002) argues that advertising practitioners from the 19th and early 20th centuries – a period that predates the cultural intermediary concept and the coming of postindustrialism by many decades – engaged in forms of mediation that we typically associate with contemporary cultural intermediaries, such as using various forms of cultural and aesthetical knowledge in their work. Her research points to the importance of historical context in examining cultural intermediary practices. As with advertising and other industries, analyzing different historical contexts reveals different forms of mediation that may serve as precursors to their cultural intermediaries today. This reality is certainly the case for the food and drink industries. My aim here is not to argue whether cultural intermediaries are new to the food and drink industry, but to identify key historical periods that either gave rise to contemporary cultural intermediary work within these industries or served as its precursors.

Overall, work within the food and drink industry has not been historically seen as glamorous or an example of cultural work. Prior to the industrial revolution food and drink production and consumption was largely regional. Goods, recipes, traditions, and rituals varied according to geographic location and by such factors as ethnicity and religion within particular areas. Along with other aspects of everyday life, modernization and industrialization transformed the practices and meanings of food and drink production and consumption. In the 19th century technologies such as railroads and refrigeration contributed to the widespread distribution of erstwhile local products, affecting such matters as price and value. Farming innovations such as in machinery, animal breeding, and the genetic engineering and chemical treatment of crops resulted in higher yields as well as homogenized products. Meanwhile cultural processes stemming from technological and economic changes redefined notions of local food and drink. Priscilla Parkhurst Ferguson (1998, 2004) argues that French cuisine emerged as a cultural field (Bourdieu, 1993) as a result of texts – chiefly cookbooks and other forms of food writing – that created and widely disseminated a distinct culinary discourse that transcended many regional distinctions and established a hierarchy of taste. In this sense, nationalized media – another modernist development – contributed to the standardization.

Political revolutions in Europe that overthrew existing aristocratic regimes and gave rise to capitalist economic systems and class structures as well as a strong division of labor redefined the relationship between status and consumption and transformed the role of work. For instance, once private servants to wealthy families, chefs became tradesmen and bearers of cultural knowledge in public restaurants. As the multiple functions of inns and taverns – lodging, food, drink, community space – divided into separate institutions, bartenders also emerged as tradesmen who specialized in drink-making and in tending the bar.

Greater transformations in the 20th century further pushed the food and drink industries beyond their humble origins as regional phenomena. The rise of fast-food outlets, supermarket chains, and microwavable meals transformed food consumption while globalization processes provided consumers with a wide array of products and cuisines. High cuisine consisted largely of French restaurants (Kamp, 2006; Kuh, 2001). Gary Alan Fine (1996) notes that other than the few who worked at upscale establishments, chefs were mainly seen as manual laborers. National prohibition, meanwhile, radically changed American drinking culture and devastated the alcohol industry. After its repeal the Great Depression of the 1930s and the First World War slowed its recovery. Emerging from the war alcohol consumption and drink-making either became simplified, spurred by technological innovations such as soda guns, ice machines, and packaged juices and sodas, in public establishments, or retreated to the private confines of the home. Alcohol companies took many decades to recover, leaving the drinks industries susceptible to corporate consolidation, particularly in the beer industry (Carroll and Swaminathan, 2000), as well as the influence of imports such as vodka, which was first introduced to the US in significant numbers in the 1950s and became its most consumed spirit by the 1970s. By the 1980s the country was in a prime position to experience a significant transformation in terms of both food and drink production and consumption, and in the mediating roles that connect the two.

# MATERIAL PRACTICES: DUAL ROLES AND NEW SERVICE PROFESSIONS

Franck Cochoy (2003) argues that to understand how consumption gets promoted we need to focus on not only producers and consumers but also the 'relational work' that occurs between them. In other words, we must examine the articulation of 'devices and dispositions', or the practices and meanings that are made at the point of mediation (also see du Gay, 2004). By focusing on the material practices and subjective outlooks of workers in food and drink industries, we can understand the roles that cultural intermediaries play within them.

An important development that has occurred in the food and drink industries is the adoption of dual roles in production and promotion by practitioners. Social network scholars typically define brokerage and mediation as those actors who exist in the middle of a triad and connect otherwise disconnected groups (Gould and Fernandez, 1989). However, actors within industries regularly inhabit multiple brokerage roles and engage in multiple practices of mediation (Foster and Ocejo, forthcoming). Beginning in the late 20th century, an expanding group of food consumers – as well as food producers and purveyors – has developed an interest in the origins of products, such as their geographical provenance and production methods (Johnston and Baumann, 2010; Kamp, 2006). As a result of their influence, workers in the food and drink industries, such as farmers, restaurateurs, and distillers, have taken on additional roles of communicating cultural understandings of the goods they provide directly to consumers. Advanced communication and information technology have led to a level of disintermediation between cultural production and consumption and given consumers more direct access to producers and their products. Digitization, for instance, has allowed musical artists to circumvent traditional corporate record labels and supply their music to fans around the world. In such cases cultural producers and their consumers are often physically disconnected from each other, despite forming direct linkages of exchange. The adoption of mediating roles by material producers within food and drink industries, however, represents a break from this trend in the sense that it is a highly interpersonal form of cultural mediation.

Technological innovations as a result of industrialization, advancements in pharmaceuticals and chemical pesticides to grow animals and crops, 'factory'-style processing of meat products, and long, corporately controlled food supply chains all contributed to an agricultural and food revolution during the 20th century (Lang, 2003). Meanwhile food retailers have become more concentrated as fewer companies own larger outlets. Many consumers have gradually grown skeptical of the sources of their food in terms of health concerns, ethical issues, and long-term environmental sustainability (Gabriel and Lang, 1995; Gross, 2009; Lang, 1996). Among the many reactions to these developments have been urban green-markets, or direct retail outlets for local farmers, that began in the 1970s and 1980s and have spread in cities across the US (McPhee, 1994; Zukin, 2009). The greenmarket provides a place for regional farmers to sell their products, which can be rarer than those found in supermarkets and are often grown using organic and more traditional techniques, directly to consumers, most of whom live within their neighborhoods. At these forums farmers circumvent wholesalers and the global food supply chain as local actors restore the ties between producer and consumer that the agricultural revolution severed. Farmers serve as both producers as well as representatives of their farms and products. They promote their goods directly to consumers by highlighting their distinctiveness and uniqueness compared to supermarket-bought products. In doing so, they construct a narrative of localness and authenticity that contrasts with inauthentic global chains (de La Pradelle, 2004).

Another example is the industry of microdistilling. Like microbrewing and the natural wine movement, microdistilling represents a niche within its larger industry. Beginning approximately in the early 1980s on the west coast of the US, microdistilling emerged as an alternative to the production processes and business models of mainstream liquor companies that make and promote popular spirits and brands. It has since spread throughout the country and in Europe. Microdistillers rediscovered seldom-used distillation practices, such as copper pot stills, which produce far smaller quantities of batch distillates than the more industrial column stills that produce distillates continuously. Their small-scale and more modest production techniques give these small companies the opportunity to experiment with their recipes and ingredients. Microdistillers have also aligned themselves with the organic food and farming movement and entered into the production chains of their regional economies. Tuthilltown Spirits in Gardiner, New York, for instance, sources most of the grains for its whiskeys and the apples for its vodkas from farmers in neighboring towns. They cite supporting the local economy of the Hudson Valley region, just north of New York City, as a significant component of their business model, company identity, and brand strategy (cf. Beverland and Luxton, 2005; Beverland, 2005). Meanwhile, Harvest Spirits in Valatie, New York, operates on an orchard that has grown and sold apples for three generations. As a small family-owned and-operated business they face financial difficulties as a result of competing against larger companies. The federal Food and Drug Administration (FDA) also regulates the apples that apple farmers can bring to market. Apples that fall on the ground during storms before being picked, for example, cannot be sold, which can add up to a significant loss in revenue for small orchards. These realities forced them to find new sources of revenue. Derek, the owner, began distilling apples for vodka and applejack (i.e. apple brandy), which he sells exclusively in New York State. As he states,

> I wanted to have a value-added product. We have a bakery at the orchard, but only so many apples go into a pie. Then a friend of mine told me, 'Hey, you know you can make vodka from apples,' and a light went off. Not that I like vodka, but I saw the potential to have a value-added product.

Prior to national prohibition (1920–1933), it was very common for small farms to distill their agricultural products for sale on the market, since distilled crops are less expensive to transport. Today microdistillers like Harvest have revived the practice, albeit within a significantly different economic environment.

As with Tuthilltown and many other members of the microdistilling movement, Derek takes pride in the provenance of his product, particularly its local nature and the handcrafted quality of their distillation process. Along with material production and brand management, they also convey their cultural knowledge directly to consumers through several practices, most important of which are tours of their distilleries. Tours benefit microdistilleries economically by allowing them to sell their products directly to consumers, thus removing the retailer or distributor from the supply chain. But they also provide them with the opportunity to show the production process to consumers and explain what makes them distinct from other companies, products, and processes. Kings County Distillery in Brooklyn, for example, holds regular tours of its production facilities on weekends. After touring the distillation room, they bring tour groups to their rickhouse (i.e. a facility for storing barrels of aging spirits), which also serves as a tasting and storage room. Kings County primarily makes bourbon, and they offer each tour member tastes of three products: an unaged, clear, corn-based distillate (i.e. white whiskey, or moonshine); the same distillate after being aged for a little over a month in a new American oak barrel, which is required by law for distillates to be called bourbon; and finally a bourbon that has been aged between seven and nine months. The purpose is to allow consumers to experience their production process by actually imbibing products at different stages of completion. Along with the tour itself these moments give microdistillers the opportunity to further their brand strategy by linking taste to provenance.

There exist strong parallels between visiting sites of drink production (also see Jamerson, 2009) and visiting places of food production and key sites in a cuisine's origin (Boniface, 2003). Rebecca Sims (2009) argues that promoting unique, local foods has become a way in which rural regions boost economic growth. Tourism industries in areas with rich food traditions strive to market the 'authenticity' of their products. Producers aim to provide savvy visitors who travel to their regions with experiences that contribute to their own authentic sense of self. As tourist destinations and engines of economic development, food and drink sources have additional meanings as embodiments of local authenticity, which has transformed the roles of their producers. While food and beverage industries feature more traditional cultural intermediaries, such as publicists and writers, producers themselves have taken on distinct roles of constructing and articulating symbolic value for their products directly to local consumers and tourists alike.

Another important development in the food and drink industries is the transformation of service workers into cultural intermediaries. As mentioned, service occupations in food and drink industries generally do not require cultural knowledge over their products or specialized forms of service. Exceptions have been wine sommeliers, or professional wine experts, who have historically served as cultural intermediaries for the wine industry. Generally found in wealthier restaurants, sommeliers use their cultural knowledge as well as a performance through the ordering process to provide customers with the 'right' drink (Smith Maguire, 2010). They mediate between the wine industry as well as their restaurant employers and relatively uninformed consumers at the point of interpersonal interaction. Today these devices are being used by other service occupations in the food and drink industries, thereby transforming them into examples of creative work (Ocejo, 2010).

An example of this transformation is cocktail bartenders. Cocktail bartenders represent a group of service workers who professionally self-identify as bartenders. They undergo a degree of professionalization, or a process by which members acquire a set of shared values and norms to apply to a particular set of cases (Abbott, 1988). Their professionalization consists of specialized training in the field of 'mixology', or a set of practices behind cocktail-making that emphasizes specific techniques, recipes, and ingredients, through formal accreditation programs as well as mentorships. They use their knowledge and skills to engage in a form of interactive service work at the point of interaction with consumers, namely the bar. Cocktail bartenders mediate between cocktail culture and, less directly, the spirits industry, and the tastes of consumers.

Through interaction and dialogue they gather information on their customers' tastes and rely on their cultural knowledge to provide them with the 'right' drink and simultaneously educate them on mixology as well as their own preferences. Their particular devices and dispositions distinguish them from other types of bartenders who do not use cultural knowledge to construct and add value to the products they sell, despite relying on interpersonal interactions (Ocejo, 2012b).

By using their knowledge and expertise in cocktails and spirits, their occupational position in specialized cocktail bars, and their professional contacts and social networks, cocktail bartenders have also expanded into other sectors of the drinks industry. In addition to specialized interactive service work, cocktail bartenders have also been hired by liquor companies to serve as 'brand ambassadors'. Cocktail bartenders engage in several practices and occupy various roles within this position (Foster and Ocejo, forthcoming). They serve as gatekeepers by connecting liquor brands to new markets in cities, bars, restaurants, and hotels around the world. It is their job to seek out consumers and discover new ways to present and market their brand. As brand ambassadors cocktail bartenders also serve as co-producers by partnering with other professionals in food and beverage industries to create new uses for their products. For instance, they regularly work with and train other bartenders how to use their brand's products (e.g. what they mix well with for cocktails and how consumers like to drink them). In addition they work with chefs on pairing cocktails and spirits with food. Most importantly they serve as tastemakers by adding value to the brands they represent by translating them to consumers through interpersonal meaning-making activities. Cocktail bartenders do so by using narratives that emphasize the uniqueness of the product's history, ingredients, or production methods. For instance, the brand ambassador for Templeton Rye emphasizes the fact that it was Al Capone's favorite liquor, while the brand ambassador for LiV Vodka, a largely regional product, promotes the fact that it is made from potatoes grown locally on Long Island. As brand ambassadors cocktail bartenders occupy a more traditional mediating role within the drink industry. They achieve this position through their own professionalization and by working in their own cultural intermediary role in specialized cocktail bars.

Another example of this transformation from the food industry is retail workers at upscale butcher shops. In reaction to 'factory'-style farming that many producers, consumers, and media members see as the unethical treatment of animals (see Pollan, 2007), many cattle and poultry farmers have rejected such practices as penning and caging, grain-feeding, and hormonal treatments, and embraced such techniques for raising and caring for cows, pigs, and chickens as free-ranging and grass-feeding. While some sell their products directly to consumers, such as through greenmarkets, most farmers distribute them through high-end butcher shops that only sell local meats from animals that were raised ethically (these shops also often count restaurants among their customers). Adopting the philosophy that the whole animal must be used, they often quickly run out of certain cuts, which distinguishes them from large supermarkets that stock large amounts of the most popular meats.

But the shops also stock rare cuts of meat. It is the job of the retail worker at the butcher shop not just to communicate the philosophy behind the meats and the farming practices that distinguishes them from those at other shops and animals from other farms to customers while also adding value to them; they also must explain analogous cuts of meat to consumers in search of more common fare. While such salesmanship contributes to the viability of the business, it also communicates the shop's values and cultural underpinnings. In these instances of high touch, inter-active service, cocktail bartenders and butcher shop workers are examples of food and beverage industry professions that have joined subsets of other occupations in service and retail as cultural intermediaries within their industries, such as fashion retailers (at select businesses) and booksellers (Pettinger, 2004; Wright, 2005a).

## ASSESSING IMPACT: NICHES AND INEQUALITY

Keith Negus (2002) argues that while scholars have examined a wide variety of occu-pations that fall under the category of cultural intermediary work, many have not connected their work to Bourdieu's larger point about their relationship to the class structure. The extent to which cultural intermediary work reinforces existing social class relations is a significant question for scholars to ask. For instance, an important impact on societies of these transformations in food and drink industries has been the reproduction and in some cases the widening of the inequality gap between the rich and poor. Farmers' greenmarkets often exemplify the latter. Lisa Markowitz (2010) documents that while greenmarkets have proliferated across the US, low-income communities have been excluded from organization efforts (Guthman, 2008) while poor neighborhoods, which have greater concentrations of unhealthy food options and higher rates of obesity and food-related health problems (Kwate et al., 2009), have far fewer markets in comparison to wealthier and whiter locales. Along with being located far from low-income neighborhoods, greenmarkets also often do not accept welfare payments. In short, the people who need the most access to fresh produce and relationships with local farmers are least likely to have them.

Related to this point is the notion of inclusion and exclusion in an array of food practices (i.e. production, meaning-making, and consumption activities) found in the food and drink industries. Josee Johnston and Shyon Baumann (2010) argue that while food has seemingly entered an era of 'cultural omnivorousness' (Peterson, 2005) (or, as mentioned earlier, when divides over highbrow-lowbrow cultural tastes have eroded), in fact food continues to serve as a strong marker of distinction for cultural elites. Instead of taken-for-granted signifiers that characterized what constituted 'good' taste in food (i.e. the gourmet quality of French food; see Ferguson, 1998; Kamp, 2006), they argue that 'foodies' today emphasize authenticity (e.g. the simple, handmade nature of its production) and level of exoticism (e.g. its cultural distance) as markers of quality. While inclusiveness is implied by the presence of a wider array of erstwhile lowbrow foods (e.g. hamburgers and tacos) under the category of 'good', they in fact exclude those versions that do not adhere to newly defined distinctions of quality (i.e. the 'inauthentic' and the familiar). In doing so, contemporary food consumers and tastemakers demonstrate hegemony over taste. Access to and acceptance within these areas of the industries become more difficult as niches within them construct symbolic boundaries that require degrees of cultural and economic capital. Despite transformations in the nature of work within their industries, for the most part the niches of food and drink that have emerged continue to produce goods and services that are out of reach for broader populations.

# FUTURE DIRECTIONS

There are several under-examined paths that researchers on cultural intermediary work in the food and drink industry can take to further understand the field. First, since non-traditional cultural workers within the industry are engaging in cultural intermediary work, there should be more research on the notion of inhabiting dual roles within the industry, such as when material producers also engage in symbolic production as well as interpersonal mediation. A second focus should be the crossover within the food and drink industries, as well as between them and other industries. The wine industry has a strong historical connection with the food industry. Today beer and spirits producers as well as cocktail purveyors are increasingly forming relationships with restaurants and hotels. Meanwhile, for many restaurateurs art and music have become fundamental elements of the meal experience that work in conjunction with food and drink. Chefs and bartenders are also using scientific techniques and technology to create products. As these practices break down conventional barriers we must start to look beyond studying single industries to understand the full scope of cultural intermediation. Further research on these crossover relationships should also examine how they shape consumer tastes and lifestyles.

Another path for inquiry is the relationship between niche and mainstream within food and drink industries. As Bourdieu (1993) documents, the field of mass production has regularly borrowed and modified content from the field of restricted production to create and promote new products and services. The rise of new service roles within food and drink industries and the marketability of such attributes as 'organic', 'local', and 'artisanal' has led to certain tensions among practitioners as large corporations seek to promote their products through these discourses. In some cases cultural intermediaries get hired by these companies to provide them with the cultural knowledge for improving and marketing their products. How are these developments influencing consumption on a wider scale? The rise of cultural intermediary work in the food and drink industries is relatively recent and still developing. Research on these industries promises to continue to reveal how both they and cultural intermediary work in general are changing.

# REFERENCES

Abbott, A. (1988) *The System of Professions: An Essay on the Division of Expert Labor.* Chicago, IL: University of Chicago Press.

Abernathy, F. A., Dunlop, J. T., Hammond, J. H. and Weil, D. (2004) 'Globalization in the apparel and textile industries: What is new and what is not?', in M. Kenney and R. Florida (eds), *Locating Global Advantage: Industry Dynamics in the International Economy.* Palo Alto, CA: Stanford University Press. pp. 23–51.

Adorno, T. and Horkheimer, M. (1979) *Dialectic of Enlightenment.* Verso: London.

Ahlkvist, J. and Faulkner, R. (2002) '"Will this record work for us?": Managing music formats in commercial radio', *Qualitative Sociology*, 25(2): 189–215.

Akrich, M., Callon, M. and Latour, B. (2002) 'The key to success in innovation part I: The art of interessement', *International Journal of Innovation*, 6(2): 187–206.

Alexander, S. (1994) *Becoming a Woman: Essays in Nineteenth- and Twentieth-Century Feminist History.* London: Virago.

Allan, S. (2004) *News Culture.* Buckingham: Open University Press.

Alvesson, M. (1994) 'Talking in organisations: Managing identity and impressions in an advertising agency', *Organisation Studies*, 15(4): 535–563.

Amin, A. and Thrift, N. (eds.) (2004) *The Blackwell Cultural Economy Reader.* Oxford: Blackwell.

Amoaku, K. (2005) *The Industry.* Chatsworth, CA: Image Entertainment. ID0628LADVD.

Anderson, T. (2006) *Making Easy Listening: Material Culture and Postwar American Recording.* Minneapolis, MN: University of Minnesota Press.

Appadurai, A. (ed.) (1986) *The Social Life of Things: Commodities in Cultural Perspective.* Cambridge: Cambridge University Press.

Arnold, M. (1993 [1867–69]) *Culture and Anarchy and Other Writings.* Cambridge: Cambridge University Press.

Arnould, E. J. and Wallendorf, M. (1994) 'Market-oriented ethnography: Interpretation building and marketing strategy formulation', *Journal of Marketing Research,* 31(4): 484–504.

Aronczyk, M. (2013) *Branding the Nation: The Global Business of National Identity.* Oxford and New York: Oxford University Press.

Aronczyk, M. and Powers, D. (eds) (2010) *Blowing Up The Brand.* New York: Peter Lang.

Arts Council England (ACE) (2010) *Achieving Great Art for Everyone.* London: Arts Council England.

Arts Council of Great Britain (1984) *Glory of the Garden.* London: Arts Council of Great Britain.

Arvidsson, A. (2006) *Brands: Meaning and Value in Media Culture.* Routledge: London.

Aspers, P. (2010) *Orderly Fashion: A Sociology of Markets.* Princeton, NJ: Princeton University Press.

Atkinson, P., Coffey, A., Delamont, S., Lofland, J. and Lofland, L. (eds) (2001) *Handbook of Ethnography*. London: Sage.

Attali, J. (2008) 'This is not America's final crisis', *New Perspectives Quarterly*, 25(2): 31–33.

Australian Academy of the Humanities (2012) *Submission in Response to Research Workforce Strategy Consultation Paper: Meeting Australia's Research Workforce Needs*. Available at: www.innovation.gov.au/Research/Documents/Submission75.pdf (accessed 1 January 2012).

Avery, D. and Crain, M. (2007) 'Branded: Corporate image, sexual stereotyping, and the new face of capitalism', *Duke Journal of Gender, Law, & Policy*, 14(1): 13–123.

Ayers, M. (ed.) (2006) *Cybersounds: Essays on Virtual Music Culture*. New York: Peter Lang.

Bagdikian, B. H. (2000) *The Media Monopoly* (6th edn). Boston, MA: Beacon Press.

Baker, S. E. (2012) 'Retailing retro: Class, cultural capital and the material practices of the (re)valuation of style', *European Journal of Cultural Studies*, 15(5): 621–641.

Bakhshi, H., Schneider, P. and Walker, C. (2008) *Arts and Humanities Research and Innovation*. London: Arts & Humanities Research Council/National Endowment for Science, Technology and the Arts.

Bakker, G. (2006) 'The making of a music multinational: PolyGram's international businesses, 1945–1998', *Business History Review*, 80(1): 81–123.

Banks, M. (2007) *The Politics of Cultural Work*. Basingstoke: Palgrave Macmillan.

Banks, S. P. (2000) *Multicultural Public Relations: A Social-Interpretive Approach* (2nd edn). Ames, IA: Iowa State University Press.

Bar, F. with Simard, C. (2006) 'From hierarchies to network firms', in L. Lievrouw and S. Livingstone (eds), *The Handbook of New Media: Updated Student Edition*. Thousand Oaks, CA: Sage. pp. 350–363.

Bardhan, N. (2003) 'Rupturing public relations metanarratives: The example of India', *Journal of Public Relations Research*, 15(3): 225–248.

Bardhan, N. and Weaver, C. K. (eds) (2011) *Public Relations in Global Cultural Contexts: Multi-Paradigmatic Perspectives*. London: Routledge.

Barnhurst, K. G. and Nerone, J. (2001) *The Form of News: A History*. London: Guilford Press.

Batchelor, A. (1998) 'Brands as financial assets', in S. Hart and J. Murphy (eds), *Brands: The New Wealth Creators*. Basingstoke: Macmillan. pp. 95–103.

Bayley, A. (2010) *Recorded Music: Performance, Culture and Technology*. Cambridge: Cambridge University Press.

Beck, U. and Beck-Gernsheim, E. (2002) *Individualization*. London: Sage.

Becker, H. (1951) 'The professional dance musician and his audience', *American Journal of Sociology*, 57(2): 136–144.

Becker, H. S. (1982) *Art Worlds*. Berkeley, CA: University of California Press.

Beeton, I. (1861) *Beeton's Book of Household Management*. London: Beeton.

Belfiore, E. (2009) 'On bullshit in cultural policy practice and research: Notes from the British case', *International Journal of Cultural Policy*, 15(3): 343–359.

Belfiore, E. and Bennett, O. (2008) *The Social Impact of the Arts: An Intellectual History*. Basingstoke: Palgrave/Macmillan.

Bell, D. (1977) 'The future world disorder: The structural context of crises', *Foreign Policy*, 27: 109–135.

Bell, D. (2007) 'Fade to grey: Some reflections on policy and mundanity', *Environment and Planning A*, 39(3): 541–554.

Bell, D. and Hollows, J. (2005) *Ordinary Lifestyles: Popular Media, Consumption and Taste*. Maidenhead: Open University Press.

Bell, D. and Hollows, J. (2006) *Historicizing Lifestyle: Mediating Taste, Consumption and Identity from the 1900s to 1970s*. Aldershot: Ashgate.

Bell, D. and Hollows, J. (2011) 'From *River Cottage* to *Chicken Run*: Hugh Fearnley-Whittingstall and the class politics of ethical consumption', *Celebrity Studies*, 2(2): 178–191.

Bell, D. and Valentine, G. (1997) *Consuming Geographies*. London: Routledge.

Bennett, T. (2000) 'Acting on the social', *American Behavioural Scientist*, 43(9): 1412–1428.

Bennett, T., Savage, M., Silva, E., Warde, A., Gayo-Cal, M. and Wright, D. (2009) *Culture, Class, Distinction*. London: Routledge.

Bensen, R. and Neveu, E. (2004) *Bourdieu and the Journalistic Field*. Cambridge: Policy Press.

Bentele, G. and Wehmeier, S. (2003) 'From literary bureaus to a modern profession: The development and current structure of public relations in Germany', in K. Sriramesh and D. Vereiè (eds), *The Global Public Relations Handbook: Theory, Research and Practice*. Mahwah, NJ: Lawrence Erlbaum. pp. 199–221.

Beverland, M. B. (2005) 'Crafting brand authenticity: The case of luxury wines', *Journal of Management Studies*, 42(5): 1003–1029.

Beverland, M. and Luxton, S. (2005) 'Managing integrated marketing communication (IMC) through strategic decoupling', *Journal of Advertising*, 34(4): 103–116.

Bielby, D. and Harrington, L. (2008) *Global TV: Exporting Television and Culture in the World Market*. New York: New York University Press.

Bielby, W. and Bielby, D. (1994) '"All hits are flukes": Institutionalized decision-making and the rhetoric of network prime time program development', *American Journal of Sociology*, 99: 1287–1313.

Bignell, J. (2005) *Big Brother: Reality TV in the Twenty-First Century*. Basingstoke: Palgrave Macmillan.

Bilton, C. (2010) 'Introduction', *International Journal of Cultural Policy*, 16(3): 231–233.

Binkley, S. (2003) 'The seers of Menlo Park: The discourse of heroic consumption in the Whole Earth Catalog', *Journal of Consumer Culture*, 3(3): 283–313.

Binkley, S. (2007) *Getting Loose: Lifestyle Consumption in the 1970s*. Durham, NC: Duke University Press.

Birtwistle, G., Clarke, I. and Freathy, P. (1999) 'Store image in the UK fashion sector: Consumer versus retailer perceptions', *International Review of Retail, Distribution and Consumer Research*, 9(1): 1–16.

Bishop, J. (2005) 'Building international empires of sound: Concentrations of power and property on the "global" music market', *Popular Music and Society*, 28(4): 443–471.

Blackburn, R. (2011) 'Crisis 2.0', *New Left Review*, 72: 33–62.

Blaszczyk, R. L. (2000) *Imagining Consumers: Design and Innovation from Wedgewood to Corning*. Baltimore, MD: Johns Hopkins University Press.

Bogart, M. H. (1995) *Artists, Advertising and the Borders of Art*. Chicago, IL: University of Chicago Press.

Böhme, G. (2003) 'Contribution to the critique of the aesthetic economy', *Thesis Eleven*, 7(3): 71–82.

Boltanski, L. and Thévenot, L. (2006) *On Justification: Economies of Worth*. Princeton, NJ: Princeton University Press.

Bondfield, M. G. (1899) 'Conditions under which shop assistants work'. *Economic Journal*, 9: 272–286.

Boniface, P. (2003) *Tasting Tourism: Travelling for Food and Drink*. Burlington, VT: Ashgate.

Bonner, F. (2011) 'Lifestyle television: Gardening and the good life', in T. Lewis and E. Potter (eds), *Ethical Consumption: A Critical Introduction*. Abingdon: Routledge. pp. 231–243.

Bookseller's Association (2011) 'UK Book Sales – Retail 1999–2009'. Available at www.booksellers.org.uk (accessed August 2011).

Bookseller's Association (2012) 'UK Book Sales – Retail 2008–2011'. Available at www.booksellers.org.uk (accessed September 2012).

Boorsma, M. (2006) 'A strategic logic for arts marketing', *International Journal of Cultural Policy*, 12(1): 73–92.

Born, G. (2005) 'On musical mediation: Ontology, technology and creativity', *Twentieth-Century Music*, 2(1): 7–36.

Born, G. (2010) 'The social and the aesthetic: For a post-Bourdieuian theory of cultural production', *Cultural Sociology*, 4(2): 171–208.

Borregaard, K. (2010) 'Size and fit in industrially produced clothes', *Encyclopedia of World Dress and Fashion: West Europe*. Oxford: Berg. pp. 123–129.

Bourdieu, P. (1984) *Distinction: A Social Critique of the Judgment of Taste*, R. Nice (trans.). Cambridge, MA: Harvard University Press.

Bourdieu, P. (1990a) *Photography: A Middle-Brow Art*. Cambridge: Polity Press.

Bourdieu, P. (1990b) *The Logic of Practice*. Cambridge: Polity Press.

Bourdieu, P. (1993) *The Field of Cultural Production: Essays on Art and Literature*. Cambridge: Polity Press.

Bourdieu, P. (1996) *The Rules of Art*. Cambridge: Polity Press.

Bourdieu, P. (1998) *On Television and Journalism*. London: Pluto Press.

Bourdieu, P. (2000) *Pascalian Meditations*. Stanford, CA : Stanford University Press/Polity Press.

Bourdieu, P. and Darbel, A. (1991) *The Love of Art: European Art Museums and Their Public*. C. Beattie and N. Merriman (trans.). Cambridge: Polity Press.

Bourdieu, P. and Passeron, J.C. (1977) *Reproduction in Education, Society and Culture*. London: Sage.

Bovone, L. (2005) 'Fashionable quarters in the post-industrial city: The Ticinese of Milan', *City and Community*, 4(4): 359–380.

Bowlby, R. (2000) 'Carried Away: The Invention of Modern Shopping. London: Faber.

Breed, W. (1955) 'Social control in the newsroom: A functional analysis', Social Forces, 33: 326–355.

Brennan, M. (2008) Writing to Reach You: An Exploration of Music Journalism in the UK and Australia. Saarbrücken: VDM.

Brint, S. G., Turk-Bicakci, L., Proctor, K. and Murphy, S. P. (2009) 'Expanding the social frame of knowledge: Interdisciplinary, degree-granting fields in American colleges and universities, 1975–2000', Review of Higher Education, 32(2): 155–183.

British Academy (2004) 'That Full Complement of Riches': The Contributions of the Arts, Humanities and Social Sciences to the Nation's Wealth. London: British Academy. Available at: www.britac.ac.uk/policy/full-complement-riches.cfm (accessed 17 December 2013).

British Design Innovation (2003) BDI Design Industry Valuation Survey 2002–03. Brighton: British Design Innovation. Available at: www.britishdesigninnovation.org (accessed 5 April 2006).

British Design Innovation (2004) BDI Design Industry Valuation Survey 2003–04. Brighton: British Design Innovation. Available at: www.britishdesigninnovation.org (accessed 20 July 2007).

Brunsdon, C. (2003) 'Lifestyling Britain: The 8–9 slot on British television', International Journal of Cultural Studies, 6(1): 5–23.

Brzezinski, Z. (1969) Between Two Ages: America's Role in the Technotronic Era. New York: Viking.

Burchell, G. (1996) 'Liberal government and techniques of the self', in A. Barry, T. Osborne and N. Rose (eds), Foucault and Political Reason: Liberalism, Neo-liberalism and Rationalities of Government. Chicago, IL: University of Chicago Press. pp. 19–36.

Bureau of Labor Statistics (2001) Comparative Labor Force Statistics, Ten Countries, 1959–2000. Washington, DC: US Department of Labor.

Bureau of Labor Statistics (2012) Public Relations Managers and Specialists. Washington, DC: Bureau of Labor Statistics. Available at: www.bls.gov/ooh/Management/Public-relations-managers-and-specialists.htm (accessed 5 August 2012).

Burkart, P. and McCourt, T. (2006) Digital Music Wars: Ownership and Control of the Celestial Jukebox. Lanham, MD: Rowman & Littlefield.

Burkitt, I. (2002) 'Technologies of the self: Habitus and capacities', Journal for the Theory of Social Behaviour, 32(2): 219–237.

Bussey, C. (2011a) 'UK PR industry worth £7.5 billion data from PR census 2011 reveals', PR Week, 14 July. London: Haymarket. Available at: http://www.prweek.com/uk/news/1080127 (accessed 12 January 2014).

Bussey, C. (2011b) 'PR Census: How much are you being paid?', PR Week, 31 August. London: Haymarket. Available at: http://www.prweek.com/article/1088355/pr-census-paid, accessed 12 January 2014.

Callon, M. (1998) The Laws of the Markets. Oxford: Blackwell.

Callon, M. (2005) 'Let's put an end on uncertainties', Sociologie du Travail, 47: 94–100.

Callon, M. and Muniesa, F. (2005) 'Peripheral vision: Economic markets as calculative collective devices', Organization Studies, 26(8): 1229–1250.

Callon, M., Méadel, C. and Rabeharisoa, V. (2002) 'The economy of qualities', *Economy and Society*, 31(2): 194–217.

Callon, M., Millo, Y. and Muniesa, F. (eds) (2007) *Market Devices*. Oxford: Blackwell. pp. 99–105.

Calýskan, K. and Callon, M. (2009) 'Economization, part 1: Shifting attention from the economy towards processes of economization', *Economy and Society*, 38(3): 369–398.

Calýskan, K. and Callon, M. (2010) 'Economization, part 2: A research programme for the study of markets', *Economy and Society*, 39(1): 1–32.

Canoy, M., van Ours, J.C. and van der Ploeg, F. (2006) 'The economics of books', in V.A. Ginsburgh and D. Throsby (eds) *Handbook of the Economics of Art and Culture*. Vol. 1. Amsterdam: Elsevier. pp. 721–761.

Carah, N. (2010) *Pop Brands: Branding, Popular Music and Young People*. New York: Peter Lang.

Carroll, G. and Swaminathan, A. (2000) 'Why the microbrewery movement? Organizational dynamics of resource partitioning in the US brewing industry', *American Journal of Sociology*, 106(3): 715–762.

Chanan, M. (1995) *Repeated Takes: A Short History of Recording and its Effects on Music*. London: Verso.

CHASS (2006) *CHASS Submission: Productivity Commission Study on Science and Innovation*. Melbourne: CHASS. Available at: www.chass.org.au/submissions/pdf/SUB20060807TG.pdf (accessed 17 December 2013).

Childress, C. (2012) 'Decision making, market logic, and the rating mindset: Negotiating BookScan in the field of US trade publishing', *European Journal of Cultural Studies*, 15(5): 604–620.

Chmielewski, D. C. (2012) 'Poptent's amateurs sell cheap commercials to big brands', *Los Angeles Times*, 8 May. Available at: http://articles.latimes.com/2012/may/08/business/la-fi-ct-poptent-20120508 (accessed 17 December 2013).

Chua, B. H. (2000) *Consumption in Asia: Lifestyles and Identities*. New York: Routledge.

Clarkin, E. (2005) 'Who makes the laws that the advertising style-police enforce? An insider's ethnographic account of the social process of advertising development and its effects on the texts it produces'. Unpublished MA thesis, Open University.

Cochoy, F. (2003) 'On the captation of publics: Understanding the market thanks to Little Red Riding Hood: Workshop on Market(-ing) Practice in Shaping Markets', Stockholm, 14–16 June.

Cochoy, F. (2007) 'A sociology of market things: On tending the garden of choices in mass retailing', in M. Callon, Y. Milo and F. Muniesa (eds), *Market Devices*. Oxford: Blackwell.

Cohen, C. (2012) 'Cultural work as a site of struggle: Freelancers and exploitation', *tripleC*, 10(2): 141–155.

Cole, H. (1884) *Fifty Years of Public Work of Sir Henry Cole, KCB, Accounted for in his Deeds, Speeches and Writings*. London: George Bell.

Coleman, M. (2005) *Playback: From the Victrola to MP3: 100 Years of Music, Machines, and Money*. Cambridge, MA: Da Capo Press.

Collins, J. (2010) *Bring on the Books for Everybody: How Literary Culture Became Popular Culture*. Durham and London: Duke University Press.

Conboy, M. (2002) *The Press and Popular Culture*. London: Sage.

Conboy, M. (2004) *Journalism: A Critical History*. London: Sage.

Conway, T. and Whitelock, J. (2005) 'Relationship marketing in the subsidized arts: The key to a strategic market focus?', *European Journal of Marketing*, 41(1–2): 192–222.

Coolidge-Consumerism (2007) Notes on 'Frederick, Christine, Consumer Celebrity', The Coolidge-Consumerism collection, US Library of Congress. Available at http://lcweb2.loc.gov:8081/ammem/amrlhtml/coolhome.html (accessed 2 January 2014).

Cooper, J. and Harrison, D. (2001) 'The social organization of audio piracy on the internet', *Media, Culture and Society*, 23(1): 71–89.

Coser, L., Kadushun, C. and Powell, W. W. (1982) *Books: The Culture and Commerce of Publishing*. New York: Basic Books.

Cottle, S. (1993) 'Taking the popular seriously: Towards a typology for the analysis of the tabloid press', *Social Science Teacher*, 22(3): 20–23.

Cottle, S. (2007) 'Ethnography and journalism: New(s) departures in the field', *Sociology Compass*, 1(1): 1–16.

Cowen, T. (2010) *Good and Plenty*. Princeton, NJ: Princeton University Press.

Crabbe, T. (2007) 'Reaching the "hard to reach": Engagement, relationship building and social control in sport-based social inclusion work', *International Journal of Sport Management and Marketing*, 2(1–2): 27–40.

Crewe, L., Gregson, N. and Brooks, K. (2003) 'The discursivities of difference: Retro retailers and the ambiguities of "the alternative"', *Journal of Consumer Culture*, 3(1): 61–82.

Cronin, A. M. (2004a) *Advertising Myths: The Strange Half-Lives of Images and Commodities*. London: Routledge.

Cronin, A. M. (2004b) 'Regimes of mediation: Advertising practitioners as cultural inter-mediaries?', *Consumption, Markets and Culture*, 7: 349–369.

Cunningham, M. (1996) *Good Vibrations: A History of Record Production*. Chessington: Castle Communications.

Cunningham, S. (2006) 'Business needs crash course in appreciation', *Australian Financial Review*, 14 August. p. 36.

Cunningham, S. (2007a) 'Oh, the humanities! Australia's innovation system out of kilter', *Australian Universities Review*, 49(1–2): 28–30.

Cunningham, S. (2007b) 'Taking arts into the digital era', *Courier Mail*, 22 June. Available at: www.onlineopinion.com.au/view.asp?article=6031 (accessed 17 December 2013).

Cunningham, S. (2009a) 'Can creativity be taught? And should it be?', *Australian Policy Online*, 7 December. Available at: www.apo.org.au/commentary/can-creativity-be-taught-and-should-it-be (accessed 17 December 2013).

Cunningham, S. (2009b) 'Creative industries as a globally contestable policy field', *Chinese Journal of Communication*, 2(1): 13–24.

Cunningham, S. (2009c) 'Trojan horse or Rorschach blot? Creative industries discourse around the world', *International Journal of Cultural Policy*, 15(4): 375–386.

Cunningham, S. (2011a) *A Conversation with Stuart Cunningham about the Creative Industries.* Podcast, available at: http://culturalstudies.podbean.com/2011/03/05/a-conversation-with-stuart-cunningham-about-the-creative-industries (accessed 17 December 2013).

Cunningham, S. (2011b) 'Developments in measuring the "creative" workforce', *Cultural Trends*, 20(1): 25–40.

Curtin, P. A. and Gaither, T. K. (2005) 'Privileging identity, difference, and power: The circuit of culture as a basis for public relations theory', *Journal of Public Relations Research*, 17(2): 91–116.

Curtin, P. A. and Gaither, T. K. (2007) *International Public Relations: Negotiating Culture, Identity, and Power.* Thousand Oaks, CA: Sage.

Dahlgren, P. and Sparks, C. (eds) (1992) *Journalism and Popular Culture.* London: Sage.

Dahlström, M. and Hermelin, B. (2007) 'Creative industries, spatiality and flexibility: The example of film production', *Norsk Geografisk Tiddskrift – Norwegian Journal of Geography*, 61(3): 111–121.

Daisey, M. (2002) *Twenty-one Dog Years: Doing Time at Amazon.Com.* London: Fourth Estate.

Dannen, F. (1991) *Hit Men: Power Brokers and Fast Money Inside the Music Business.* London: Vintage.

Datamonitor (2010) *Books in the United Kingdom.* London: Datamonitor Europe.

Davis, A. (2003) 'Whither mass media and power? Evidence for a critical elite theory alternative', *Media, Culture and Society*, 25(5): 669–690.

Daymon, C. and Hodges, C. E. M. (2009) 'Researching occupational culture of public relations in Mexico City', *Public Relations Review*, 35: 429–433.

de La Pradelle, M. (2004) *Market Day in Provence.* Chicago, IL: University of Chicago Press.

de Sola Pool, I. (1983) *Technologies of Freedom.* Cambridge, MA: Harvard University Press.

de Valck, M. (2008) *Film Festivals: From European Geopolitics to Global Cinephilia.* Amsterdam: Amsterdam University Press.

Demetrious, K. (2011) 'Bubble wrap: Social media, public relations, culture and society', in L. Edwards and C. E. M. Hodges (eds), *Public Relations Society and Culture: Theoretical and Empirical Exploration.* Abingdon: Routledge.

DeNora, T. (2000) *Music in Everyday Life.* New York: Cambridge University Press.

DeNora, T. and Belcher, S. (2000) 'When you're trying something on you picture yourself in a place where they are playing this kind of music' – musically sponsored agency in the British clothing retail sector', *The Sociological Review*, 48 (1): February 80–101(22).

Department for Culture, Media and Sport (DCMS) (1999) *Policy Action Team 10 Report.* London: DCMS.

Department for Culture, Media and Sport (DCMS) (2000) *Centres for Social Change: Museums, Galleries and Archives for All.* London: DCMS.

Department for Culture, Media and Sport (DCMS) (2007) *Changing Lives and Places: Lessons from Cultural Pathfinders.* London: DCMS.

Design Council (2005) *The Business of Design.* London: Design Council.

Dewey, J. and Bentley, A. (1991 [1949]) 'Knowing and the known', In Boydston, J. (ed.) *The Later Works, 1925–1953*. Carbondale: Southern Illinois University Press.

Di Maggio, P. (1977) 'Market structure, the creative process and popular culture: Towards an organizational reinterpretation of mass culture theory', *Journal of Popular Culture*, 11(2): 436–452.

Dicken, P. (2007) *Global Shift: Mapping the Changing Contours of the World Economy* (5th edn). Los Angeles: Sage.

DiCola, P. and Thomson, K. (2002) *Radio Deregulation: Has It Served Citizens and Musicians?* Washington, DC: The Future of Music Coalition.

DiMaggio, P. (1987) 'Classification in art', *American Sociological Review*, 52(4): 440–455.

Dichter, E. (1957) *Advertiser's Weekly*, 8 November. pp. 22–24.

Doane, R. (2009) 'Bourdieu, cultural intermediaries and good housekeeping's George Marek: A case study of middlebrow musical taste', *Journal of Consumer Culture*, 9(2): 155–186.

Donnelly, K. (2005) *The Spectre of Sound: Music in Film and Television*. London: BFI Publishing.

Dowling, E., Nunes, R. and Trott, B. (2007) 'Immaterial and affective labour explored', *Ephemera: Theory & Politics in Organization*, 7(1): 1–7.

du Gay, P. (1996) *Consumption and Identity at Work*. London: Sage.

du Gay, P. (2004) 'Devices and dispositions: promoting consumption', *Consumption, Markets and Culture*, 7(2): 99–105.

du Gay, P. (2010) 'Performativities: Butler, Callon and the moment of theory', *Journal of Cultural Economy*, 3(2): 171–179.

du Gay, P. and Pryke, M. (eds) (2002a) *Cultural Economy*. London: Sage.

du Gay, P. and Pryke, M. (2002b) 'Cultural economy: An introduction', in P. du Gay and M. Pryke (eds), *Cultural Economy: Cultural Analysis and Commercial Life*. London: Sage. pp. 1–19.

du Gay, P., Hall, S., Janes, L., Mackay, H. and Negus, K. (1997) *Doing Cultural Studies: The Story of the Sony Walkman*. London: Sage.

Durrer, V. (2008) 'An Interdisciplinary Examination of the Interpretation and Delivery of Social Inclusion in the Arts'. PhD thesis, University of Liverpool.

Durrer, V. and Miles, S. (2009) 'New perspectives on the role of cultural intermediaries in social inclusion in the UK', *Consumption, Markets & Culture*, 12(3): 225–241.

Dutta, M. (2008) *Communicating Health: A Culture-Centred Approach*. London: Polity Press.

Dutta, M. J. and Pal, M. (2011) 'Public relations and marginalization in a global context: A postcolonial critique', in N. Bardhan and C. Kay Weaver (eds), *Public Relations in Global Cultural Contexts: Multi-Paradigmatic Perspectives*. London: Routledge. pp. 195–225.

Dyson, E., Gilder, G., Keyworth, G. and Toffler, A. (1994) *Cyberspace and the American Dream: A Magna Carta for the Knowledge Age*. Version 1.2. Washington, DC: Progress and Freedom Foundation. Available at: http://pff.org/issues-pubs/futureinsights/fi1.2magnacarta.html (accessed 17 December 2013).

Edwards, L. (2006) 'Rethinking power in public relations', *Public Relations Review*, 32(3): 229–231.

Edwards, L. (2008) 'PR practitioners' cultural capital: An initial study and implications for research and practice', *Public Relations Review*, 34: 367–372.

Edwards, L. (2010) '"Race" in public relations', in R. Heath (ed.), *The Sage Handbook of Public Relations*, 2nd edn. Thousand Oaks, CA: Sage. pp. 205–222.

Edwards, L. (2011) 'Public relations and society: A Bourdieuvian perspective', in L. Edwards and C. E. M. Hodges (eds), *Public Relations Society and Culture: Theoretical and Empirical Explorations*. Abingdon: Routledge. pp. 61–74.

Edwards, L. (2012) 'Exploring the role of public relations as a cultural intermediary occupation', *Cultural Sociology*, 6(4): 438–454.

Edwards, L. and Hodges, C. E. M. (2011) 'Introduction: Implications of a (radical) socio-cultural "turn" in public relations scholarship', in L. Edwards and C. E. M. Hodges (eds), *Public Relations Society and Culture: Theoretical and Empirical Explorations*. Abingdon: Routledge. pp. 1–14.

Edwards, L. and Pieczka, M. (2013) 'Public relations and "its" media: Exploring the role of trade media in the enactment of public relations' professional project', *Public Relations Inquiry*, 2(1): 5–25.

Ehrenreich, B. and English, D. (2005) *For Her Own Good: Two Centuries of the Experts' Advice to Women*. New York: Anchor Books.

Eide, M. and Knight, G. (1999) 'Public/private service: Service journalism and the problems of everyday life', *European Journal of Communication*, 14(4): 525–547.

Eikhof, D. and Haunschild, A. (2007) 'For art's sake! Artistic and economic logics in creative production', *Journal of Organizational Behaviour*, 28(5): 523–538.

Eldridge, J., Kitzinger, J. and William, K. (1997) *The Mass Media and Power in Modern Britain*. Oxford: Oxford University Press.

Elliott, J. (2005) 'From demo to hit: The biography of three songs by country songwriter Tom Douglas', *Popular Music and Society*, 28(1): 3–13.

Elliott, R. (1996) 'Discourse analysis: Exploring action, function and conflict in social texts', *Marketing Intelligence and Planning*, 14(6): 65–68.

Elliott, R. (1997) 'Existential consumption and irrational desire', *European Journal of Marketing*, 31(3/4): 285–296.

Elmer, P. (2011) 'Public relations and storytelling', in L. Edwards and C. E. M. Hodges (eds), *Public Relations, Society and Culture: Theoretical and Empirical Explorations*. Abingdon: Routledge. pp. 47–59.

Emerson, R. W. (1909–14). *Essays and English Traits*. Cambridge, MA: Harvard Classics.

English, J. F. (2005) *The Economy of Prestige: Prizes, Awards, and the Circulation of Cultural Value*. Cambridge, MA: Harvard University Press.

Ennis, A. (2005) 'Graphic Design Practice: Impersonation, Invocation and Multiple Audiences'. Unpublished MA thesis, Concordia University.

Entman, R. M. (2004) *Projections of Power: Framing News, Public Opinion and US Foreign Policy*. London: University of Chicago Press.

Entwistle, J. (2006) 'The cultural economy of fashion buying', *Current Sociology*, 54(5): 704–724.

Entwistle, J. (2009) *The Aesthetic Economy of Fashion: Markets and Values in Clothing and Modelling*. Oxford: Berg.

Entwistle, J. and Rocamora, A. (2006) 'The field of fashion materialized: A study of London fashion week', *Sociology*, 40(4): 735–751.

Ericson, R. V., Baranek, P. M and Chan, J. B. (1991) *Representing Order: Crime, Law and Justice in the News Media*. Milton Keynes: Open University Press.

Ettema, J. S., Whitney, D. C. and Wackman, D. B. (1987) 'Professional mass communicators', in C. H. Berger and S. H. Chaffee (eds), *Handbook of Communication Science*. London: Sage.

Ewenstein, B. and Whyte, J. (2007) 'Beyond words: Aesthetic knowledge and knowing in design', *Organization Studies*, 28(5): 689–708.

Eymard-Duvernay, F. (2005) 'Qualifying goods', *Sociologie du Travail*, 47: 100–104.

Fairchild, C. (2008) *Pop Idols and Pirates: Mechanisms of Consumption and the Global Circulation of Popular Music*. Aldershot: Ashgate.

Fairchild, C. (2012) *Music, Radio and the Public Sphere: The Aesthetics of Democracy*. Basingstoke and New York: Palgrave.

Fairchild, C. (2014 – forthcoming) *DJ Danger Mouse's The Grey Album*. London: Bloomsbury/Continuum.

Featherstone, M. (1991) *Consumer Culture and Postmodernism*. London: Sage.

Fenton, N. (ed.) (2010) *New Media, Old News: Journalism and Democracy in the Digital Age*. London: Sage.

Fenton, N., Bryman, A., Deacon, D. and Birmingham, P. (1998) *Mediating Social Science*. London: Sage.

Ferguson, P. P. (1998) 'A cultural field in the making: Gastronomy in 19th-century France', *American Journal of Sociology*, 104(3): 597–641.

Ferguson, P. P. (2004) *Accounting for Taste: The Triumph of French Cuisine*. Chicago, IL: University of Chicago Press.

Filene, B. (2000) *Romancing the Folk: Public Memory and American Roots Music*. Chapel Hill, NC: University of North Carolina Press.

Fine, B. and Leopold, E. (1993) *The World of Consumption*. London: Routledge.

Fine, G. A. (1996) *Kitchens: The Culture of Restaurant Work*. Berkeley, CA: University of California Press.

Fletcher, L. and Lobato, R. (2013) 'Living and labouring as a music writer', *Cultural Studies Review*, 19(1): 155–176.

Florida, R. (2002) *The Rise of the Creative Class: And How it's Transforming Work, Leisure, Community and Everyday Life*. London: Basic Books.

Fonarow, W. (2005) *Empire of Dirt: The Aesthetics and Rituals of British Indie Music*. Middletown, CT: Wesleyan University Press.

Forde, E. (2001) 'From polyglottism to branding: On the decline of personality journalism in the British music press', *Journalism*, 2(1): 23–43.

Forde, E. (2003) 'Journalists with a difference: Producing music journalism', in S. Cottle (ed.), *Media Organization and Production*. London: Sage.

Foster, P. and Ocejo, R. E. (forthcoming) 'Cultural intermediaries in an age of disintermediation: Brokerage and the production and consumption of culture', in C. Jones (ed.), *Handbook of Creative Industries*. Oxford: Oxford University Press.

Fox, M. (2005) 'Market power in music retailing: The case of Wal-Mart', *Popular Music and Society*, 28(4): 501–519.

Fox, S. (1997) *The Mirror Makers: A History of American Advertising and its Creators*. Chicago, IL: University of Illinois Press.

Frank, T. (1997) *The Conquest of Cool: Business Culture, Counterculture, and the Rise of Hip Consumerism*. Chicago, IL: University of Chicago Press.

Franssen, T. and Kuipers, G. (2013) 'Coping with uncertainty, abundance and strife: Decision-making processes of Dutch acquisition editors in the global market for translations', *Poetics*, 41(1): 48–74.

Freeman, A. (2007) *London's Creative Sector: 2007 Update*, Working Paper 22. London: Greater London Authority.

Frederick, C. (1913) *The New Housekeeping: Efficiency Studies in Home Management*. London: Doubleday.

Friedman, S. (2012) 'Cultural omnivores or culturally homeless? Exploring the shifting cultural identities of the socially mobile', *Poetics*, 40(5): 467–489.

Fuller, M. and Goffey, A. (2012) *Evil Media*. Cambridge, MA: MIT Press.

Furgason, A. (2008) 'Afraid of technology? Major label response to advancements in technology', *Popular Music History*, 3(2): 149–170.

Gabatt, A. (2011) 'Amazon and Waterstones report downloads eclipsing printed book sales', *The Guardian*, 19 May.

Gabriel, Y. and Lang, T. (1995) *The Unmanageable Consumer*. London: Sage.

Gadda, C. (2000 [1957]) *That Awful Mess on the Via Merulana*. New York: New York Review Books.

Gains, F. (2011) 'Elite ethnographies: Potential pitfalls and prospects for getting "up close and personal"', *Public Administration*, 89(1): 156–166.

Gans, H. (1980) *Deciding What's News: A Study of CBS Evening News, NBC Nightly News, Newsweek and Time*. New York: Pantheon.

Garnham, N. (1986) 'Extended review: Bourdieu's *Distinction*', *Sociological Review*, 34(2): 423–433.

Garnham, N. (2005) 'From cultural to creative industries: An analysis of the implications of the "creative industries" approach to arts and media policy making in the United Kingdom', *International Journal of Cultural Policy*, 11(1): 15–29.

Garofalo, R. (1999) 'From music publishing to MP3: Music and industry in the 20th century', *American Music*, 17(3): 318–354.

Gay, L. (1999) 'Before the deluge: The technoculture of song-sheet publishing viewed from late nineteenth-century Galveston', *American Music*, 17(4): 396–421.

Gee, J. (2005) *Introduction to Discourse Analysis*, 2nd edn. New York: Routledge.

Geertz, C. (1973) *The Interpretation of Cultures*. Basic Books: New York.

Gelber, S. M. (1999) *Hobbies: Leisure and the Culture of Work in America*. Ithaca, NY: Columbia University Press.

George, M. (2008) 'Interactions in expert service work: Demonstrating professionalism in personal training', *Journal of Contemporary Ethnography*, 37(1): 108–131.

Gibson, C. and Klocker, N. (2004) 'Academic publishing as "creative" industry and recent discourses of "creative economies": Some critical reflections', *Area*, 36(4): 423–434.

Giddens, A. (1991) *Modernity and Self-identity: Self and Society in the Late Modern Age*. Polity Press: Cambridge.

Giertz-Mårtensen, I. (2010) 'Fashion forecasting', *Encyclopedia of World Dress and Fashion, West Europe*. Oxford: Berg. p. 137.

Gill, R. (2003) 'Power and the production of subjects: A genealogy of the new man and the new lad', in B. Benwell (ed.), *Masculinity and Men's Lifestyle Magazines*. Oxford: Blackwell. pp. 34–56.

Gillespie, T. (2007) *Wired Shut: Copyright and the Shape of Digital Culture*. Cambridge, MA: MIT Press.

Ginsberg, L. (2000) 'The hard work of working out: Defining leisure, health and beauty in a Japanese health club', *Journal of Sport and Social Issues*, 34(3): 260–281.

Gitlin, T. (1995) 'Media sociology: The dominant paradigm', in O. Boyd-Barrett and C. Newbold (eds), *Approaches to Media: A Reader*. London: Arnold. pp. 21–33.

Godart, F. and Mears, A. (2009) 'How do cultural producers make creative decisions? Lessons from the catwalk', *Social Forces*, 88(2): 671–692.

Godbout, T. M. (1993) 'Employment change and sectoral distribution in 10 countries, 1970–1990', *Monthly Labor Review*, October: 3–20.

Goffman, E. (1959) *The Presentation of Self in Everyday Life*. Garden City, NY: Anchor.

Goldman, R. and Papson, S. (1998) *Nike Culture*. London: Sage.

Gorz, A. (2004) 'Économie de la connaissance, exploitation des savoirs: Entretien réalisé par Yann Moulier Boutang and Carlo Vercellone', *Multitudes*, 15. Available at: http://multitudes.samizdat.net/Economie-de-la-connaissance (accessed 17 December 2013).

Gough-Yates, A. (2003) *Understanding Women's Magazines*. London: Routledge.

Gould, R.V. and Fernandez, R. M. (1989) 'Structures of mediation: A formal approach to brokerage in transaction networks', *Sociological Methodology*, 19: 89–126.

Graham, B., Ashworth, G. and Tunbridge, J. (2005) 'The uses and abuses of heritage', in G. Corsane (ed.), *Heritage Museums and Galleries: An Introductory Reader*. London: Routledge.

Graham, M. (2008) 'Warped geographies of development: The Internet and theories of economic development', *Geography Compass*, 2(3): 771–789.

Gray, C. (2004) 'Joining-up or tagging on? The arts, cultural policy and the view from below', *Public Policy and Administration*, 19(2): 38–49.

Green, H. (1986) *Fit for America: Health, Fitness, Sport and American Society*. New York: Pantheon.

Green, N. (1997) *Ready-to-Wear and Ready-to-Work: A Century of Industry and Immigrants in Paris and New York*. Durham, NC: Duke University Press.

Greenberg, M. (2008) *Branding New York: How a City in Crisis was Sold to the World*. New York: Routledge.

Greenleaf, C., McGreer, R. and Parham, H. (2006) 'Physique attitudes and self-presentational concerns: Exploratory interviews with female group aerobic exercisers and instructors', *Sex Roles*, 54(3/4): 189–199.

Griffiths, D., Miles, A. and Savage, M. (2008) 'The end of the English cultural elite', in M. Savage and K. Williams (eds), *Remembering Elites*. Oxford: Blackwell. pp. 189–210.

Gross, J. (2009) 'Capitalism and its discontents: Back to the Lander and Freegan foodways in rural Oregon', *Food and Foodways*, 17(2): 57–79.

Grugulis, I. and Bozkurt, Ö. (eds) (2011) *Retail Work*. Basingstoke: Palgrave Macmillan.

Guthman, J. (2008) 'If they only knew: Color blindness and universalism in California alternative food institutions', *The Professional Geographer*, 60: 387–397.

Hackley, C. (1999) 'An epistemological odyssey: Towards social construction of the advertising process', *Journal of Marketing Communications*, 5(3): 157–168.

Hackley, C. (2000) 'Silent running: Tacit, discursive and psychological aspects of management in a top UK advertising agency', *British Journal of Management*, 11(3): 239–254.

Hackley, C. (2002) 'The panoptic role of advertising agencies in the production of consumer culture', *Consumption, Markets & Culture*, 5(3): 211–229.

Hackley, C. (2003) 'How divergent beliefs cause account team conflict', *International Journal of Advertising*, 22(3): 313–331.

Hackley, C. and Kover, A. J. (2007) 'The trouble with creatives ... negotiating creative identity in advertising agencies', *International Journal of Advertising*, 26(1): 63–78.

Hall, S., Critcher, C., Jefferson, T., Clarke, J. and Roberts, B. (1978) *Policing the Crisis*. London: Macmillan.

Hallin, D. C. and Mancini, P. (2010) 'Western media systems in comparative perspective', in J. Curran (ed.), *Media and Society*. London: Bloomsbury. pp. 103–122.

Hamilton, M. (2008) *In Search of the Blues: Black Voices, White Visions*. New York: Basic Books.

Hannigan, J. (1998) *Fantasy City: Pleasure and Profit in the Postmodern Metropolis*. London: Routledge.

Hanser, A. (2008) *Service Encounters: Class, Gender, and the Market for Social Distinction in Urban China*. Palo Alto, CA: Stanford University Press.

Haravon Collins, L. (2002) 'Working out the contradictions: Feminism and aerobics', *Journal of Sport and Social Issues*, 26(1): 85–109.

Hardt, M. and Negri, A. (2000) *Empire*. Cambridge: Harvard University Press.

Haring, B. (2000) *Beyond the Charts: MP3 and the Digital Music Revolution*. Los Angeles, CA: Off the Charts.

Harker, D. (1997) 'The wonderful world of IFPI: Music industry rhetoric, the critics and the classical Marxist critique', *Popular Music*, 16(1): 45–79.

Harvey, D. (2000) *Spaces of Hope*. Edinburgh: Edinburgh University Press.

Hatch, M. J. and Shultz, M. (2010) 'Toward a theory of brand co-creation with implications for brand governance', *Journal of Brand Management*, 17(8): 590–604.

Haynes, J. (2005) 'World music and the search for difference', *Ethnicities*, 5(3): 365–385.

Hebdige, D. (1988) *Hiding in the Light: On Images and Things*. London and New York: Routledge.

Hendy, D. (2000) 'Pop music radio in the public service: BBC Radio 1 and new music in the 1990s', *Media, Culture and Society*, 22(6): 743–761.

Hennion, A. (1989) 'An intermediary between production and consumption: The producer of popular music', *Science, Technology, & Human Values*, 14(4): 400–424.

Hennion, A. (2003) 'Music and mediation: Toward a new sociology of music', in M. Clayton, T. Herbert and R. Middleton (eds), *The Cultural Study of Music: A Critical Introduction*. London: Routledge. pp. 80–91.

Henrion, F. H. K. and Parkin, A. (1967) *Design Coordination and Public Image*. London: Studio Vista.

Hesmondhalgh, D. (2002) *The Cultural Industries*. London: Sage.

Hesmondhalgh, D. (2005) 'The production of media entertainment', in J. Curran and M. Gurevtich (eds), *Mass Media and Society*. London: Hodder Arnold.

Hesmondhalgh, D. (2006a) 'Media and cultural policy as public policy', *International Journal of Cultural Policy*, 11(1): 95–109.

Hesmondhalgh, D. (2006b) 'Bourdieu, the media and cultural production', *Media, Culture & Society*, 28(2): 211–231.

Hesmondhalgh, D. (2007) *The Cultural Industries* (2nd edn). London: Sage.

Hesmondhalgh, D. and Baker, S. (2011) *Creative Labour: Media Work in Three Cultural Industries*. London: Routledge.

Hesmondhalgh, D. and Pratt, A. C. (2005) 'Cultural industries and cultural policy', *International Journal of Cultural Policy*, 11(1): 1–13.

Heying, C. (2011) *Brew to Bikes: Portland's Artisan Economy*. Portland, OR: Ooligan Press.

Hickman, M. (2008) 'The campaign that changed the eating habits of a nation', *The Independent*, 28 February.

Higgins, D. (2003) *The Art of Writing Advertising: Conversations with William Bernbach, George Gribbin, Rosser Reeves, David Ogilvy, Leo Burnett*. London: McGraw Hill.

Hill, S. (2006) '*Q* and *The Face*: Narratives of consumption in the UK music press in the 1980s', *Popular Music History*, 1(2): 189–212.

Hinde, S. and Dixon, J. (2007) 'Reinstating Pierre Bourdieu's contribution to cultural economy theorizing', *Journal of Sociology*, 43(4): 401–20.

Hirsch, P. M. (1972) 'Processing fads and fashions: An organization-set analysis of cultural industry systems', *American Journal of Sociology*, 77: 639–659.

Hirschman, E. C. (1983) 'Aesthetics, ideologies and the limits of the marketing concept', *Journal of Marketing*, 47(3): 45–55.

Hirschman, E. C. (1989) 'Role-based models of advertising creation and production', *Journal of Advertising*, 18(4): 42–59.

Hochschild, A. R. (1983) *The Managed Heart: Commercialization of Human Feeling*. Berkeley, CA: University of California Press.

Hochschild, A. (2003) *The Managed Heart: The Commercialization of Human Feeling* (2nd edn). Berkeley, CA: University of California Press.

Hodges, C. E. M. (2006) '"PRP culture": A framework for exploring public relations practitioners as cultural intermediaries', *Journal of Communication Management*, 10(1): 80–93.

Hodges, C. E. M. (2011) 'Public relations in the postmodern city: An ethnographic account of PR occupational culture in Mexico City', in L. Edwards and C. E. M. Hodges (eds), *Public Relations Society and Culture: Theoretical and Empirical Exploration.* Abingdon: Routledge. pp. 33–46.

Hodges, C. E. M. (2012) 'The meaning(s) and making(s) of PR: The potential for ethnography within public relations research', in A. Frame and V. Carayol (eds), *Studying Communication Practices from a Cross-Cultural Standpoint: Practical and Methodological Issues.* New York: Peter Lang.

Hodges, C. E. M. and McGrath, N. (2011) 'Communication for social transformation', in L. Edwards and C. E. M. Hodges (eds), *Public Relations Society and Culture: Theoretical and Empirical Explorations.* Abingdon: Routledge. pp. 90–104.

Hoggart, R. (2004) *Mass Media in a Mass Society: Myth and Reality.* London: Continuum.

Hollows, J. (2003) 'Oliver's twist: Leisure, labour and domestic masculinity in the Naked Chef', *International Journal of Cultural Studies*, 6(2): 229–248.

Hollows, J. and Jones, S. (2010) '"At least he's doing something": Moral entrepreneurship and individual responsibility in Jamie's Ministry of Food', *European Journal of Cultural Studies*, 13(3): 307–322.

Holt, D. B. (2004) *How Brands Become Icons: The Principles of Cultural Branding.* Boston, MA: Harvard Business School Publishing.

Holt, D. B. (2006) 'Jack Daniel's America: Iconic brands as ideological parasites and pros- elytizers', *Journal of Consumer Culture*, 6(3): 355–377.

Hopkins, C. C. (1998 [1923]) *My Life in Advertising and Scientific Advertising.* Chicago, IL: NTC Business Books.

Horowitz, D. (2004) *Anxieties of Affluence, Critiques of American Consumer Culture, 1939–1979.* Boston, MA: University of Massachusetts Press.

Howe, S. (2003) 'The NBC music appreciation hour: Radio broadcasts of Walter Damrosch, 1928–1942', *Journal of Research in Music Education*, 51(1): 64–77.

Hoyer, S. and Lauk, E. (2003) 'The paradoxes of the journalistic profession: A historical perspective', *Nordicom Review*, 24(2): 3–18.

Huijgh, E. (2007) 'Diversity united? Towards a European cultural industries policy', *Policy Studies*, 28(3): 209–224.

Hutson, D. J. (2012) 'Training Bodies, Building Status: Health, Physical Capital, and the Negotiation of Difference in the US Fitness Industry'. Unpublished dissertation, University of Michigan.

Ihlen, O. (2009) 'On Bourdieu: Public relations in field struggles', in O. Ihlen, B. van Ruler and M. Fredriksson (eds), *Public Relations and Social Theory.* Routledge: London. pp. 62–82.

Independent Publishers Association (IPA) (2007) 'UK Advertising Statistics'. Available at: www.ipa.co.uk/resource_centre/ukstatistics.cfm (accessed 20 July 2007).

Inglis, I. (2003) '"Some kind of wonderful": The creative legacy of the Brill Building', *American Music*, 21(2): 214–235.

Ingold, T. (2000) *The Perception of the Environment: Essays in Livelihood, Dwelling and Skill.* London: Routledge.

Intellectual Property Office (IPO) (2009) 'Branding in a Modern Economy'. Newport: Intellectual Property Office.

Iosifidis, P. (2011) *Global Media and Communication Policy*. Basingstoke: Palgrave Macmillan.

Jackall, R. and Hirota, J. M. (2000) *Image Makers: Advertising, Public Relations and the Ethos of Advocacy*. Chicago, IL: University of Chicago Press.

Jackson, D. (2001) Interview with Dan Jackson, London, 5 December.

Jamerson, H. (2009) 'Intoxicators, educators, and gatekeepers: The enactment of symbolic boundaries in Napa Valley wineries', *Poetics*, 37(4): 383–398.

Janssen, S., Verboord, M. and Kuipers, G. (2011) 'Comparing cultural classification: High and popular arts in European and US elite newspapers', *Kölner Zeitschrift für Soziologie und Sozialpsychologie*, 63 (special issue 51): 139–168.

Jenkins, R. (1992) *Pierre Bourdieu*. London: Routledge.

Johnson, A. and Sandberg, J. (2008) 'Controlling service work: An ambiguous accomplishment between employees, management and customers', *Journal of Consumer Culture*, 8(3): 389–417.

Johnston, J. and Baumann, S. (2007) 'Democracy versus distinction: A study of omnivorousness in gourmet food writing', *American Journal of Sociology*, 113(1): 165–204.

Johnston, J. and Baumann, S. (2010) *Foodies: Democracy and Distinction in the Gourmet Foodscape*. New York: Routledge.

Jones, S. (ed.) (2002a) *Pop Music and the Press*. Philadelphia, PA: Temple University Press.

Jones, S. (2002b) 'Music the moves: Popular music, distribution and network technologies', *Cultural Studies*, 16(2): 213–232.

Jones, S. and Taylor, B. (2013) 'Food Journalism', in B. Turner and R. Orange (eds), *Specialist Journalism*. London: Routledge.

Joy, T. (1952) *Bookselling*. London: Pitman.

Joy, T. (1974) *The Bookselling Business*. Oxford: Alden Press.

Julier, G. (2000) *The Culture of Design*. London: Sage.

Kamp, D. (2006) *The United States of Arugula: How We Became a Gourmet Nation*. New York: Broadway Books.

Kaneva, N. (2011) 'Nation branding: Toward an agenda for critical research', *International Journal of Communications*, 5: 117–141.

Karpik, L. (2005) 'What is to be done with singularities?', *Sociologie du Travail*, 47: S89–S123.

Karpik, L. (2010) *Valuing the Unique: The Economics of Singularities*. Princeton and Oxford: Princeton University Press.

Katz, M. (2004) *Capturing Sound: How Technology Has Changed Music*. Berkeley, CA: University of California Press.

Kawashima, N. (1997) *Museum Management in a Time of Change: Impacts of Cultural Policy on Museums in Britain 1979–1997*. Warwick: Centre for Cultural Policy Studies, University of Warwick.

Kawashima, N. (2006) 'Audience development and social inclusion in Britain', *International Journal of Cultural Policy*, 12(1): 55–72.

Keane, J. (1991) *Media and Democracy*. Cambridge: Polity Press.

Keane, M. (2006) 'From made in China to created in China', *International Journal of Cultural Studies*, 9(3): 285–296.

Kelly, A., Lawlor, K. and O'Donohoe, S. (2008) 'A fateful triangle? Tales of art, commerce and science from the Irish advertising field', *Advertising & Society Review*, 9(3): 1–48. Available at: http://muse.jhu.edu/journals/asr/ (accessed 5 July 2008).

Kenney, W. (1999) *Recorded Music in American Life: The Phonograph and Popular Memory, 1890–1945*. New York: Oxford University Press.

Kent, M. K. and Taylor, M. (2002) 'Toward a dialogic theory of public relations', *Public Relations Review*, 28: 21–37.

Killmeier, M. (2001) 'Voices between the tracks: Disk jockeys, radio and popular music, 1955–60', *Journal of Communication Inquiry*, 25(4): 353–374.

Kim, J. E., Ju, H. W. and Johnson, K. K. P. (2009) 'Sales associate's appearance: Links to consumers' emotions, store image, and purchases', *Journal of Retailing and Consumer Services*, 16: 407–413.

Kirk, M. (2004) *The Way the Music Died*. Boston, MA: WGBH Educational Foundation.

Kitzinger, J. (2000) 'Media templates: Patterns of association and the (re)construction of meaning over time', *Media, Culture and Society*, 22(1): 64–84.

Klein, B. (2009) *As Heard on TV: Popular Music in Advertising*. Farnham: Ashgate.

Klein, N. (1999) *No Logo: Taking Aim at the Brand Bullies*. New York: Picador.

Klepp, I. G. (2001) *Hvorfor går klær ut av bruk? Avhending sett i forhold til kvinners klesvaner*, SIFO Rapport nr. 3–001. Oslo: Statens Institutt For Forbruksforskning.

Kloosterman, R. and Quispel, C. (1990) 'Not just the same old show on my radio: An analysis of the role of radio in the diffusion of black music among whites in the south of the United States of America, 1920 to 1960', *Popular Music*, 9(2): 151–164.

Knorr-Cetina, K. and Preda A. (2001) 'The epistemization of economic transactions', *Current Sociology*, 49(4): 27–44.

Korczynski, M. (2002) *Human Resource Management in Service Work*. Basingstoke: Palgrave Macmillan.

Korczynski, M. (2005) 'The point of selling: capitalism, consumption and contradictions', *Organization*, 12(1): 69–88.

Kornberger, M. (2010) *Brand Society: How Brands Transform Management and Lifestyle*. Cambridge: Cambridge University Press.

Kotkin, J. (2001) *The New Geography: How the Digital Revolution is Reshaping the American Landscape*. New York: Random House.

Kraidy, M. and Sender, K. (eds) (2011) *The Politics of Reality Television: Global Perspectives*. London: Routledge.

Kramer, M. (2002) '"Can't forget the motor city": Creem Magazine, rock music, Detroit identity, mass consumerism, and the counterculture', *Michigan Historical Review*, 28(2): 43–77.

Kuh, P. (2001) *The Last Days of Haute Cuisine*. New York: Viking.

Kuipers, G. (2006) *Good Humor, Bad Taste: A Sociology of the Joke*. Berlin/New York: Mouton de Gruyter.

Kuipers, G. (2011) 'Cultural globalization as the emergence of a transnational cultural field: Transnational television and national media landscapes in four European countries', *American Behavioral Scientist*, 55(5): 541–557.

Kuipers, G. (2012) 'The cosmopolitan tribe of television buyers: Professional ethos, personal taste and cosmopolitan capital in transnational cultural mediation', *European Journal of Cultural Studies*, 15(5): 581–603.

Kwate, N. O. A., Yau, C. Y., Loh, J. M. and Williams, D. (2009) 'Inequality in obesigenic environments: Fast food density in New York City', *Health & Place*, 15(1): 364–373.

L'Etang, J. (2004) *Public Relations in Britain: A History of Professional Practice in the 20th Century*. Mahwah, NJ: Lawrence Erlbaum.

L'Etang, J. (2006) 'Public relations and sport in promotional culture', *Public Relations Review*, 34(4): 453–457.

L'Etang, J. (2007) *Public Relations: Concepts, Practice and Critique*. London: Sage.

L'Etang, J. (2008) 'Public relations, persuasion and propaganda: Truth, knowledge, spirituality and mystique', in A. Zerfass, B. van Ruler and K. Sriramesh (eds), *Public Relations Research: European and International Perspectives*. Wiesbaden: Verlag fur Sozialwissenschaft. pp. 251–270.

L'Etang, J. (2009) 'Public relations and diplomacy in a globalized world: An issue of public communication', *American Behavioral Scientist*, 53(4): 607–626.

L'Etang, J. and Pieczka, M. (eds) (2006) *Critical Perspectives in Public Relations* (2nd edn). London and Boston: International Thomson.

L'Etang, J., Falkheimer, J. and Lugo, J. (2007) 'Public relations and tourism: Critical reflections and a research agenda', *Public Relations Review*, 33: 68–76.

Laing, D. (2006) 'Anglo-American music journalism: Texts and ontexts', in A. Bennett, B. Shank and J. Toynbee (eds), *The Popular Music Studies Reader*. London: Routledge. pp. 333–343.

Laitala, K., Grimstad Klepp, I. and Hauge, B. (2011) 'Materialised ideals: Sizes and beauty', *Culture Unbound: Journal of Current Cultural Research*, 3: 19–42.

Lakshman, N. (2008) 'Copyediting? Ship the work out to India', *Business Week*, 8 July. Available at: www.businessweek.com/globalbiz/content/jul2008/gb2008078_678274. htm (accessed 17 December 2013).

Lamont, M. and Thevenot, L. (2000) *Rethinking Comparative Cultural Sociology: Repertoires of Evaluation in France and the United States*. Cambridge: Cambridge University Press.

Land, C. and Taylor, S. (2010) 'Surf's up: Work, life, balance and brand in a new age capitalist organization', *Sociology*, 44(3): 395–413.

Lang, T. (1996) 'Going public: Food campaigns during the 1980s and 1990s', in D. Smith (ed.), *Nutrition Scientists and Nutrition Policy in the Twentieth Century*. London: Routledge. pp. 238–236.

Lang, T. (2003) 'Food industrialization and food power: Implications for food governance', *Development Policy Review*, 21(5–6): 555–568.

Langer, J. (1998) *Tabloid Television: Popular Journalism and 'Other News'*. London: Routledge.

Langland, E. (1995) *Nobody's Angels: Middle-class Women and Domestic Ideology in Victorian Culture*. Ithaca, NY: Cornell University Press.

Lanza, J. (1994) *Elevator Music: A Surreal History of Muzak, Easy-Listening, and Other Moodsong*. New York: St. Martin's Press.

Larner, W. and Molloy, M. (2009) 'Globalization, the "new economy" and working women: Theorizing from the New Zealand designer fashion industry', *Feminist Theory*, 10(1): 35–59.

Lash, S. and Urry, J. (1987) *The End of Organized Capitalism*. Madison, WI: The University of Wisconsin Press.

Lash, S. and Urry, J. (1994) *Economies of Signs and Space*. London: Sage.

Latour, B. (1991) 'Technology is society made durable', in J. Law (ed.), *A Sociology of Monsters: Essays on Power, Technology, and Domination*. London: Routledge. pp. 103–131.

Law, J. (2002) 'Economics as interference', in P. du Gay and M. Pryke (eds), *Cultural Economy*. London: Sage. pp. 23–40.

Lawson, T. (2001) Interview with Timothy Lawson, London, 13 March.

Lazzarato, M. (1997) 'Immaterial labor', in P. Virno and M. Hardt (eds), *Radical Thought in Italy: A Potential Politics*. Minneapolis, MN: University of Minnesota Press. pp. 133–147.

Lears, J. (1994) *Fables of Abundance: A Cultural History of Advertising in America*. New York: Basic Books.

Leavitt, S.A. (2002) *From Catharine Beecher to Martha Stewart: A Cultural History of Domestic Advice*. Chapel Hill, NC: University of North Carolina Press.

Lee, H. K. (2012) 'Cultural consumers as "new cultural intermediaries": Manga scanlators', *Arts Marketing: An International Journal*, 2(2): 231–243.

Leidner, R. (1999) 'Emotional labor in service work', *Annals of the American Academy of Political Social Science*, 561: 81–95.

Leiss, W., Klein, S., Jhally, S. and Botterill, J. (2005) *Social Communication in Advertising: Consumption in the Mediated Marketplace*. New York: Routledge.

Leopold, E. (1993) 'The manufacture of the fashion system', in J. Ash and E. Wilson (eds), *Chic Thrills*. Berkeley, CA: California University Press. pp. 101–118.

Levenstein, H. (1989) 'Two hundred years of French food in America', *Journal of Gastronomy*, 5(Spring): 67–89.

Lewis, T. (2008a) *Smart Living: Lifestyle Media and Popular Expertise*. New York: Peter Lang.

Lewis, T. (2008b) 'Transforming citizens: Green politics and ethical consumption on lifestyle television', *Continuum*, 2(2): 227–240.

Lewis, T. (2009) *TV Transformations*. London: Routledge.

Lewis, T. (2012) '"There grows the neighbourhood": Green citizenship, creativity and life politics on eco-TV', *International Journal of Cultural Studies*, 15(3): 315–326.

Lewis, T. and Potter, E. (2011) 'Introducing ethical consumption', in T. Lewis and E. Potter (eds), *Ethical Consumption: A Critical Introduction*. Abingdon: Routledge. pp. 12–44.

Lewis, T., Martin, F. and Sun, W. (2012) 'Lifestyling Asia? Shaping modernity and selfhood on life advice programming', *International Journal of Cultural Studies*, 15(6): 537–566.

Leyshon, A., Webb, P., French, S., Thrift, N. and Crewe, L. (2005) 'On the reproduction of the musical economy after the internet', *Media, Culture and Society*, 27(2): 177–209.

Lien, M. E. (1997) *Marketing and Modernity*. Oxford: Berg.

Lindevang, T. (2012) 'Young Entrepreneurs in Africa's Emerging Fashion Industry'. Unpublished working paper presented in the Business in Development Countries Seminar Series, Copenhagen Business School.

Linklater, M. (2006) 'I don't want to spoil the party …' *The Times*, 8 November. Accessible at: www.timesonline.co.uk/tol/comment/columnists/magnus_linklater/article629022.ece (accessed 1 January 2008).

Lipovetsky, G. (1994) *The Empire of Fashion: Dressing Modern Democracy*. Princeton, NJ: Princeton University Press.

Lipsky, M. (1980) *Street-level Bureaucracy: Dilemmas of the Individual in Public Services*. New York: Russell Sage Foundation.

Littler, J. (2009) *Radical Consumption: Shopping for Change in Contemporary Culture*. Maidenhead and New York: Open University Press.

Lloyd, M. (1996) 'Feminism, aerobics and the politics of the body', *Body & Society*, 2(2): 79–98.

Lloyd, R. (2006) *Neo-Bohemia: Art and Commerce in the Postindustrial City*. New York: Routledge.

Lodziak, C. (2002) *The Myth of Consumerism*. London: Pluto.

Löfgren, O. (2005) 'Catwalking and coolhunting: The production of newness', in O. Löfgren and R. Willim (eds), *Magic, Culture and the New Economy*. Oxford: Berg. pp. 57–71.

Lury, C. (2004) *Brands: The Logos of the Global Economy*. London and New York: Routledge.

Lury, C. and Moor, L. (2010) 'Brand valuation and topological culture', in M. Aronczyk and D. Powers (eds), *Blowing Up The Brand*. New York: Peter Lang. pp. 29–52.

Lury, C. and Warde, A. (1997) 'Investments in the imaginary consumer: Conjectures regarding power, knowledge and advertising', in M. Nava, A. Blake, I. MacRury and B. Richards (eds), *Buy This Book: Studies in Advertising and Consumption*. London: Routledge. pp. 87–102.

Luxford, J. (2010) 'Art for art's sake – was it ever thus? A historical perspective', in N. Beech and B. Townley (eds), *Managing Creativity: Exploring the Paradox*. Cambridge: Cambridge University Press. pp. 87–105.

Lynch, B. (2011) *Whose Cake is it Anyway?* London: Paul Hamlyn Foundation.

Mabry, D. (1990) 'The rise and fall of Ace Records: A case study in the independent record business', *Business History Review*, 64(3): 411–450.

Macdonald, S. (1998) 'Exhibitions of power and powers of exhibitions: An introduction to the politics of display', in S. Macdonald (ed.), *The Politics of Display: Museums, Science, Culture*. London: Routledge. pp. 1–24.

Maher, T. (1994) *Against My Better Judgement*. London: Mandarin.

Malefyt, T. (2003) 'Models, metaphors and client relations: The negotiated meanings of advertising', in T. Malefyt and B. Moeran (eds), *Advertising Cultures*. Oxford: Berg. pp. 139–163.

Malefyt, T. and Moeran, B. (eds) (2003) *Advertising Cultures*. Oxford: Berg.

Mann, C. (2000) 'The heavenly Jukebox', *The Atlantic Monthly*, 286(3): 39–59.

Marazzi, C. (2011) *The Violence of Financial Capital*. Los Angeles, CA: Semiotext(e).

Marcus, C. (2005) *Future of Creative Industries: Implications for Research Policy*. Brussels: European Commission Foresight Working Documents Series.

Marcus, G. E. (1995) 'Ethnography in/of the world system: The emergence of multi-sited ethnography', *Annual Review of Anthropology*, 24: 95–117.

Marcus, J. (2004) *Amazonia*. New York and London: New Press.

Markowitz, L. (2001) 'Finding the field: Notes on the ethnography of NGOs', *Human Organization*, 60(1): 40–46.

Markowitz, L. (2010) 'Expanding access and alternatives: Building farmers' markets in low-income communities', *Food and Foodways*, 18(1–2): 66–80.

Marks, S. (1991) 'Introduction', in M. Sudy (ed.), *Personal Trainer Manual: The Resource for Fitness Instructors*. San Diego, CA: American Council on Exercise.

Markula, P. and Pringle, R. (2006) *Foucault, Sport and Exercise*. London: Routledge.

Marshall, L. (2003) 'For and against the music industry: An introduction to bootleg collectors and traders', *Popular Music*, 22(1): 57–72.

Marx, K. (1980/1857–8) *Marx's Grundrisse*, Selected and Edited by David McLellan. London: Paladin.

Mason, R. (2004) 'Conflict and complement: An exploration of the discourses informing the concept of the socially inclusive museum in contemporary Britain', *International Journal of Heritage Studies*, 10(1): 49–73.

Mattelart, A. (2002) 'An archaeology of the global era: Constructing a belief', *Media, Culture & Society*, 24 (5): 591–612.

Mattern, S. (2008) 'Font of a nation: Creating a national graphic identity for Qatar', *Public Culture*, 20(3): 479–496.

Matthews, J. (2010) *Producing Serious News for Citizen Children: A Study of the BBC's Children's Programme, Newsround*. New York: Edwin Mellen.

Matthews, J. and Brown, A. R. (2012) 'Negatively shaping the asylum agenda? The representational strategy and impact of a tabloid news campaign', *Journalism Criticism, Theory and Practice*, 13(6): 802–881.

Matthews, J. and Cottle, S. (2012) 'Television news ecology in the United Kingdom: A study of communicative architecture, its production and meanings', *Television and New Media*, 13(2): 103–223.

Matthews, J. and Fisher, A. (forthcoming) 'Growing attachments? War correspondents, habitus and professional reflections on the experience of conflicts and reporting practices'.

Maxwell, R. and Miller, T. (2012) *Greening the Media*. New York: Oxford University Press.

McChesney, R. W. (2004) *The Problem of the Media*. New York: Monthly Review Press.

McChesney, R. and Schiller, D. (2003) *The Political Economy of International Communication: Foundations for the Emerging Global Debate About Media Ownership and Regulation*. Geneva: United Nations Research Institute for Social Development.

McCourt, T. and Burkart, P. (2003) 'When creators, corporations and consumers collide: Napster and the development of on-line music distribution', *Media, Culture and Society*, 25(3): 333–350.

McCourt, T. and Rothenbuhler, E. (1997) 'SoundScan and the consolidation of control in the popular music industry', *Media, Culture and Society*, 19(2): 201–218.

McCracken, G. (1986) 'Culture and consumption: A theoretical account of the structure and movement of the cultural meaning of consumer goods', *Journal of Consumer Research*, 13(1): 71–84.

McCracken, G. (1988) *Culture and Consumption*. Bloomington and Indianapolis, IN: Indiana University Press.

McCracken, G. D. (2005) *Culture and Consumption II: Markets, Meaning and Brand Management*. Bloomington, IN: Indiana University Press.

McFall, L. (2002) 'What about the old cultural intermediaries? An historical review of advertising producers', *Cultural Studies*, 16(4): 532–552.

McFall, L. (2004) *Advertising: A Cultural Economy*. London: Sage.

McFall, L. (2011) 'Advertising: Structure, agency or agencement?', in M. Deuze (ed.), *Managing Media Work*. London: Sage.

McFall, L., du Gay, P. and Carter, S. (2008) *Conduct: Sociology and Social Worlds*. Manchester: Manchester University Press.

McGuigan, J. (1996) *Culture and the Public Sphere*. London: Routledge.

McGuigan, J. (2010) 'Creative labour, cultural work and individualisation', *International Journal of Cultural Policy*, 16(3): 323–335.

McKay, S. (2008) 'Advice columns as cultural intermediaries', *Australian Journal of Communication*, 35(2): 93–103.

McLeod, C., O'Donohoe, S. and Townley, B. (2011) 'Pot Noodles, placements and peer regard: Creative career trajectories and communities of practice in the British advertising industry', *British Journal of Management*, 22(1): 114–131.

McLeod, K. (2005) 'MP3s are killing home taping: The rise of internet distribution and its challenge to the major label music monopoly', *Popular Music and Society*, 28(4): 521–531.

McNair, B. (1999) *News and Journalism in the UK*. London: Routledge.

McPhee, J. (1994) *Giving Good Weight*. New York: Farrar, Straus and Giroux.

McRobbie, A. (1998) *British Fashion Design: Rag Trade or Image Industry?* London: Routledge.

Méadel, C. and Rabeharisoa, V. (2001) 'Taste as a form of adjustment between food and consumers', in R. Coombs, K. Green, V. Walsh and A. Richards (eds), *Technology and the Market: Demand, Users and Innovation*. Cheltenham: Edward Elgar. pp. 234–253.

Mears, A. (2012) 'Transnational Circuits in the Global Cultural Economy: The Case of Talent Scouts in Fashion'. Paper presented in a panel on 'Emergence and innovation in markets and organizations'. International Economic Sociology Conference, Higher School of Economics, Moscow, October, 2012.

Mechling, J. (2003) 'Advice literature', in B. E. Carroll (ed.), *American Masculinities: A Historical Encyclopedia*. London: Sage. pp. 13–15.

Meier, L. (2011) 'Promotional ubiquitous musics: Recording artists, brands, and "rendering authenticity', *Popular Music and Society*, 34(4): 399–415.

Mellor, N. (2008) 'Arab journalists as cultural intermediaries', *International Journal of Press/Politics*, 13(4): 465–483.

Mick, D. G. and Buhl, C. (1992) 'A meaning-based model of advertising experience', *Journal of Consumer Research*, 19(3): 317–338.

Mickey, T. J. (2008) *Deconstructing Public Relations: Public Relations Criticism*. London: Lawrence Erlbaum.

Miles, A., Savage, M. and Bühlmann, F. (2011) 'Telling a modest story: Accounts of men's upward mobility from the national child development study', *British Journal of Sociology*, 62(3): 418–441.

Miller, B. (1994) 'A mirror of ages past: The publication of music in domestic periodicals', *Notes*, 50(3): 883–901.

Miller, D. (1997) *Capitalism: An Ethnographic Approach*. Oxford: Berg.

Miller, D. and Dinan, W. (2000) 'The rise of the PR industry in Britain 1979–98', *European Journal of Communication*, 15(1): 5–35.

Miller, D. and Dinan, W. (2007) *Thinker, Faker, Spinner, Spy: Corporate PR and the Assault on Democracy*. London: Pluto.

Miller, L. J. (2001) 'Saving books from the market: Price maintenance policies in the United States and Europe', in P. Pendakur and R. Harris (eds), *Citizenship and Participation in the Information Age*. Ottawa: Department of Canadian Heritage.

Miller, L. J. (2006) *Bookselling and the Culture of Consumption*. Chicago and London: University of Chicago Press.

Miller, P. and Rose, N. (1997) 'Mobilizing the consumer: Assembling the subject of consumption', *Theory, Culture and Society*, 14(1): 1–36.

Miller, T. (2007) *Cultural Citizenship: Cosmopolitanism, Consumerism and Television in a Neoliberal Age*. Philadelphia, PA: Temple University Press.

Miller, T. (2009) 'From creative to cultural industries: Not all industries are cultural, and no industries are creative', *Cultural Studies*, 23(1): 88–99.

Miller, T. (2012) *Blow Up the Humanities*. London: Temple.

Mirza, M. (2006) *Culture Vultures*. London: Policy Exchange.

Moeran, B. (2005a) *The Business of Ethnography*. New York: Berg.

Moeran, B. (2005b) 'Tricks of the trade: The performance and interpretation of authenticity', *Journal of Management Studies*, 4(5): 901–922.

Mol, J. and Wijnberg, N. (2007) 'Competition, selection and rock and roll: The economics of payola and authenticity', *Journal of Economic Issues*, 41(3): 701–714.

Molleda, J. C. (2001) 'International paradigms: The Latin American School of Public Relations', *Journalism Studies*, 2(4): 513–530.

Molleda, J. C. and Ferguson, M. A. (2004) 'Public relations roles in Brazil: Hierarchy eclipses gender differences', *Journal of Public Relations Research*, 16(4): 327–351.

Molloy, M. and Larner, W. (2010) 'Who needs cultural intermediaries indeed? Gendered networks in the designer fashion industry', *Journal of Cultural Economy*, 3(3): 361–377.

Moloney, K. (2006) *Rethinking Public Relations: PR Propaganda and Democracy*. Abingdon: Routledge.

Molotch, H. (2003) *Where Stuff Comes From: How Toasters, Toilets, Cars, Computers, and Many Other Things Come to Be as They Are*. New York: Routledge.

Moor, L. (2007) *The Rise of Brands*. Oxford: Berg.

Moor, L. (2008) 'Branding consultants as cultural intermediaries', *The Sociological Review*, 56(3): 408–428.

Moor, L. (2012) 'Beyond cultural intermediaries? A socio-technical perspective on the market for social interventions', *European Journal of Cultural Studies*, 15(5): 563–580.

Moore, J. (2004) 'The art of philanthropy and the formation and development of the Walker Art Gallery in Liverpool', *Museum and Society*, 2(2): 68–83.

Moore, J. and Julier, G. (2009) *Design and Creativity: Policy, Management and Practice*. Oxford: Berg.

Moorefield, V. (2005) *The Producer as Composer: Shaping the Sounds of Popular Music*. Cambridge, MA: MIT Press.

Moorman, M. (2003) *Tom Dowd and the Language of Music*. Force Entertainment. FV1812.

Mora, E. (2000) 'Small entrepreneurs, cultural intermediaries in a metropolitan context', *Polis*, 14(2): 235–254.

Morley, D. (1980) *The 'Nationwide' Audience: Structure and Decoding*. London: British Film Institute.

Mort, F. (1996) *Cultures of Consumption: Masculinities and Social Space in Late Twentieth-Century Britain*. London: Routledge.

Morton, D. (2006) *Sound Recording: The Life Story of a Technology*. Baltimore, MD: Johns Hopkins University Press.

Mumby, F. (1910) *The Romance of Bookselling: A History From the Earliest Times to the Twentieth Century*. London: Chapman and Hall.

Muniesa, F., Millo, Y. and Callon, M. (2007) 'An introduction to market devices', *The Sociological Review*, 55(Issue Supplement S2): 1–12.

Murdock, G. (2003) 'Back to work: Cultural labor in altered times', in A. Beck (ed.), *Cultural Work: Understanding the Cultural Industries*. London and New York: Routledge.

Murphy, J. M. (1998) 'What is branding?', in S. Hart and J. Murphy (eds), *Brands: The New Wealth Creators*. Basingstoke: Macmillan.

Musselin, C. and Paradeise, C. (2005) 'Quality: A debate', *Sociologie du Travail*, 47: 89–123.

Nathan, M. (2005) *The Wrong Stuff: Creative Class Theory, Diversity and City Performance*. Centre for Cities, Institute for Public Policy Research Discussion Paper 1. Available at: http://cjrs-rcsr.org/archives/30–/NATHAN.pdf (accessed 17 December 2013).

Naylor, D. and Toope, S. (2010) 'Don't swallow these innovation nostrums', *Globe and Mail*, 31 August. Available at: www.theglobeandmail.com/news/opinions/dont-swallow-these-innovation-nostrums/article1688275 (accessed 17 December 2013).

Negri, A. (2007) *Goodbye Mister Socialism*. Paris: Seuil.

Negus, K. (1992) *Producing Pop Culture and Conflict in the Popular Music Industry*. London: Hodder.

Negus, K. (1993) 'Plugging and programming: Pop radio and record promotion in Britain and the United States', *Popular Music*, 12(1): 57–68.

Negus, K. (1995) 'Where the mystical meets the market: Creativity and commerce in the production of popular music', *The Sociological Review*, 47(2): 316–341.

Negus, K. (1997) 'The production of culture', in P. du Gay (ed.), *Production of Culture / Cultures of Production*. London: Sage. pp. 67–118.

Negus, K. (1999) *Music Genres and Corporate Cultures*. London: Routledge.

Negus, K. (2002) 'The work of cultural intermediaries and the enduring distance between production and consumption', *Cultural Studies*, 16(2): 501–515.

Newman, A. and McLean, F. (2006) 'The impact of museums upon identity', *International Journal of Heritage Studies*, 12(1): 49–68.

Newsinger, J. (2013) 'The politics of regional audio-visual policy in England: Or, how we learnt to stop worrying and get "creative"', *International Journal of Cultural Policy*, 18(1): 111–125.

Nickson, D., Warhurst, C., Commander, J., Hurrell, S. A. and Cullen A. M. (2012) 'Soft skills and employability: Evidence from UK retail', *Economic and Industrial Democracy*, 33(1): 65–84.

Nixon, S. (1996) *Hard Looks: Masculinities, Spectatorship and Contemporary Consumption*. London: UCL Press.

Nixon, S. (1997) 'Circulating culture', in P. Du Gay (ed.), *Production of Culture / Cultures of Production*. London: Sage. pp. 177–220.

Nixon, S. (2002) 'Re-imagining the ad agency: The cultural connotations of economic forms', in P. du Gay and M. Pryke (eds), *Cultural Economy: Cultural Analysis and Commercial Life*. London: Sage. pp. 132–149.

Nixon, S. (2003) *Advertising Cultures, Gender, Commerce, Creativity*. London: Sage.

Nixon, S. (2006) 'The pursuit of newness: Advertising, creativity and the "narcissism of minor differences"', *Cultural Studies*, 20(1): 89–106.

Nixon, S. (2012) *Hard Sell: Advertising, Affluence and Trans-Atlantic Relations circa 1951–69*. Manchester: Manchester University Press.

Nixon, S. and du Gay, P. (2002) 'Who needs cultural intermediaries?', *Cultural Studies*, 16(4): 495–500.

Nixon, S., Hall, S. and Evans, S. (2012) *Representation: Cultural Representation and Signifying Practices* (2nd edn). London: Sage.

O'Boyle, N. (2011) *New Vocabularies, Old Ideas: Culture, Irishness and the Advertising Industry*. Bern: Peter Lang.

O'Brien, D. (2010) *Measuring the Value of Culture*. London: Department for Culture, Media and Sport.

O'Brien, D. (2013) *Cultural Policy: Value, Management and Modernity*. London: Routledge.

O'Connor, J. (2005) 'Creative exports: Taking cultural industries to St Petersburg', *International Journal of Cultural Policy*, 11(1): 45–60.

O'Donohoe, S. (1997) 'Raiding the postmodern pantry: Advertising intertextuality and the young adult audience', *European Journal of Marketing*, 31(3/4): 234–253.

O'Hara, K. and Brown, B. (eds) (2006) *Consuming Music Together: Social and Collaborative Aspects of Music Consumption Technologies*. Dordrecht: Springer.

O'Reilly, D. (2006) 'Commentary: Branding ideology', *Marketing Theory*, 6(2): 263–271.

Oakley, K. (2004) 'Not so cool Britannia: The role of the creative industries in economic development', *International Journal of Cultural Studies*, 7(1): 67–77.

Oakley, K. (2006) 'Include us out – economic development and social policy in the creative industries', *Cultural Trends*, 15(4): 255–273.

Oakley, K. (2010) *A Conversation with Kate Oakley*. Podcast, available at: http://culturalstudies.podbean.com/2010/09/17/a-conversation-with-kate-oakley (accessed 17 December 2013).

Ocejo, R. E. (2010) 'What'll it be? Cocktail bartenders and the redefinition of service in the creative economy', *City, Culture and Society*, 1(4): 179–14.

Ocejo, R. (ed.) (2012a) *Ethnography and the City: Readings on Doing Urban Fieldwork*. London: Routledge.

Ocejo, R. (2012b) 'At your service: The meanings and practices of contemporary bartenders', *European Journal of Cultural Studies*, 15(5): 642–658.

Ocejo, R. (2014) *Upscaling Downtown: Bars and Conflicts on the Lower East Side, East Village, and Bowery*. Princeton: Princeton University Press.

Ogilvy, D. (1997) *David Ogilvy: An Autobiography*. New York: Wiley.

Ogilvy, D. (2004 [1963]) *Confessions of an Advertising Man*. London: Southbank Publishing.

Olins, W. (1978) *The Corporate Personality: An Inquiry into the Nature of Corporate Identity*. London: Design Council.

Olsen, B. (2009) 'Rethinking marketing's evolutionary paradigm and advertiser's role as cultural intermediary', in J. F. Sherry and E. Fischer (eds), *Explorations in Consumer Culture Theory*. New York: Routledge. pp. 57–82.

Orsi, C. (2009) 'Knowledge-based society, peer production and the common good', *Capital & Class*, 33: 31–51.

Orwell, G. (1968) *The Collected Essays, Journals and Letters Vol. 1: An Age Like This*. London: Secker and Warburg.

Ostrander, S. (1993) '"Surely you're not in this just to be helpful": Access, rapport and interviews in three studies of elites', *Journal of Contemporary Ethnography*, 22: 17–27.

Ouellette, L. and Hay, J. (2008) *Better Living Through Television*. Oxford: Palgrave.

Palmer, G. (2003) *Discipline and Liberty: Television and Governance*. Manchester: Manchester University Press.

Palmer, G. (2004) '"The new you": Class and transformation in lifestyle television', in S. Holmes and D. Jermyn (eds), *Understanding Reality Television*. London: Routledge. pp. 173–90.

Palmer, G. (2008) *Exposing Lifestyle Television: The Big Reveal*. Aldershot: Ashgate.

Patterson, R. A. (1985) 'Six constraints on the production of literary works', *Poetics*, 14: 45–67.

Peck, J. (2007) 'The creativity fix', *Fronesis 24*. Available at: www.eurozine.com/articles/2007–6–8-peck-en.html (accessed 17 December 2013).

Pecknold, D. (2007) *The Selling Sound: The Rise of the Country Music Industry*. Durham, NC: Duke University Press.

Peichi, C. (2008) 'New media for social change: Globalisation and the online gaming industries of South Korea and Singapore', *Science, Technology & Society*, 13(2): 303–323.

Peterson, R. (1997) 'The rise and fall of highbrow snobbery as a status marker', *Poetics*, 25(2): 75–92.

Peterson, R. (2005) 'Problems in comparative research: The example of omnivorousness', *Poetics*, 33(5–6): 257–282.

Peterson, R. A. and Kern, R. M. (1996) 'Changing highbrow taste: From snob to omnivore', *American Sociological Review*, 61(5): 900–907.

Pettinger, L. (2004) 'Brand culture and branded workers: Service work and aesthetic labor in fashion retail', *Consumption, Markets and Culture*, 7: 165–184.

Pettinger, L. (2008) 'Developing aesthetic labour: The importance of consumption', *International Journal of Work, Organisation and Emotion*, 2(4): 327–343.

Philips, D. (2005) 'Transformation scenes: The television interior makeover', *International Journal of Cultural Studies*, 8(2): 213–229.

Pickton, D. and Broderick, A. (2005) *Integrated Marketing Communications* (2nd edn). Harlow: Prentice Education.

Pieczka, M. (2006) 'Public relations expertise in practice', in J. L'Etang and M. Pieczka (eds), *Public Relations: Critical Debates and Contemporary Practice*. Mahwah, NJ: Lawrence Erlbaum. pp. 279–302.

Pilditch, J. (1970) *Communication by Design: A Study in Corporate Identity*. New York: McGraw-Hill.

Pine, B. J., II and Gilmore, J. H. (1998) 'Welcome to the experience economy', *Harvard Business Review*, 76(4): 97–105.

Piore, M. J. and Sabel, C. (1984) *The Second Industrial Divide*. New York: Basic Books.

Political Economy Research Institute (2004) *The Misfortune 100: Top Corporate Air Polluters in the United States*. Amherst, MA: University of Massachusetts.

Pollan, M. (2007) *The Omnivore's Dilemma: A Natural History of Four Meals*. New York: Penguin.

Porter Benson, S. (1992) '"The clerking sisterhood": Rationalization and the work culture of sales women in American department stores 1890–1960', in A. J. Mills and P. Tancred (eds), *Gendering Organizational Analysis*. Newbury Park, CA: Sage. pp. 167–184.

Porter-Benson, S. (1998) *Counter Cultures: Saleswomen, Managers and Customers in American Department Stores 1890–1940*. Chicago, IL: University of Illinois Press.

Powell, H. and Prasad, S. (2010) '"As seen on TV." The celebrity expert: How taste is shaped by lifestyle media', *Cultural Politics*, 6(1): 111–124.

Powell, J. and Gilbert, T. (2007) 'Performativity and helping professions: Social theory, power, and practice', *International Journal of Social Welfare*, 16(3): 193–201.

Powers, D. (2010) 'Rock criticism's public intellectuals', *Popular Music and Society*, 33(4): 533–548.

*PR Week*/PRCA (2011) *2011 PR Census*. London: Public Relations Consultants' Association.

Pray, D. (1996) *Hype! Fabulous Sounds*. NW1159.

Preston, P. and Rogers, J. (2011) 'Social networks, legal innovations and the "new" music industry', *Info*, 13(6): 8–19.

Prior, N. (2011) 'Critique and renewal in the sociology of music: Bourdieu and beyond', *Cultural Sociology*, 5(1): 121–138.

Public Relations Society of America (2012) *Industry Facts and Figures*. Available at: http://media.prsa.org/prsa+overview/industry+facts+figures/ (accessed 5 August 2012).

Puddefoot, S. (1970) 'The women complex', in R. Boston (ed.), *The Press We Deserve*. London: Routledge. pp.73–87.

PwC (2011) *Cover to Cover: A Market Analysis of the Australian Book Industry*. Melbourne: Department of Innovation, Industry, Science and Research. Available at: www.innovation.gov.au/Industry/BooksandPrinting/BookIndustryStrategyGroup/Documents/PwCCovertoCover.pdf (accessed September 2012).

Ramanathan, S. (2006) 'The creativity mantra', *The Hindu*, 29 October. Available at: www.hindu.com/mag/2006/10/29/stories/2006102900290700.htm (accessed 17 December 2013).

Randazzo, S. (1993) *Mythmaking on Madison Avenue*. Chicago, IL: Probus.

Rappaport, E. D. (2000) *Shopping for Pleasure: Women in the Making of London's West End*. Princeton, NJ: Princeton University Press.

Reagan, R. (1966) 'The Creative Society', speech at the University of Southern California, 19 April. Available at: www.freerepublic.com/focus/news/742041/posts (accessed 17 December 2013).

Redden, G. (2008) 'Economy and reflexivity in makeover television', *Continuum: Journal of Media and Cultural Studies*, 22(4): 485–494.

Reese, S. D., Gandy, O. H. and Grant, A. G. (eds) (2001) *Framing Public Life: Perspectives on Media and Our Understanding of the Social World*. London: Lawrence Erlbaum.

Riess, S. A. (1989) *City Games: The Evolution of American Urban Society and the Rise of Sports*. Urbana, IL: University of Illinois Press.

Ritson, M. and Elliott, R. (1999) 'The social uses of advertising: An ethnographic study of adolescent advertising audiences', *Journal of Consumer Research*, 26(3): 260–277.

Ritzer, G. and Jurgenson, N. (2010) 'Production, consumption, prosumption: The nature of capitalism in the age of the digital "prosumer"', *Journal of Consumer Culture*, 10(1): 13–36.

Rock, P. (1983) 'News as eternal recurrence', in S. Cohen and J. Young (eds), *Manufacture of News*. London: Constable.

Rose, N. (1996) *Inventing Our Selves: Psychology, Power, and Personhood*. Cambridge: Cambridge University Press.

Ross, A. (2006–07) 'Nice work if you can get it: The mercurial career of creative industries policy', *Work Organisation, Labour and Globalisation*, 1(1): 1–19.

Ross, A. (2011) *Bird on Fire: Lessons from the World's Least Sustainable City*. New York: Oxford University Press.

Rushkoff, D. (2001) *Merchants of Cool*. WGBH Educational Foundation. FROL-6909.

Sanjek, R. (1996) *Pennies from Heaven: The American Popular Music Business in the Twentieth Century*. New York: Da Capo Press.

Sargent, C. (2009) 'Playing, shopping, and working as rock musicians: Masculinities in "de-skilled" and "re-skilled" organization', *Gender and Society*, 23(5): 665–687.

Sayers, S. (2007) 'The concept of labor: Marx and his critics', *Science & Society*, 71(4): 431–454.

Scannell, P. and Cardiff, D. (1991) *A Social History of British Broadcasting: Serving the Nation*, Vol. 1 (1922–39). Oxford: Blackwell.

Schlesinger, P. (2007) 'Creativity: From discourse to doctrine', *Screen*, 48(3): 377–387.

Schlesinger, P. and Tumber, H. (1994) *Reporting Crime: The Media Politics of Criminal Justice*. Oxford: Clarendon.

Schulz, S. (2008) 'Our lady hates viscose: The role of the customer image in high street fashion production', *Cultural Sociology*, 2(3): 385–405.

Scott, L. M. (1994) 'Images in advertising: The need for a theory of visual rhetoric', *Journal of Consumer Research*, 21(2): 252–273.

Segrave, K. (1994) *Payola in the Music Industry: A History, 1880–1991*. Jefferson, NC: McFarland.

Serazio, M. (2008) 'The apolitical irony of generation mash-up: A cultural case study in popular music', *Popular Music and Society*, 31(1): 79–94.

Shaw, G. (1992) 'The evolution and impact of large-scale retailing in Britain', in J. Benson and G. Shaw (eds), *The Evolution of Retail Systems c1800–1914*. Leicester: Leicester University Press. pp. 135–165.

Sherman, R. (2011) 'The production of distinctions: Class, gender, and taste work in the lifestyle management industry', *Qualitative Sociology*, 34: 201–219.

Sherry, J. F. J. (1987) 'Advertising as a cultural system', in J. Umiker-Sebeok (ed.), *Marketing and Semiotics: New Directions in the Study of Signs for Sale*. Berlin: Mouton de Gruyter. pp. 441–461.

Shiga, J. (2007) 'Copy-and-persist: The logic of mash-up culture', *Critical Studies in Media Communication*, 24(2): 93–114.

Shove, E. (2004) *Comfort, Cleanliness and Convenience*. Oxford: Berg.

Siebert, F. S., Peterson, T. and Schramm, W. (1956) *Four Theories of the Press*. Urbana, IL: University of Illinois Press.

Silverstone, R. (1999) *Why Study the Media?* London: Sage.

Sims, R. (2009) 'Food, place, and authenticity: Local food and the sustainable tourist experience', *Journal of Sustainable Tourism*, 17(3): 321–336.

Skeggs, B. (2009) 'The moral economy of person production: The class relations of self-performance on "reality" television', *Sociological Review*, 57(4): 626–44.

Skov, L. (2002) 'Hong Kong fashion designers as cultural intermediaries: Out of global garment production', *Cultural Studies*, 16(4): 553–569.

Skov, L. (2006) 'The role of trade fairs in the global fashion business', *Current Sociology*, 54(4): 764–783.

Skov, L. (2011) 'Dreams of small nations in a polycentric fashion world', *Fashion Theory*, 15(2): 137–156.

Skov, L. and Cumming, V. (eds) (2010) *Encyclopedia of World Dress and Fashion*, Vol. 8 – West Europe. Oxford: Oxford University Press.

Skov, L. and Melchior, M. R. (2010) 'Research approaches to the study of dress and fashion', *Encyclopedia of World Dress and Fashion*. Oxford: Berg. pp. 11–16.

Slater, D. (1997) *Consumer Culture and Modernity*. Cambridge: Polity Press.

Slater, D. (2002) 'Capturing markets from the economists', in P. du Gay and M. Pryke (eds), *Cultural Economy: Cultural Analysis and Commercial Life*. London: Sage. pp. 57–77.

Slater, D. (2010) 'Marketing as monstrosity: The impossible place between culture and economy', in D. Zwick and J. Cayla (eds), *Inside Marketing: Practices, Ideologies, Devices*. Oxford: Oxford University Press. pp. 23–41.

Smith, J. (1998) *The Sounds of Commerce: Marketing Popular Film Music*. New York: Columbia University Press.

Smith Maguire, J. (2001) 'Fit and flexible: The fitness industry, personal trainers and emotional service labor', *Sociology of Sport Journal*, 18(4): 379–402.

Smith Maguire, J. (2008a) *Fit for Consumption: Sociology and the Business of Fitness*. London: Routledge.

Smith Maguire, J. (2008b) 'The personal is professional: Personal trainers as a case study of cultural intermediaries', *International Journal of Cultural Studies*, 11(2): 203–221.

Smith Maguire, J. (2010) 'Provenance and the liminality of production and consumption: The case of wine promoters', *Marketing Theory*, 10(3): 269–282.

Smith Maguire, J. (2013) 'The construction of an urban, middle-class Chinese consumer culture: The case of cultural intermediaries in the Shanghai wine market'. Paper presented at the Habitable City in China, Centre for Urban History, University of Leicester.

Smith Maguire, J. and Matthews, J. (2010) 'Cultural intermediaries and the media', *Sociology Compass*, 4(7): 405–16.

Smith Maguire, J. and Matthews, J. (2012) 'Are we all cultural intermediaries now?', *European Journal of Cultural Studies*, 15(5): 551–562.

Soar, M. (2000) 'Encoding advertisements: Ideology and meaning in advertising production', *Mass Communication and Society*, 3(4): 415–437.

Sommerlund, J. (2008) 'Mediations in fashion', *Journal of Cultural Economy*, 1(2): 165–180.

Sparks, C. (1992) 'Popular journalism: Theories and practice', in P. Dahlgren and C. Sparks (eds), *Journalism and Popular Culture*. London: Sage. pp. 24–44.

Sparks, E. and Watts, M. J. (2011) *Degrees for What Jobs? Raising Expectations for Universities and Colleges in a Global Economy*. Washington, DC: National Governors Association Center for Best Practices.

Spielvogel, L. (2003) *Working Out in Japan: Shaping the Female Body in Tokyo Fitness Clubs*. Durham, NC: Duke University Press.

Spiggle, S. (1994) 'Analysis and interpretation of qualitative data in consumer research', *Journal of Consumer Research*, 21(3): 491–503.

Squires, C. (2007) *Marketing Literature*. London: Palgrave Macmillan.

Stevenson, N., Jackson, P. and Brooks, K. (2003) 'Reading men's lifestyle magazines: Cultural power and the information society', in B. Benwell (ed.), *Masculinity and Men's Lifestyle Magazines*. Oxford: Blackwell. pp. 112–131.

Stevenson, R.W. (1993) 'Bank for East Europe lives well in London', *New York Times*, 21 April. Available at www.nytimes.com/1993/04/21/business/bank-for-east-europe-lives-well-in-london.html?n=Top%2fClassifieds%2fReal%20Estate%2fColumns%2fLiving%20In (accessed 17 December 2013).

Stratton, J. (2010) 'Chris Blackwell and "my boy lollipop": Ska, race and British popular music', *Journal of Popular Music Studies*, 22(4): 436–465.

Striphas, T. (2009) *The Late Age of Print*. New York and Chichester: Colombia University Press.

Sturdy, A. (1998) 'Customer care in a consumer society: Smiling and sometimes meaning it', *Organization*, 5(1): 27–53.

Sudy, M. (1991) *Personal Trainer Manual: The Resource for Fitness Instructors*. San Diego, CA: American Council on Exercise.

Suisman, D. (2009) *Selling Sounds: The Commercial Revolution in American Music*. Cambridge, MA: Harvard University Press.

Sutton, M. (2002) Interview with Michelle Sutton, London, 15 February.

Tasgal, A. (2003) 'The science of the brands: Alchemy, advertising and accountancy', *International Journal of Market Research*, 45(2): 133–166.

Thebérge, P. (2004) 'The network studio: Historical and technological paths to a new ideal in music making', *Social Studies of Science*, 34(5): 759–781.

Thomas, L. (2008) '"Ecoreality": The politics and aesthetics of "green" television', in G. Palmer (ed.), *Exposing Lifestyle Television: The Big Reveal*. Aldershot: Ashgate. pp. 177–188.

Thompson, C. J. (2004) 'Marketing mythology and discourses of power', *Journal of Consumer Research*, 31(1): 162–180.

Thompson, C. J. and Haytko, D. L. (1997) 'Speaking of fashion: Consumer's uses of fashion discourses and the appropriation of countervailing cultural meanings', *Journal of Consumer Research*, 24(2): 15–42.

Thompson, E. (1995) 'Machines, music and the quest for fidelity: Marketing the Edison Phonograph in America, 1877–1925', *The Musical Quarterly*, 79(1): 131–171.

Thompson, J. B. (2000) *Political Scandal: Power and Visibility in the Media Age*. Cambridge: Polity.

Thompson, J. B. (2005) *Books in the Digital Age*. Cambridge: Polity.

Thompson, J. B. (2010) *Merchants of Culture*. Cambridge: Polity.

Thornton, S. (1996) *Club Cultures: Music, Media, and Subcultural Capital*. Hanover, NH: University Press of New England.

Thrift, N. (2005) *Knowing Capitalism*. Thousand Oaks, CA: Sage.

Timoner, O. (2004) *Dig!* Interloper Films. MMA2260.

Toffler, A. (1983) *Previews and Premises*. New York: Morrow.

Tschmuck, P. (2009) 'Copyright, contracts and music production', *Information, Communication and Society*, 12(2): 251–266.

Tuchman, G. (1972) 'Objectivity as strategic ritual: An examination of newsmen's notions of objectivity', *American Journal of Sociology*, 77(4): 660–679.

Tunstall, J. (1972) *Journalists at Work: Specialist Correspondents: Their News Organisations, News Sources and Competitor Colleagues*. London: Constable.

Turner, B. and Orange, R. (eds) (2012) *Specialist Journalism*. London: Routledge.

Turner, G. (2009) *Ordinary People and the Media: The Demotic Turn*. Sage: London.

Turner, G. (2012) *What's Become of Cultural Studies?* London: Sage.

Turner-Riggs (2007) *Book Retail in Canada, Department of Canadian Heritage*. Ottawa: Turner-Riggs. Available at: www.pch.gc.ca/pgm/padie-bpidp/rep/rapp-rep_07/rapport-pdf-report-eng.pdf (accessed September 2012).

Turnstall, J. (1964) *The Advertising Man in London Advertising Agencies*. London: Chapman and Hall.

Twitchell, J. B. (2004*) Branded Nation*. New York: Simon and Schuster.

United Nations (2010) *The Creative Economy Report 2010*. Available at: www.unctad.org/creative-economy (accessed December 2012).

United Nations Conference on Trade and Development (2004) *Creative Industries and Development*, Eleventh Session, São Paolo. TD(XI)/BP/13.

United Nations Educational, Scientific and Cultural Organization (2002) *Culture and UNESCO*. Paris: United Nations Educational, Scientific and Cultural Organization.

Ursell, G. (2000) 'Television production: Issues of exploitation, commodification and subjectivity in UK television labour markets', *Media, Culture and Society*, 22(6): 805–825.

Ursell, G. (2004) 'Changing times, changing identities: A case study of British journalists', in T. E. Jensen and A. Westenholz (eds), *Identity in the Age of the New Economy*. Cheltenham: Edward Elgar.

Van Maanen, J. (2011) *Tales of the Field: On Writing Ethnography*. Chicago, IL: University of Chicago Press.

Van Wijk, E. (2006) 'The myth of individuated creativity: The ties that bind creative professionals in advertising agencies', 7th International Conference on Organisational Discourse: Identity, Ideology and Idiosyncrasy. Free University, Amsterdam, 26–28 July.

Vancour, S. (2009) 'Popularizing the classics: Radio's role in the American music appreciation movement, 1922–34', *Media, Culture and Society*, 31(2): 289–307.

Vargo, S. L. and Lusch, R. F. (2004) 'Evolving a new dominant logic for marketing', *Journal of Marketing*, 68(1): 1–17.

Warfield, P. (2009) 'John Philip Sousa and "The menace of mechanical music"', *Journal of the Society for American Music*, 3(4): 431–463.

Waterstones (2012) 'James Daunt announces Waterstones Kindle deal'. Available at www.waterstones.com/waterstonesweb/pages/kindle-press-release/2414/ (accessed September 2012).

Weaver, C. K., Motion, J. and Roper, J. (2006) 'From propaganda to discourse (and back again): Truth, power and public relations', in J. L'Etang and M. Pieczka (eds), *Critical Perspectives in Public Relations* (2nd edn). London and Boston: International Thomson. pp. 7–22.

Weber, M. (1946a) *From Max Weber: Essays in Sociology*. New York: Oxford University Press.

Weber, M. (1946b) 'Class, status, party', in H. Gerth and C. W. Mills (eds), *From Max Weber*. Oxford: Oxford University Press. pp. 180–195.

Wehmeier, S. (2004) 'From capitalist public relations to socialist *oeffentlichkeitsarbeit* and back: Public relations in East Germany', in J. C. Garcia-Zamor (ed.), *Bureaucratic, Societal and Ethical Transformation of the Former East Germany*. Lanham, MD: University Press of America. pp. 147–174.

Wernick, A. (1991) *Promotional Culture: Advertising, Ideology and Symbolic Expression*. London: Sage.

Westhoff, B. (2011) 'Bud Bundy, original gangsta', *LA Weekly*, 34(2): 16–22.

White, C. L. (1970) *Women's Magazines, 1693–1968*. London: Joseph.

Whitehead, C. (2005) 'Visiting with suspicion: Recent perspectives on art and art museums', in G. Corsane (ed.), *Heritage Museums and Galleries: An Introductory Reader*. London: Routledge. pp. 89–101.

Wikström, P. (2009) *The Music Industry: Music in the Cloud*. Cambridge: Polity.

Wilensky, H. L. (1964) 'The professionalization of everyone?', *American Journal of Sociology*, 70(September): 137–158.

Williams, C. L. and Connell, C. (2010) '"Looking good and sounding right": Aesthetic labor and social inequality in the retail industry', *Work and Occupations*, 37(3): 349–377.

Williamson, J. (1978) *Decoding Advertisements: Ideology and Meaning in Advertising*. London: Marion Boyars.

Williamson, J. and Cloonan, M. (2007) 'Rethinking the music industry', *Popular Music*, 26(2): 305–322.

Willmott, H. (2010) 'Creating "value" beyond the point of production: Branding, financialization and market capitalization', *Organization*, 17(5): 1–26.

Wilson, E. (1985) *Adorned in Dreams: Fashion and Modernity*. London: Virago.

Winship, J. (2000) 'Culture of restraint: The British chain store 1920–39', in P. Jackson, M. Lowe, D. Miller and F. Mort (eds), *Commercial Cultures: Economies, Practices, Spaces*. Oxford: Berg. pp. 15–34.

Witz, A., Warhurst, C. and Nickson, D. (2003) 'The labour of aesthetics and the aesthetics of organisation', *Organization*, 10(1): 33–54.

Wolfsfeld, G. (1997) *Media and Political Conflict: News from the Middle East*. Cambridge: Cambridge University Press.

Woo, B. (2012) 'Alpha nerds: Cultural intermediaries in a subcultural scene', *European Journal of Cultural Studies*, 15(5): 659–676.

Woodham, J. (1997) *Twentieth-Century Design*. Oxford: Oxford University Press.

Work Foundation (2007) *Staying Ahead: The Economic Performance of the UK's Creative Industries*. London: Department for Culture, Media and Sport. Available at: www.culture.gov.uk/reference_library/publications/archive_2007 (accessed July 2007).

Wright, D. (2004) '"You're part of the package": Rationalization and the status of expert knowledge in the retail book trade', *Savoir, Travail et Société*, 2(3): 17–37.

Wright, D. (2005a) 'Mediating production and consumption: Cultural capital and "cultural workers"', *British Journal of Sociology*, 56(1): 106–121.

Wright, D. (2005b) 'Commodifying respectability: Distinctions at work in the bookshop', *Journal of Consumer Culture*, 5(3): 295–314.

Wright, D. (2012) 'List-culture and literary taste in a time of "endless choice"', in A. Lang (ed.), *From Codex to Hypertext*. Cambridge, MA: University of Massachusetts Press.

Wyatt, R. and Badger, D. (1990) 'Effects of information and evaluation in film criticism', *Journalism Quarterly*, 67(2): 359–368.

Xu, J. H. (2007) 'Brand-new lifestyle: Consumer-oriented programmes on Chinese television', *Media, Culture and Society*, 29(3): 363–376.

Zak, A. (2010) *I Don't Sound Like Nobody: Remaking Music in 1950s America*. Ann Arbor, MI: University of Michigan Press.

Zukin, S. (2009) *Naked City: The Death and Life of Authentic Urban Places*. New York: Oxford University Press.

Zwaan, K. and Bogt, T. F. M. T. (2009) 'Research note: Breaking into the popular record industry: An insider's view on the career entry of pop musicians', *European Journal of Communication*, 24(1): 89–101.

# INDEX

actor network theory 1, 3, 15, 40, 60, 175, 179
advertising 9, 17, 19, 21, 25, 34–41, 42, 44, 45, 51, 53, 55, 67–76, 78, 80–1, 86, 91–3, 132, 137–8, 147–8, 168–9, 170, 173, 175, 178, 192, 194
  account team 68, 70–2, 74
  agency 28, 34–5, 36, 67, 68–9, 72–4, 75, 80–1, 86, 87
  agency-client relationship 68, 72–6
  art directors 36, 51, 70–2, 74
  assessing impact 75–6
  conceptualization of 35–6, 41
  creatives 68, 69, 71, 72, 73, 74
  executives 20, 24 n.5, 43
  historical development 39, 68–9, 73–4, 80, 91, 137–8, 147–8, 170, 194
  as a market device 35, 37–40
  material practices 9, 35, 45, 68, 69–75, 80, 173, 175
  see also agencement; brands/branding; copywriters; market research; music, and advertising; public relations/PR, compared with advertising self-advertising
advice manuals 9, 85, 87, 136–8, 149, 158–9, 161, 194
  see also lifestyle media
aesthetics 29, 68, 75, 111, 114, 123, 133, 137, 138, 142, 165, 173, 176, 189, 190
  bourgeois 138
  definition of culture 43, 45
  freedom 172
  identity 172
  occupations 20
  postmodern 138
  products 74
  see also dispositions; knowledge
aestheticization 86, 136
aesthetic labour 20, 175–8
affect 7, 11, 23, 60, 175–7
affective labour 175, 177
affordance 126, 129
agencement 38, 40, 48–9
agency (of actors) 6, 7, 11, 24, 38, 40, 69, 99, 127, 137, 145, 146, 154, 168
algorithms 49, 190
Amazon.com 182, 186, 190, 191
anxiety 11, 24, 39–40, 171, 189
  and class 18–9, 22
  producer 74
apprenticeship 116, 184

art 31, 97, 100–12, 120, 123, 133, 156, 201
  and commerce 68, 72, 75–6
  degree, study of 83, 106–7, 109, 116
  field 100–10
  of living 19
  marketing 104
  participation programmes 100–11
  and science 75
  worlds 103, 109, 111–12, 133
  see also art galleries/museums; value, artistic
art galleries/museums 100–3 105–6 111–2
artisan 25, 36, 193, 201
artists and repertoire/A&R division 52, 131
  see also popular music industry
arts promotion 100–12
  assessing impact 108–11
  historical development 102–3
  material practices 103–8
audience 27, 54, 79, 80, 92–4, 104, 109, 111–12, 130, 138, 139, 142, 149–51, 154
  target 71, 83–5, 104, 110
  values 92
  see also knowledge, of audience
authority 2, 6, 8, 10, 20–1, 27, 36, 60, 85, 114, 143, 144, 158, 161–2, 164, 185
  of legitimation 21
authenticity 184, 189, 193, 196–8, 200
  see also sincerity
autonomy 2, 6, 117, 123, 148, 150, 152, 165, 166, 173, 185
  creative 116, 118, 123

bartenders 21, 195, 198–200, 201
belief 15, 22–3, 29–31, 60, 77, 86, 92, 102, 107–9, 118, 163–5, 180, 183–4
  see also sincerity
Blaszczyk, R.L. 113–4, 121, 123
book retail 45, 53, 56, 180–91, 200
  assessing impact 186–89
  diploma 184
  field 186–9, 191 n.1
  historical development 181–3, 186, 189, 190
  management cultures of 184–5
  and marketing 180–1, 189–90
  material practice 56, 183–6, 190
  see also brands/branding, and book selling; chain retailing; value, literary

Bourdieu, P. on cultural intermediaries 1–4, 15–24,
    35–7, 40–1, 42–4, 63 n.3, 68, 102, 111, 113–14,
    133, 164, 168, 180, 191, 200–1
    *see also* bourgeois/bourgeoisie; dispositions; habitus;
        petite bourgeois/petite bourgeoisie; taste
bourgeois/bourgeoisie 3, 17–22, 24 n.5, 63 n.3, 69,
    108, 138
    aspiring 136
    bohemian 69
    established 21
    occupations 18
    *see also* middle class
brands/branding 2, 9, 42, 44–5, 48–50, 77–88, 89, 92,
    94, 114, 116, 131, 168–79, 190, 197–9
    abstract dimensions 80, 88
    and advertising 69, 72, 75, 80–1, 86
    assessing impact 77, 82, 84–6
    and book selling 187
    and celebrities 30, 134, 139–40
    consultants 45, 82, 84–6, 178
    and drinks 196–7
    and fashion 115, 118, 168–79
    historical development 78–80, 170
    management 77, 85, 87, 197
    material practices 80–4, 171–7
    and music 83
    personality 80–3, 87
    spatial scope 80–1, 172, 175
    workers 174
    *see also* brand valuation; brand values; lifestyle: brands/
        goods; translation of values into material form
branded garment retail/BGR 168–79
brand valuation 88
brand values 79, 81, 84, 87, 168
bureaucracy 5, 25–6, 30, 33, 73, 103, 130, 147
bureaucratization 19, 165
burnout 23, 157, 165–67
butchers 199–200

calculation 38, 49–50
    *see also* algorithms; evaluation, work of; judgement
        devices; market research
capital
cultural 3, 9–10, 16, 21–3, 36, 72, 96, 102, 108, 135,
    139, 162, 166, 169, 188, 192, 201
    economic 1, 29, 72, 102, 122, 183, 188, 201
    educational 16, 18, 21, 22, 27, 37, 59, 95, 162,
        165–7, 176
    field 21, 151, 161, 167, 184, 193
    human 31
    institutional 162
    journalistic 190
    physical 9, 10, 121, 139, 156–60, 162, 164–7, 172, 175–8
    *see also* knowledge

capitalism 26, 30, 78, 96, 122–3, 136, 141–2, 144, 178, 194
Callon, M. 3, 35–41, 46–50, 116, 118
    *see also* agencement; calculation; economization;
        professional qualifiers of goods; qualification;
        singularization
catwalk economy 114
celebrity 30, 93, 134–5, 139–41, 143, 144, 158, 189
    *see also* brands/branding, and celebrities; chefs,
        celebrity; personal trainers, celebrity
chain retailing 114, 140, 169–70, 181–91, 195
    *see also* supply chain; value chain
chains of actors *see* networks
chefs 193–5, 199, 201
    celebrity 134–5, 140–1
circuit of culture 90–9, 169
clothing retail 114, 168–79
    assessing impact 177–78
    historical development 122, 169–72
    material practices 172–7
    *see also* fashion
co-creation 27–8, 55, 67, 72, 76, 103–5, 108, 199
cognitariat 26–33
    *see also* creative class
commodity chain *see* value chain
consumerism 86, 96, 127, 170–1, 178, 188, 190
consumption *see* production and consumption;
    promotion of consumption
consumer
    culture 7, 18, 20, 23, 75–6, 85, 134, 138, 140,
        168–71, 176–8
    experience 76, 81, 93–4, 96, 129–30, 157, 178,
        189–90, 198, 201
    lifestyle 94, 122, 138, 140, 143–4
    market 3, 9–11, 113, 117–21, 124, 136, 158
    *see also* audience; knowledge, of consumers;
        knowledge, of audience; mobilization, of
        consumers
cookbooks *see* advice manuals
cool 1, 21, 32, 118–19
co-production *see* co-creation
copywriters
    in advertising 36, 51, 70–4
    in journalism 149
creativity 4–5, 25, 27, 29, 31, 39, 71–5, 84, 119
creative class 4, 29–30, 32
    *see also* Florida, R.
creative economy 25, 28–9, 33 n.3
creative industries 4–6, 11, 25–6, 28–33, 54–76, 101, 123
    *see also* cultural industries
creative occupations/work 4–6, 31, 119, 168
    *see also* advertising creative; autonomy, creative;
        cultural work; cultural workers
credibility 7, 10, 20, 50, 54, 131, 140, 152, 154–5,
    156–7, 159, 161–4, 166

critics (non-academic) 17, 22, 25, 49, 55, 109, 123, 127, 131, 145, 149, 151–2
cultural economy 1, 3–4, 6, 10, 15, 68, 135, 178, 192
cultural field 1–2, 9–10, 57, 90, 94–5, 98, 123, 135, 156, 162, 167, 194
cultural industries 5, 18, 29–30, 54, 75, 79, 91, 113, 181, 192
cultural omnivorousness 193, 200
cultural policy 5, 54, 100–3, 108, 123, 127
cultural production 2–3, 5–7, 41, 52–3, 86, 129, 133, 180, 183, 186, 191, 196
cultural work 3–6, 11, 25–8, 32, 85, 194
cultural workers 5–6, 26, 145, 201
culture and commerce 181, 186
curators 25, 101, 109, 112, 123, 190
customer service 85, 168, 174–5, 191
 see also service work
cybertarianism 25–33

democratization 28, 109, 136, 170, 193
designers 25, 39, 43, 46, 81–3, 93, 96, 178, 180
 branded garment retail 172–3
 fashion 115–21, 123, 170
design industry 77–8, 80, 114
desire
 on the part of consumers/clients 11, 20, 23–4, 35–6, 40, 44, 47, 123, 134, 159, 164, 169, 171, 174–5
 on the part of cultural intermediaries 11, 24, 29, 41, 100, 102, 106–8, 134, 163, 166, 174–6, 183–4, 188–9, 191
de-skilling 188
devices 2–4, 7, 9–11, 22–4, 34–41, 48–51, 87–8, 114, 146–7, 149, 151–4, 157–63, 167, 169, 173–5, 179, 185, 195, 198–9
 assemblages of 40–1, 48
 see also advertising, as a market device; algorithms; judgement devices; market research
Dichter, E. 39–40
digital
 artefacts 179
 capitalism 30
 cultures 133
 *Magna Carta* 27
 media 27, 44, 46, 53–4, 57–8, 81, 87, 93, 125, 131–2, 140, 173, 178, 188, 190
 retailing 188
 technologies 4, 11, 25–8, 31–2, 44, 51, 60, 79–80, 94, 102, 115, 128, 130, 179, 180, 183, 185, 189, 190–1, 196
disintermediation 25–7, 132, 196
 see also intermediation mediation
dispositions 2, 3, 7, 9, 11, 15–6, 22–3, 36–7, 39, 84–7, 128, 139, 146–7, 149–54, 157, 161, 164–5, 172, 174, 176–7, 195, 199

dispositions *cont.*
 aesthetic 22
 of consumer 39, 85–6, 159, 177
 cultural 36–7
 idealized 9
 professional 150, 152, 161, 166
 sincere 22
 vocational 163–4, 166
 see also habitus; subjectivity of cultural intermediaries
distinction see taste
Don Draper 34–5, 37, 39–41

economic rationality 50, 163, 167
economization 46
editors 25, 52, 56, 149, 151, 180
education see capital, educational
electronic point of sale (EPOS) 185
Elias, N. 136
elite culture 16, 24 n.3, 104, 109–12, 138, 183
 see also legitimate culture; taste
elite institutions 101–2, 111, 153
elites 10, 57–9, 63 n.3, 102, 109, 112, 146, 153, 158, 183, 185, 200–1
 see also ethnography, of elites
elitism 100, 106
embodiment 11, 23, 31, 60, 79, 81, 98, 135, 139–40, 157, 159, 162, 164, 166, 174–6, 178, 185, 189, 198
emotion see affect; anxiety; desire; fear; pleasure
emotional connection 83, 93, 121, 141, 153, 165, 173, 175
emotional labour 164–5, 175
entrepreneurs/entrepreneurship 30, 131, 138, 141–2, 156, 161, 163
environmental sustainability 32–3, 113, 121–2, 141–2, 193, 196
ethical consumption 87–8, 141–3, 193, 196, 199
ethnography 7, 38, 52–63, 69, 71, 73, 75, 95, 98, 150
 of elites 58–9
evaluation, work of 48–50, 55, 68, 73–5, 81, 113–14, 119, 150
 see also algorithms; calculation; judgement devices; market research
expertise 2, 9–10, 21–2, 27, 39–40, 95, 117–19, 134–44, 148, 154–5, 156–64, 167, 170, 176, 184–5, 188–91, 198–9
 see also lifestyle experts; ordinary experts; professionals

fashion 17, 19, 36–7, 44, 45, 113–24, 149, 151, 170, 172, 176, 179, 181, 200
 assessing impact 118–19, 120–3
 field 123
 historical development 115–18, 121
 learning/training 116–19, 172

fashion *cont.*
    marketing 114–5, 119, 168–9, 173, 180
    material practices 56–7, 114, 118–20
    orientation 10, 21, 162, 169, 176
    product development 114–15, 118, 123–4
    *see also* brands/branding, and fashion; clothing retail;
        cool designers; fast fashion
fast fashion 118, 170, 172
fear 11, 44, 75, 132, 164, 188
fieldwork (as method) 55–8, 61–2, 101
fitness
    as field 156–59, 161, 162, 164
    historical development 159–60
    occupations 44, 156
    *see also* personal trainers
Florida, R. 29–30
food 39, 139, 142
    campaigns 134, 141–2
    culture 53, 142, 200
    local food 142, 193–4, 196–9, 201
    marker of taste 16, 192–3, 200–1
    *see also* provenance
food and drink industry 192–201
    assessing impact 200–1
    historical development 192–5
    material practices 195–200
    *see also* bartenders; brands/branding, and drinks;
        butchers; greenmarkets
food journalism/writing 149, 194, 198
food personalities 134–5, 140, 143
    *see also* chefs; Jamie Oliver
Foucault, M. 136, 141
frames/framing 9–11, 15, 20–1, 37–8, 39, 42, 45, 50,
    53–5, 61–2, 68, 71, 95, 132, 134–5, 144, 146–7,
    150–4, 156, 161, 169, 173
freelance work 82–3, 116, 118, 149
future directions for research 11, 23–4, 60–1, 76, 87–8,
    97–9, 111–12, 123–4, 133, 143–4, 154–5, 166–7,
    178–9, 189–91, 201

gatekeeper 5, 7, 26–7, 52, 54, 94, 101, 110, 199
gender 8, 95, 98, 114–5, 122, 135–9, 149, 154, 171, 177
globalization 6, 8, 26, 28–9, 51, 79, 112, 114–16, 118,
    121–3, 129–32, 142–4, 157, 168–70, 177, 179,
    195–6
governmentality 10, 23, 31, 141, 164
greenmarkets 196, 200

habitus 10, 22–4, 39, 55, 85, 128–9, 155, 166
handbooks *see* advice manuals
hermeneutic pinball machine 7, 61–2
higher education, expansion of 3, 18, 22, 116

ideology 25–6, 67–76, 91, 108, 144, 163
ideological intermediaries 67

immaterial labour 6, 59–61, 177, 179
impression management 73, 159, 167
inauthenticity 196, 201
individualization 6, 135, 138, 143–4
    *see also* lifestyle culture
innovation 5, 28–32, 46–7, 49, 83–5, 115, 120–2, 169,
    182, 194–6
instrumentalism 22, 30, 100, 108, 119, 167
intermediation 25–6, 29, 31, 33, 42–3, 46, 48–9,
    51, 94–6, 99, 112, 132–3, 168, 172–3, 178,
    193, 201
    *see also* disintermediation; mediation; production
        and consumption
intertextuality 71–2
interviewing (as method) 39, 53–61, 70–3, 86, 100–8,
    117, 124 n.1, 144, 162, 171
invisible labour 52–3, 59, 174, 179, 191

Jamie Oliver 134–6, 138, 139–42
journalists 17, 22, 25, 28, 44, 46, 52, 93, 96, 124,
    145–55, 190
    assessing impact 153–4
    and editors 151
    freelance 149
    historical development 147–9
    material practices 146–8, 149–53
    and media organizations 149–59
    and personalization 148–52
    and sources 146, 149–50, 155
    tabloid 148, 151
    *see also* capital, journalistic; copywriters; food
        journalism/writing; music journalists/critics;
        news values
journalistic field 147–55
journalistic forms 147–54
judgement devices 49–50

Karpik, L. 47, 49–50
    *see also* judgement devices; singularization
knowledge
    abstract 21, 150, 160
    aesthetic 194
    of audience 67, 71, 85
    of consumer 9–10, 36, 39, 67, 71, 84–5, 113,
        117–20, 150
    *see also* capital

labour, forms of 18, 24 n.4, 130–2, 137, 159, 171,
    174–7, 179, 181, 191
    *see also* aesthetic labour; affective labour; emotional
        labour; immaterial labour; service work
labour market 5–6, 27, 54, 115, 159, 178
legitimacy 1–11, 16, 21–4, 54–5, 92, 95–6, 132, 139,
    145–6, 156–67
    *see also* authority of legitimation

legitimate culture 11, 16, 21, 36–7, 85, 103, 153
    *see also* elite culture; taste
lifestyle
    brands/goods 138, 170, 176, 190
    of cultural intermediaries 20, 36–7, 139–40,
        163–6, 176
    ethic 20, 136, 140–1
    promotion of 20, 96–7
    of social groups 20–1, 32, 137–8, 144, 149, 192–3
    *see also* consumer lifestyle
lifestyle culture 89, 98, 134–44
lifestyle experts 134–44, 160, 163
    assessing impact 140–3
    historical development 135–8
    material practices 139–40
lifestyle media 134–44, 156, 159
    *see also* advice manuals
Lipovetsky, G. 115, 123–4

*Mad Men* 34–6, 39
magazines 17, 44, 53, 87–8, 115, 125, 137–8, 143,
    148–9, 156, 158–9, 170
marketing 19, 21, 49, 56, 59, 67–8, 76, 80, 87, 92, 136,
    153, 201
    executives 19
    strategies 48, 86, 127, 158
    *see also* art, marketing; book retail, marketing;
        fashion, marketing
market research 39–40, 49, 54, 68, 71, 74–5, 88, 94, 119–20
Marx/Marxism 42–4, 46, 177
mediation 2, 17, 42–5, 49–51, 52–3, 60–1, 67, 69,
    75–6, 115, 146, 168–9, 171–5, 177, 179, 180–1,
    185–6, 188–91, 193–6, 201
    mediation-at-a-distance 190–1
    regimes of mediation 2, 23, 56, 61, 69, 75
    *see also* disintermediation; intermediation;
        production and consumption
middle class 36, 63 n.3, 95, 144, 158, 170–2, 192
    *see also* bourgeois/bourgeoisie; petite bourgeois/
        petite bourgeoisie
mixology 21, 198–9
mobilization 11, 36, 122
    of consumers 10, 39–40, 44, 157, 164
models (fashion) 56–7, 119, 173
modern
    art/music 16
    fashion/goods 82, 84
    people 39, 137
Molotch, H. 114
music 126–9, 132
    and advertising 72, 132
    -based reality television 131–2
    classical 49
    and media 127, 132
    and retail 127, 131, 173, 201

music *cont.*
    *see also* affordance; brands/branding, and music;
        popular music industry
music journalists/critics 127, 131, 149, 151
musical subjects 126–8
musicians 25, 125, 131–2, 176
myth 10, 35, 67, 69, 72, 75, 85, 182

narratives *see* storytelling
Net Book Agreement/NBA 182–3
networks 10, 26, 29, 46–50, 60, 94, 109, 114–16, 122–3,
    146, 152–3, 155, 172–3, 177, 186, 191, 195, 199
    *see also* circuit of culture
new middle class
    *see* bourgeois/bourgeoisie; petite bourgeois/petite
        bourgeoisie
new occupations/professions 1,3, 11, 17–24, 36, 52, 133
newspapers 17, 28, 125, 138, 143, 147–8, 151, 154
news values 148, 151
novelty 10, 121–3

occupational identity 161, 182, 198–9
Ogilvy, D. 41, 70, 73
Oliver, J. 134–6, 138–42
ordinary experts 135–6, 139–40
organizational values 77, 97–8, 110, 150, 200
    *see also* professional knowledge, norms, skills, values
Orwell, G. 181

passion *see* desire
pedagogic role 17, 20, 85, 102, 105, 110, 113–14, 116–18,
    122, 134–44, 142, 157, 160, 164, 185, 188
    *see also* advice manuals; lifestyle experts;
        recommendations, work of making
personal and professional, relationship between 20,
    22–3, 56, 70–1, 85, 101, 105–9, 119, 123, 126,
    139–40, 155, 157, 160, 162–6, 176–7
personal trainers 52–3, 139, 156–67
    assessing impact 164–6
    celebrity 158
    historical development 157–60
    material practices 160–4
    *see also* fitness
petite bourgeois/petite bourgeoisie 3, 17–22, 36–7,
    42, 68, 192
    established 21, 26, 36
    occupations 19, 21
Pilditch, J. 79–80
pleasure 11, 20, 27, 31, 39–40, 104, 117, 120, 134, 138,
    164, 176, 189–90
popular music industry 37, 52, 125–33, 190, 196
    assessing impact 126, 132
    historical development 129–30
    material practices 130–2
    specific intermediaries 131

popular music industry *cont.*
  *see also* artists and repertoire/A&R division; music:
    music journalists/critics
postindustrialism/post-Fordism 25, 27, 29, 136–8,
  170, 194
precariousness and work 5–6, 26–7, 165–6
  *see also* freelance work; self-employment
PremierVision 120, 124 n.2
prestige 16, 96, 123, 145, 156
  *see also* social status
production and consumption, relationship between 1,
  4, 6, 11, 19, 24 n.4, 36, 42–6, 49–51, 67–8, 90, 94,
  104, 113–15, 121, 133, 156, 168, 175, 194–6
  *see also* intermediation; mediation
professional knowledge, norms, skills, values 2, 8–9, 22,
  30, 53–5, 57, 90, 92, 95, 113, 131, 135, 146–50,
  152–5, 157, 161–3, 198–9
  *see also* dispositions, professional; expertise; personal
    and professional, relationship between;
    professionalization; professional status
professionalization 8–9, 18–19, 21, 23, 78–9, 91, 95,
  116, 147–8, 157–8, 161, 184, 198–200
professional status 60, 103, 148, 152, 158, 161–2, 164, 184
professional qualifiers of goods 1, 4, 38–9, 41,
  48–51, 53
  *see also* new occupations/professions
promotion 9, 11, 23, 25, 31, 44, 77, 80, 86, 90–3, 96,
  116, 132, 140, 156, 159–60, 163, 165, 167, 185,
  190, 193, 195
  of consumption 1, 8, 11, 23, 44, 175
provenance 193, 196–8
public relations/PR 9, 17, 20, 44, 52, 68, 87, 89–99, 153
  assessing impact 96–7
  and clients 92–5
  compared with advertising 92, 93
  field 90–8
  historical development 90–2
  and lifeworlds 92, 95, 98
  material practises 92–7
  and participatory communication 97
  practitioners/PRPs 89–99
  and social change 97

qualification 1, 4, 8, 11, 23, 38–40, 42–51, 53, 116,
  118, 169, 175

ratings *see* market research
rational consumer 181, 185, 189
rationalization 81, 102, 113, 137, 182–3, 185–6,
  188–91
recommendations, work of making:
  in book retail 188–90
  in clothing retail 174–5, 179
  in fashion 113

relationship building 89, 95, 97, 101–12, 116–17, 119,
  126–9, 153, 160, 173, 184–5, 200–1
reputation 10, 79, 81, 89, 96, 121, 123, 150, 152

saleability 119–20, 201
self-advertising 162
self-branding 140
self-employment 165
service work 56, 159, 163, 166, 171, 174, 193, 198–200
  frontline 10, 156, 158, 160, 166
sincerity 22–3, 70, 107, 164, 166, 184
  *see also* authenticity; belief
singularization 47–50
social class 3, 4, 16, 22–4, 26, 36–7, 52, 103, 109,
  136–8, 159, 171, 173, 175, 200
  downward mobility 18, 37
  *see also* anxiety; bourgeois/bourgeoisie; creative
    class; middle class; petite bourgeois/petite
    bourgeoisie; working class
social status
  of individuals/groups 29, 57–9, 63 n.3, 110–11,
    135, 137, 139, 161, 165, 171–8, 192–4
  of goods 54, 75, 82, 132, 137, 159, 173, 193
  *see also* professional status; status competition
status competition 20, 24, 41
storytelling 36, 70, 72, 75, 92, 98, 131, 169, 177, 188,
  196, 199
street-level bureaucrats 6
studying up 58–9
subjectivity of cultural intermediaries 3–7, 9, 11,
  18–19, 22–3, 31, 35–6, 39, 41, 87, 94–5, 98, 117,
  166, 174, 177, 179, 195
  *see also* dispositions; habitus
supermarkets 38, 71, 114, 117, 119, 140, 142, 186–8,
  195–6, 199
supply chain 132, 169, 189, 196–7
  *see also* chain retailing; value chain
symbolic
  boundaries 120, 123, 193, 201
  goods and services 15, 17, 19, 55, 59, 67–8, 89, 180
  imposition 20, 22
  meaning 39, 69, 72, 86, 93–4, 138, 168, 192–3
  mediation 43–5, 49–51, 168, 191
  production 53, 56–7, 201
  realm 137
  rehabilitation strategies 21
  *see also* value, symbolic

tabloid journalism 148, 151
  *see also* journalists, and personalization
taste 2, 10, 15–24, 32, 36–7, 45, 48, 85–6, 96, 108–9,
  113–14, 119, 135–7, 139, 142–3, 162, 164–6,
  170, 174, 176, 178, 183, 185–6, 190, 192–4,
  198–201

taste *cont.*
   cultural intermediaries' own 22–3, 96, 108–9, 119,
      139, 164, 166, 176, 188, 199, 201
   and distinction 22, 136, 171–2, 175, 200–1
   republic of 186, 190
   *see also* elite culture; legitimate culture
taste brokers *see* taste makers
taste makers 1, 3, 15, 24, 36–7, 45, 50, 69, 85, 96–7,
      112, 114, 123, 126, 136, 143, 148, 168, 173, 179,
      195, 199, 201
   television 40, 52–3, 80, 125, 127, 132, 134–44, 150,
      156, 159, 179, 189, 190
   buyers 52–4, 57
   *see also* lifestyle media; music-based reality television
textbooks *see* advice manuals
translation of values into material form 81–4
triangulation 53, 55, 61–2
trust 49, 58, 95, 101, 104–5, 108, 110, 140, 184

value
   abstract 82
   artistic 102, 104–5, 110, 112
   cultural 7, 10, 25, 32, 35–6, 54, 82, 137, 139, 156–7,
      164, 176, 186, 188

value *cont.*
   economic 128
   exchange 47, 162
   literary 190
   social 100
   surplus 177
   symbolic 1, 54, 60, 73, 96, 159, 178,
      184, 198
   use 47, 54
   *see also* artistic value; audience, values; brand
      valuation; brand values; news values;
      organizational values; translation of
      values into material form; value
      formation/production
value chain 1–2, 6, 10, 94, 116–17, 119, 146, 153,
      155, 186
value formation/production 1–2, 4, 6, 10–11,
      15, 35–6, 44, 54–6, 60–1, 108, 124, 128,
      158, 166, 169, 173, 177–8, 193, 197,
      199–200

working class 108, 142, 170–1, 192
   *see also* bourgeois/bourgeoisie; middle class; petite
      bourgeois/petite bourgeoisie